ALL-STAR BASE-BALL

SINCE 1933

Also by Robert Obojski:

Bush League: A History of Minor League Baseball
The Rise of Japanese Baseball Power

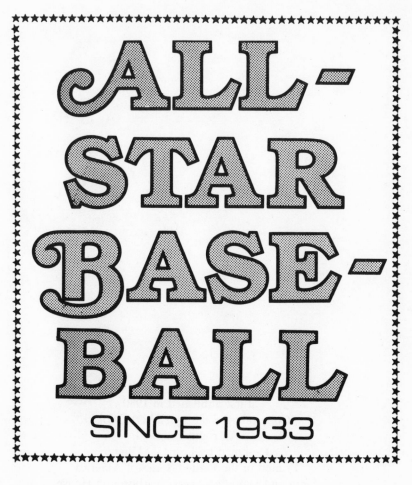

ALL-STAR BASEBALL

SINCE 1933

Robert Obojski

STEIN AND DAY/*Publishers*/New York

First published in 1980
Copyright © 1980 by Robert Obojski
All rights reserved
Designed by Louis A. Ditizio
Printed in the United States of America
Stein and Day/*Publishers*/Scarborough House
Briarcliff Manor, N.Y. 10510

Library of Congress Cataloging in Publication Data

Obojski, Robert.
  All-star baseball since 1933.

  Bibliography: p. 179
  Includes index.
  1. All-Star Baseball Game—History.   I.   Title.
GV863.A1026   796.357'784   79-20961
ISBN 0-8128-2694-9

Acknowledgments

SPECIAL thanks go to Clifford Kachline and John Redding, historian and librarian respectively, at the National Baseball Hall of Fame Museum and Library, Cooperstown, New York, for supplying both information and photos.

I must also single out for special mention Mike Ryan, public relations director for the San Diego Padres, who was so kind during my stay in San Diego for the 1978 All-Star Game.

Baseball executives who helped in one way or another include: Bill Veeck, president of the Chicago White Sox; Al Rosen, president of the New York Yankees; Hank Peters, executive vice-president and general manager of the Baltimore Orioles; Monte Irvin, assistant director of information in Commissioner Bowie Kuhn's office; Charles S. "Chub" Feeney, president of the National League; and Lee MacPhail, president of the American League.

Contents

Foreword by Ralph Kiner xi

1. The Birth of Baseball's All-Star Game 1
2. Voting for the All-Stars 5
3. The Bambino Belts One and Catches One: 1933 7
4. Hubbell, the Screwball Maestro,
   Mystifies the Maulers: 1934 14
5. Foxx Bites: 1935 19
6. Joe DiMaggio Wears Goat Horns: 1936 22
7. The Downfall of Dizzy Dean: 1937 27
8. Durocher Bunts a "Homer": 1938 30
9. Rapid Robert Rescues Damn Yankees: 1939 32
10. Two All-Star Games: 1940 34
    A Winter Game for a Winter War 34
    The First Shutout 35
11. The Saga of a Third-Story Man: 1941 37
12. Baseball Goes to War 41
    Bombed in the First: 1942 42
    The First All-Star Night Game: 1943 43
    Cavarretta's Big Day: 1944 45

13. The Americans Own the Postwar Diamond 47
    Terrible Ted Rips Rip's Eephus: 1946 47
    Pitchers' Battle: 1947 50
    Walking Wounded Win: 1948 51
    The End of the All-Star Color Bar: 1949 52
14. The Tables Turn 56
    Five Extra Innings: 1950 56
    Home Run Derby: 1951 58
    Short and Wet: 1952 60
    E. Slaughter = A Slaughter: 1953 60
    Blasts and a Bloop: 1954 62
15. The Mid-Fifties 66
    Messiah at the Bat: 1955 66
    Ballot Stuffing for Foggy Bottom Honors: 1956 68
    Minnie's Squeaker: 1957 70
    Silver Anniversary Singles: 1958 71
16. Let's Play Two! 73
    Willie Whips Whitey: 1959 (I) 74
    Transcontinental Doubleheader: 1959 (II) 75
    A Day in the Furnace: 1960 (I) 75
    "Twin Bill" Sweep: 1960 (II) 77
    The Cave of the Winds: 1961 (I) 77
    Deadlock: 1961 (II) 79
    Maury Wills Steals the Show: 1962 (I) 80
    Homers Make the Difference: 1962 (II) 81
17. Vengeance 83
    Wonderful Willie (I): 1963 83
    Two Strikes, Two Outs, in the Bottom of
        the Ninth: 1964 85
    Wonderful Willie (II): 1965 86
    A Hot Time in St. Louis: 1966 87
    Thirty, Count 'Em, Thirty Strikeouts: 1967 89
    Wonderful Willie (III): 1968 90
    The Washington Massacre: 1969 91
    A Thorny Rose: 1970 92
18. Every Dog Has His Day: 1971 94
19. Business As Usual 96
    Little Big Man: 1972 96
    The Kansas City Stomp: 1973 97
    The Write-In Hero: 1974 98
    Madlock and Matlack: 1975 99
    The Juniors Saw Red: 1976 100
    Right Where It Hurts: 1977 101
    Disappearing Act: 1978 102
20. A Pirate Reigns in the Kingdome: 1979 112

21. National League Supremacy: What Does It Mean?   116
22. "I Remember the Glory"   126
    Box Scores   129
    Bibliography   179
    Index   181

Illustrations between pages 46 and 47, 128 and 129.

Foreword by Ralph Kiner

MILLIONS of American boys would like to become big league ball-players, but there are only a little more than 600 at a time who are privileged to wear the uniform of one of the 26 teams in the majors.

Then only 50 or so of "The 600" are chosen for the annual All-Star Game. When you consider the long odds against being named to an All-Star team, you can better appreciate the sense of pride a player takes when he represents his league in the midsummer classic.

Methods of choosing players for the All-Star teams have varied during the past half-century, and though selection techniques have been subject to criticism from time to time, we know for a fact that the sport's greatest players take the field for this contest. And because the top diamond stars compete, the All-Star Game has become a baseball classic.

Many of the greatest deeds on the diamond have been performed in All-Star competition: Carl Hubbell's five consecutive strikeouts in 1934; Ted Williams's dramatic homer in the 1941 game and his four-for-four batting spree in 1946; Al Rosen's two homers in 1954; Willie Mays's six-for-eight performance in the two 1960 games; Johnny Callison's game-winning homer in 1964; Willie McCovey's brace of homers in 1969; Reggie Jackson's tape-measure shot in 1971; and Steve Garvey's batting heroics in the 1974 and 1978 games.

Personally, I remember the 1950 game played at Chicago's Comiskey Park most vividly. Ted Williams robbed me of an extra-base-hit in the first inning when he leaped high and picked off my line drive against the fence in left center field. Ted fractured his left elbow in the process, but through sheet grit and determination he remained in the game until the ninth inning. He didn't realize at first that he had suffered a break.

In the top of the ninth, I was lucky enough to catch hold of one of Art Houtteman's pitches and pop a homer to tie the score for the National League—that remains one of the biggest thrills I ever had in baseball, coming through in the clutch.

It remained for Red Schoendienst to win the game for us with his dramatic fourteenth-inning homer. The game was a long one, but the fans seemed to enjoy every minute of it, for they watched, I believe, baseball at its very best.

The major league baseball All-Star Game now has enough tradition behind it so that it has become not only an integral part of baseball lore but an important part of American folklore in general.

In this book, Robert Obojski covers the history of All-Star play from its beginnings through to the present. It is the most comprehensive account of the midsummer classic that I have ever seen.

Ralph Kiner, who hit 369 homers during his ten years in the major leagues, was elected to baseball's Hall of Fame in 1975. In addition, he slammed out three homers in All-Star competition.

Kiner's feat of leading the league in home runs for seven consecutive seasons (1946-52) is a major league record, and his 101 homers in 1949-50 still stands as a National League mark for two successive years. He was named by The Sporting News *as the N.L.'s Top Player in 1950.*

Ralph has been a member of the broadcasting team of the New York Mets since they entered the N.L. in 1962.

The Birth of Baseball's All-Star Game

THE 1930s ushered in the most severe economic depression in our history. Professional baseball wasn't immune to the malady. Even though fans continued to flock to the World Series, regular season attendance and receipts dropped off alarmingly, and salaries were scaled down. Commissioner Kenesaw Mountain Landis, whose contract had been renewed at $65,000 annually, voluntarily took a $25,000 salary cut.

The minor leagues were particularly hard hit during the depression; some of them collapsed. The minor circuits that survived in those years did it by dint of struggle.

It was during those trying times that the All-Star Game was launched, the proceeds devoted to a fund to take care of former professional players who found themselves without resources in their declining years. Bringing together picked teams of standout players in an interleague contest, the All-Star Game was conceived by Arch Ward, the imaginative sports editor of *The Chicago Tribune.* That newspaper sponsored the inaugural game of 1933 as an adjunct to the Chicago Century of Progress Exposition.

It was Ward's contention that baseball, too, should have a role to play in depicting the country's development prior to 1933. Many special promotions were arranged in connection with the Exposition, but Ward's original contribution—arranging the "Game of the Century"—was clearly the best and certainly the longest lived.

There is no indication that Ward had anything so permanent in mind. He focused his attention on a one-year "spectacular" (long before that word came to be used as a noun).

Comiskey Park was chosen as the setting for the game, and arrangements were made to have fans across the country vote for the participating players by ballot. For the managers, Ward wanted the two biggest names in baseball: John McGraw, who had recently retired after piloting the New York Giants for 31 years, and Connie Mack, still very much the manager of the Philadelphia Athletics, a post he had held since the American league was organized in 1901. Actually, McGraw and Mack began their big league managing careers in the National League back in the 1890s (the "Stone Age" of baseball), McGraw with the Baltimore Orioles, and Mack with the Pittsburgh Pirates.

The World Series confrontations of John McGraw and Connie Mack in the early years of the century had done much to fan the flames of intense baseball interest.

From 1934 on managers for the midsummer classic were chosen automatically: the pennant-winning pilots from each league would direct the All-Stars. Each manager was also given a free hand in selecting the coaches of his choice for the "dream game."

Arch Ward: Super Promoter

Arch Ward, born in Irwin, Illinois on December 27, 1896, and raised in Council Bluffs, Iowa, rose from small beginnings to become one of the most enterprising and successful promoters and writers in the history of American athletics. He took his first two years of college at St. Joseph's College and Academy in Dubuque, helping to pay his own way by serving as a correspondent for Dubuque newspapers, waiting on tables, and doing odd jobs.

Ward then switched to Notre Dame University as a junior in 1919, and during his two years at South Bend he served as the school's athletic publicity director. Following his graduation from Notre Dame, Ward went to Rockford, Illinois, as sports editor of *The Morning Star.*

He joined *The Chicago Tribune* sports department in 1925 as a copyreader and in quick succession was named editor of the early Sunday sports editions, assistant sports editor, and, in 1930, sports editor. In that position he inherited the "In the Wake of the News" column, the oldest continuous sports column in the country. Ring Lardner had started it, and Ward was about the fifth in line.

Once Ward took command of the *Tribune* sports department, his great flare for promotion came to the fore, and he often became so deeply involved in special projects that he found it necessary to assign members of his staff to ghost his column for him. Whenever he got around to it, Arch could do a good story or column, but being a promoter—that was his thing.

While he is best remembered for the creation of the All-Star Baseball Game, he also conceived the College All-Star Football Game, first played in 1934, developed the Golden Gloves boxing tournaments, and promoted ice skating competitions, championship horse racing, track and field meets, and various other types of sporting events too numerous to mention. In virtually every type of event he promoted, the net proceeds were donated to charitable institutions of one type or another, and in this regard he served as vice-president for many years of Chicago Tribune Charities, Inc. In fact, the Chicago Tribune Charities poured many millions of dollars raised from Ward's myriad of sporting events into Protestant, Jewish, and Roman Catholic charitable organizations.

The National Football League offered Ward the commissionership in the early 1940s. He turned them down, but he suggested that they hire Elmer Layden as commissioner, and they did.

Ward reached his peak as a promoter in 1946 when he almost single-handedly organized the All-America Football Conference. Ed Prell, then a *Tribune* sports writer, recalled recently:

> I can still remember the moment—Arch came up to me in our sports department and he says, "Ed, I wish I had enough time to go out and organize a new football league. I would do it."
>
> Well, he did. Believe it or not, he organized the All-American Conference, what some of the Chicago writers later were to call the Arch-America Conference. Arch got all kinds of people, moneyed people, together and passed out the franchises. And when the All-American Conference got started, the *Tribune* was its house organ.

Prell, who worked with Ward for many years, also said: "To be honest, I think Arch was actually self-centered, a bit on the cold side. He could simulate being the good guy, the big promoter, but basically he was a country boy. Remember he was from Council Bluffs and Dubuque. Going into the big hotels, being a big shot, were things he took on almost unnaturally. He dressed and acted the part, but he still seemed the small-town guy who had been caught up in this thing."

Nevertheless, during the 1930s and 1940s, the small-town boy had no peer as a big-time sports promoter.

Arch Ward died at the age of 58, on July 9, 1955, just as he was getting ready to leave for a look at the 22nd All-Star Game scheduled for Milwaukee three days hence.

A special memorial tribute was paid to Ward just before the start of the game at Milwaukee. As the players, managers, and coaches lined up along the base lines with heads bared, the crowd stood up for a few moments of silent prayer to honor the memory of the originator of the

All-Star classic. Many of the game's dignitaries attended Ward's funeral the morning of the contest, then drove to Milwaukee for the belated start of the game, which was set back half an hour.

The success of the major league All-Star Baseball Game has made a significant impact upon sports in general. Since the introduction of this blue-ribbon event, numerous U.S. minor leagues have made their own All-Star games an annual affair. And All-Star encounters are staged regularly in the Mexican, Caribbean, and Japanese baseball leagues.

And All-Star games are now major features in other sports, including ice hockey, basketball, football, and even soccer. This all evolved from Arch Ward's conception of an All-Star major league baseball game.

2

Voting for
the All-Stars

ARCH Ward felt strongly that the fans should vote for the players who would play on the All-Star team. The 1933 election was conducted by *The Chicago Tribune,* with the fans being allowed to vote for 18 players in each league by clipping special ballots and returning them to the newspaper.

The ballots were to have appeared in newspapers published in all the major league cities, but a number of them were apparently missed since the voting was light and centered mainly in the Chicago area. Babe Ruth led all the players in the balloting, polling just over 10,000 votes.

While the fan voting was respected, the managers actually could have chosen any players they preferred, since the popular balloting was officially classified as advisory—that is, it would serve to "guide" Messrs. Mack and McGraw.

The same fan-manager selection method was utilized again in 1934, and though nearly everyone agreed that the best players were named as All-Stars, the light voting caused the baseball establishment to look for another way to pick the teams.

The size of each team was increased to 20 players in 1934 and then to 21 in 1936, to 23 in 1937, and to 25 in 1939. With the expansion to 24 clubs in 1969, the squad size was boosted to its present 28.

From 1935 through 1946 the eight managers from each league selected all the players for the All-Star squads. The All-Star pilot, however, could use his own discretion in choosing a starting lineup. (The only exception came in 1937 when the two All-Star managers picked the entire rosters.) During this period, Joe McCarthy, the New York Yankee manager, got the most opportunity to pick starting lineups; he piloted seven American League teams.

5

The All-Star voting procedure underwent a full circle of changes over the next 23 years. Fans again elected the starting players from 1947 through 1957, with the Associated Press handling most of the tabulation of the public's votes. However, the overenthusiasm by Cincinnati rooters in 1957 led to another temporary abandonment of fan balloting. (See the section on the 1957 game for details on the Cincinnati ballot box stuffing.)

In 1958, Commissioner Ford Frick delegated the All-Star voting chores to the players, managers, and coaches, with all votes restricted to ballplayers in the voter's own league. There was a barrage of criticism with this system too, as players were frequently accused of voting for their friends. This major-league-wide poll was employed through 1969 when the new commissioner, Bowie Kuhn, acted to return the voting to the public. Kuhn, a lifelong and avid fan, said of the All-Star rivalry, "The fans should be permitted to pick the players they want to see."

Fully satisfied that sufficient safeguards had been found to prevent another occurrence of ballot box stuffing, Kuhn returned the voting to the public for the 1970 game with the cooperation of the Gillette Company, which underwrites and helps promote the fan balloting. At the heart of the new system was a punch-card ballot with the names of the player nominees at each starting position except pitcher and a write-in space for players not listed.

Early critics complained that some players who were off to flaming starts in 1970 were not on the ballot. Fans pretty well defused the issue by choosing heavy-hitting Rico Carty to the N.L. starting lineup as a write-in candidate. Over the years there have been other prominent write-in candidates. In 1974, for example, Steve Garvey was picked as starting N.L. first baseman on the strength of write-in votes, and he proceeded to demonstrate how wise the fans were by emerging as the game's MVP.

Perhaps the best yardstick of the success of the present system is that in the past decade baseball's All-Star fan balloting has become by far the largest nonpolitical election in the United States. In 1970 just over 2 million votes were cast, and that number had increased to nearly 8.4 million in 1976. More than 12.5 million fans voted in 1977, over 12.2 million in 1978, and the figure went to 12.3 million in 1979. From 1970 through 1979, approximately 70 million All-Star votes were recorded.

The leading vote-getter for each league wins the "Gillette Trophy," an award that is presented to the players in a special ceremony conducted on the day before the All-Star Game. In recent years such stars as Rod Carew and Steve Garvey have been pulling in more than 4 million votes each; in a popular election that would have been enough to make them the governor of virtually any state in the union!

3

The Bambino
Belts One and
Catches One: 1933

BABE Ruth, the broad-shouldered, big-bellied, spindle-legged, fantastic superman of swat, was clearly the major attraction at the 1933 All-Star Game, a star among stars.

The Bambino, now 38 (some said he was 39 or even older) and in his 20th season of major league baseball, was clearly past his prime, however. When he broke in with the Boston Red Sox in 1914, he packed a lean and hard 205 pounds of bone and muscle on his 6'2" frame, but his weight had ballooned up to 240 or so, and his eyes were no longer what they used to be. He was still hitting .300, but years of hard living were finally beginning to take their toll. The reflexes weren't as quick as they once were.

George Herman Ruth bestrode the big league playing fields like a colossus, and at midseason 1933 he had belted nearly 700 homers, a truly amazing figure, since no other player had even come close to hitting *half* his total at that point. Ruth, a legend in his own time, had done nothing less than to revolutionize baseball by hammering out home runs in bunches and almost single-handedly sending "inside baseball" (clawing and scratching for one run) the way of the extinct carrier pigeon.

The colossus, unfortunately, was showing telltale signs of crumbling. One Chicago writer looked out over the field during pregame practice, saw Ruth chasing a fly ball, and commented: "The Babe can still hit—no doubt about it—but he looks slow and sluggish." Then after the Babe caught the ball, he pulled up at the end of the short sprint huffing and puffing.

The game attracted a capacity crowd of more than 47,000 fans at

Chicago's Comiskey Park that July 6th, and a buzz of excitement filled the air for this was to be the battle of the giants, the "Game of the Century," as some called it. On the American League squad were such stalwarts as Ben Chapman, Bill Dickey, Lou Gehrig, Lefty Gomez, Tony Lazzeri, and Babe Ruth, of course, of New York; Rick Ferrell of Boston; Jimmy Dykes and Al Simmons of Chicago; Earl Averill, Wes Ferrell, and Oral Hildebrand of Cleveland; Charlie Gehringer of Detroit; Jimmie Foxx and Lefty Grove of Philadelphia; Sammy West of St. Louis; and Joe Cronin and "General" Alvin Crowder of Washington.

Representing the senior circuit were such notable diamond figures as Wally Berger of Boston; Tony Cuccinello of Brooklyn; Woody English, Gabby Hartnett, and Lon Warneke of Chicago; Chick Hafey of Cincinnati; Carl Hubbell, Frank "Lefty" O'Doul, Hal Schumacher, and Bill Terry of New York; Dick Bartell and Chuck Klein of Philadelphia; Pie Traynor and Paul Waner of Pittsburgh; Frankie Frisch, "Wild Bill" Hallahan, Pepper Martin, and Jimmy Wilson of St. Louis.

The American Leaguers wore their regular home uniforms, but National League president John Heydler dressed up his players in special uniforms for the occasion. They were steel gray with "National League" inscribed in blue letters across the shirts.

The National League was particularly anxious to win this game, since it had been doing badly in recent World Series. In fact, the Nationals had dropped five of the last six series at the hands of the New York Yankees and Philadelphia Athletics, both great powerhouse teams of the era. The St. Louis Cards, representing the N.L. in the 1931 fall classic, did edge out the Athletics four games to three, and they took the laurels largely on the heroics of Pepper Martin who batted a phenomenal .500 (12 for 24) while running wild on the base paths with five steals.

Vernon Gomez, the Yankees' brilliant southpaw who possessed a blazing fastball and a baffling curve, and at 22 already a two-time 20-game winner, was chosen as starting pitcher for the A.L. By pregame agreement no hurler was to go more than three innings (except if the contest went into overtime). Gomez had no problems with the Nationals in the first, retiring them in order.

Bill Hallahan, ace of the Cardinals' staff and victor in two games in the 1931 World Series, also a left-hander, started for the Nationals, and induced leadoff batter Ben Chapman to ground out to third. Charlie Gehringer walked and that brought up the Babe. Hallahan had to wait until the long ovation for Ruth died down—then, working carefully, he threw the first ball well outside, and Gehringer, going with the pitch, slid into second safely with a steal. Ruth now had a man in scoring position.

The Sultan of Swat proceeded to strike out on three straight pitches, swinging hard and missing the third, a fastball, as the fans groaned. Gehrig grounded out to end the inning.

Gomez retired the N.L. again in the second without a score.

Al Simmons opened the bottom half by flying out to center. Then Jimmy Dykes and Joe Cronin both walked. Rick Ferrell flied out to right to bring up Gomez, one of the weakest hitting pitchers in baseball. For the entire 1933 season, in fact, Lefty managed 9 singles in 80 at bats for a puny .113 average. Gomez, however, laid the wood to one of Hallahan's curves and drove the ball into left center, scoring Dykes with the first run in All-Star history.

"That base hit gave me as much satisfaction as anything I've done in baseball," Gomez said recently. "Nobody expected me to deliver in that situation, and I was as much surprised as anybody in the ball park."

Lefty felt like he was walking on air when he went back to the mound . . . he worked rapidly and retired the Nationals in one-two-three order. The 1–0 lead still held.

In the last of the third, Gehringer opened with a walk. They didn't call Hallahan "Wild Bill" for nothing. Ruth now came to the plate for the second time with Gehringer on base.

The American League fans cheered lustily for the old home run king while the National League boosters gave him some loud hoots.

Hallahan mopped his brow and curved in his first pitch, a little inside for a ball. Then a fastball just nipped the outside corner. One-and-one. Ruth casually stepped out of the box, filled his hands with dirt—nobody wore fancy batting gloves in those days—and wiped off the residue on his pants.

Ruth waved his big bat menacingly, measuring Hallahan's every movement. The pitch rode into the plate . . . Ruth took his patented semiuppercut swing—and craaack!, the bat and ball met squarely. The ball was blasted as if shot from a cannon and crashed hard into the bleachers in right field for a two-run homer!

Thunderous applause reverberated throughout the stadium as Ruth, head down, circled the bases in his familiar short-stepped gait. The Bambino had risen to the occasion as he had so many times in his career.

Hallahan, obviously shaken by the Babe's blast, walked Gehrig, and at this point manager McGraw decided the Cardinals' left-hander had had enough and derricked him in favor of Lon Warneke, the "Arkansas Hummingbird." Wild Bill had walked five men in his short stint on the mound, and that still stands as an All-Star record after nearly 50 years.

Warneke succeeded in retiring the Americans without further scoring in the inning.

Writers in the press box kept chattering about Ruth and his heroics. "I said all along he could still murder the ball," snapped a New York scribe.

"Yeah, yeah," said a hard-boiled Chicago reporter. "But let's wait to see what he does if he gets a tough chance in the field. If he has to run more than 10 or 15 feet, he'll never make it . . . he'll let in more runs than he's driven in."

Both teams failed to score in the fourth and fifth. Alvin Crowder was now on the mound for the Americans.

The A.L. did mount a mild threat in their half of the fifth, however. With one out, Ruth lined a single into center. Gehrig fanned, but Simmons singled to left, and Ruth, breathing a bit hard, pulled up at second.

"Ruth's wheels are gone," sniffed the cynical Chicago writer. "A fast runner could have made it to third on that hit." Dykes made the third out, and the rally was aborted.

The sixth inning, however, turned out to be a small disaster for the Bambino. As he stood out in right field, getting his wind back, Lefty O'Doul, a pinch hitter, grounded out to Gehringer.

That brought up Warneke, not a bad hitting pitcher—he batted an even .300, in fact, during the 1933 season. (Warneke was actually allowed to pitch four innings since the inning in which he came out to relieve Hallahan was not counted as one of the regulation three.) Lon hit under one of Crowder's pitches and sliced a short fly into right. Ruth came barreling in for the ball like an old steam locomotive and tried to snag it with his gloved hand . . . but the ball bounced a couple of feet in front of him, took a wicked little hop, got past the Babe, and rolled out to the base of the bleacher wall.

Before the embarrassed Babe could retrieve the pesky horsehide and heave it back to the infield, the grinning Warneke was perched on third base. The kindly official scorer awarded Warneke a triple rather than giving him only a single and charging a two-base error to the right fielder who was cursing furiously under his breath. Ruth said later that he wasn't really sure if he had misjudged the ball—something he seldom did—or if his legs just gave out at the wrong time.

The cynical Chicago typewriter jockey just couldn't resist sticking in his two cents worth. "Toldja. That Ruth runs like an old lady . . . any half-decent fielder would have put away that fly ball with no trouble."

Pepper Martin grounded out to Dykes, Warneke scoring easily on the throw to first. Switch-hitter Frankie Frisch, batting left-handed against the right-handed Crowder, leaned into a hanging curve and lined a drive directly over Ruth's head and into the right field seats.

"I suppose he should have caught up with that one too," barked the harried New York writer.

The Americans now led by a single run, 3–2.

Joe Cronin opened the bottom of the sixth with a single to center. Rick Ferrell sacrificed perfectly, moving Cronin to second.

At this point, with a man in scoring position, Connie Mack called on Earl Averill to bat for Alvin Crowder. Crowder had to leave the game regardless, since he had pitched his three innings. Averill came through with a single up the middle to score Cronin, and the A.L. now enjoyed a more comfortable 4–2 advantage.

Ben Chapman kept the rally going with a neat bunt single, but Gehringer flied out to right. Two out, runner on first, and Babe Ruth came ambling up to the plate.

While his homer still stuck out as the key swat for the Americans, the Babe was still miffed about the fly he had messed up in the top of the inning. Another blast into the bleachers would atone for it, he thought, especially against Warneke, the man who hit the fluke triple.

Ruth took Warneke's first pitch, a fastball, for a strike. Thinking the next pitch would be a curve, Ruth swung a little late and missed . . . Warneke had given him another fastball.

The Babe, now as angry as a bull, stepped out of the box, walked around in a little circle, knocked some specks of dirt out of his spikes, and moved back in. He waved his big 42-ounce bat, cocked it over his left shoulder, waited for the pitch. This time Warneke served up a sharp-breaking curve. Ruth took a wide sweeping powerful swing—and missed the ball by a foot.

A groan went up from the crowd. The mighty Ruth had struck out.

The old behemoth trotted out slowly to his position in right field, not fully satisfied with his performance in the game.

The two finest left-handed pitchers in baseball entered the contest in the seventh: Robert Moses "Lefty" Grove, ace of the Philadelphia A's for the A.L., and Carl Hubbell, the brilliant screwball artist of the New York Giants for the N.L. The pair went on to hurl scoreless ball for the balance of the game.

In the eighth, however, the Nationals seriously threatened to get right back into the game. Grove struck out leadoff hitter Pepper Martin, but Frisch, batting right-handed this time, rifled a single past first baseman Gehrig. Chuck Klein swung under a pitch a little too much and lofted a high fly to Simmons in left. With two out and a runner on first, Chick Hafey, Cincinnati outfielder and 1931 National League batting champion, came up.

Grove's first pitch was a blazing fastball, and the right-handed-hitting Hafey swung, got around a trifle late, but hit the ball squarely and sent a towering drive deep into right field.

The New York writer in the press box gasped. "Oh, oh! this is it—that one is going into the bleachers, or at least up against the screen."

Ruth instinctively turned with the crack of the bat and hustled back to the right field barrier, looking up for a split second through the sun's glare to judge the ball's trajectory.

With his broad back positioned against the wall, he saw the ball was going to fly over his head and that he'd have to time his leap perfectly to have any chance at all of catching it. Then the Babe sprang into the air with a catlike grace, all 240 pounds of him, and miraculously the horse-hide hit into the webbing of his well-worn glove, with the force of the drive knocking him up against the barrier.

The ball remained in the glove!

The crowd broke out into a spontaneous cheer. Ruth had robbed Hafey of an almost certain homer and saved the game for the Americans.

"How'd you like that play?" the New York press box denizen asked his Chicago counterpart.

"I'll have to admit Ruth is a great ballplayer—always has been," came the answer. "He comes through when the chips are down. Forget what I said before."

The balance of the game was an anticlimax. The Nationals went out quietly in their half of the ninth, and the game ended at 4–2.

Everyone in the press box agreed that Ruth's catch of Hafey's drive was the game's best defensive play—interestingly, it was the Babe's only putout of the day.

When John McGraw was interviewed in the clubhouse after the game, he said, "I thought sure Hafey's ball was going into the seats. You have to give Ruth credit . . . he was marvelous."

Connie Mack said from the outset that he was out to win rather than to see how many players he could get into the game. He made only one lineup change aside from the pitchers. John McGraw, on the other hand, used 17 players. Consequently, American League stars like Jimmie Foxx, Tony Lazzeri, and Bill Dickey sat on the bench for the entire game.

A Conversation with Joe Cronin

At the 1978 New York Mets' "Old-Timers Day" staged at Shea Stadium I had the rare opportunity to conduct a lengthy interview with Joe Cronin, still hale at 72 and wearing his old Boston Red Sox uniform. Cronin did not play in the two-inning Old-Timers exhibition game, but he did coach at third base and wigwagged all kinds of signals to his batters and base runners.

Cronin, Hall of Fame shortstop, distinguished himself as player-manager for both the Washington Senators and Boston Red Sox, and served as Red Sox general manager until he was named American League president in 1959. Cronin spent 14 years as the A.L.'s chief executive, retired at the end of 1973, and then was given the honorary post as the league's chairman.

Cronin reminisced about the 1933 All-Star Game:

When I stepped onto the field at Comiskey Park, I remembered that it was only five or six years earlier that I was trying to establish myself in the majors—and here I was the starting shortstop for the American League. I didn't have time to get nervous either, because in that first inning I accepted the first three fielding chances. (Pepper Martin and Frankie Frisch both grounded out to Cronin, and then the big shortstop made a sensational catch of Chuck Klein's line smash.)

It was also a nice feeling to know I had a hand in helping the American League score the first run in this game. . . .

The All-Star Game was to be tried for one year on an experimental basis, and if it went over, another would be played in 1934. The interleague competition was a smash success from the start, and over the years it's become an extremely important part of baseball. Babe Ruth's performance had a lot to do with the success of the 1933 game—no doubt about it.

Then the All-Star idea caught on eventually with all other major team sports. Still the All-Star Baseball Game has always been something extra special, and for that reason draws far more attention than all-star events in other sports. We certainly have more tradition behind us.

There was a certain magic appeal of pitting the best players in the American and National Leagues against each other in a classic baseball duel. This was Arch Ward's idea of perfection on the diamond where every player at every position would be the best.

4

Hubbell,
the Screwball Maestro,
Mystifies the
Maulers: 1934

THE National League played host for the 1934 All-Star Game at New York's storied Polo Grounds on July 10th. Bill Terry of the Giants and Joe Cronin of the Washington Senators, rival managers in the 1933 World Series, masterminded the two teams, and both men were further honored by being selected to the starting lineups by the fans. No one at the time considered that unusual because the 1930s were the era of the player-manager.

Lefty Gomez, on his way to a brilliant 26–5 season, gained the starting nod for American League mound duties for the second year in a row, while "Memphis Bill" Terry called on Carl Hubbell, the left-handed screwballing wizard from the Ozarks, to stop the fearsome array of A.L. sluggers. Hubbell was en route to a 21–12 season's record and a league-leading ERA of 2.30.

"King Carl" got off to a shaky start as Charlie Gehringer led off the first inning with a single and grabbed an extra base as center fielder Wally Berger bobbled the ball. Heinie Manush drew a walk, and an uneasiness gripped the National League rooters as the mighty Babe Ruth lumbered into the batter's box. The Bambino worked the count to one ball and two strikes, then watched with a puzzled expression as a screwball nipped the outside corner for the third strike.

Lou Gehrig was next. It took Ol' Hub six pitches to strike him out, but at least Larrupin' Lou got his money's worth, swinging at and missing three pitches with great flourishes. On the first pitch to Jimmie Foxx, a strike, Gehringer and Manush worked a double steal right under catcher Gabby Hartnett's nose. Two pitches later the crowd broke out into a roar as the "Maryland Strong Boy" went down swinging.

Hartnett later confessed he had become so enthralled by the power of Hubbell's pitching he hardly noticed there were any runners on base. Hub himself said, "That double steal didn't bother me none 'cause I knew I'd get Jimmie."

Frankie Frisch, batting right-handed, opened the bottom of the first by belting a homer into the left field bleachers, staking the Nationals to a quick 1-0 lead. That gave Frisch two homers for the first two All-Star Games, one left-handed and one right-handed, not bad for a man who never had hit for the circuit more than 12 times in a whole season.

As the second inning opened, Hubbell continued his magic. Al Simmons, twice American League batting champion and a man who hit .380 or better four times, whiffed on four pitches. Next came Joe Cronin, an MVP winner and one of baseball's most dependable clutch hitters. He, too, whiffed on four pitches, giving Hubbell five strikeouts in a row.

Bill Dickey came to bat. The hard-hitting Yankee catcher took two strikes and a ball, and then broke the spell by rapping out a single. Lefty Gomez ended the inning by swinging at a third strike.

This was a demonstration of pitching never equaled before or since. The 30-year-old left-hander had struck out in succession the flower of the American League hitters, Ruth, Gehrig, Foxx, Simmons, and Cronin—with only one, Foxx, managing to even nick him for a foul. After more than 45 years, the five strikeouts in succession still stands as a record for the midsummer classic, though three other pitchers have fanned six in a single All-Star appearance.

Hubbell retired the A.L. in order in the third, on two fly balls and a grounder, and, as he left the field, his three-inning stint completed, the crowd of nearly 50,000 rose to give him an ovation that shook the rafters of the Polo Grounds. It was, after all, Hub's home park.

Joe Medwick got hold of a Gomez fastball in the bottom of the third and blasted a three-run homer, giving the N.L. a 4-0 lead. It appeared almost certain that Hubbell would gain credit for a pitching victory.

Once King Carl was gone, however, the American League bounced back ferociously to score eight runs off Lon Warneke and Van Lingle Mungo in the fourth and fifth innings. In fact, the A.L.'s six runs in the fifth still remains as the one-inning All-Star high. It was a day of records.

Earl Averill of Cleveland delivered key extra base blows in each of those two innings—he lined a run-scoring triple in the fourth and then unloaded a two-run double in the fifth.

The Nationals refused to roll over, for in their half of the fifth they scored three runs and kayoed Red Ruffing before he could retire a single batter. But Mel Harder came in and shut the door on the senior circuit almost completely. In his five innings on the mound, Master Melvin bottled up the National Leaguers with his mixture of sharp-breaking curves and fastballs. A pitcher was still allowed to go more than three innings in a relief situation. Before Harder began to be plagued by arm trouble in the late 1930s, he was one of the A.L.'s supreme curveball artists.

The Americans went on to score one more run in the sixth and won the game 9–7. Scarcely anyone remembers the 1934 game's final score, however, or even that the A.L. emerged victorious in that slugfest, but no one has forgotten Carl Hubbell's record-breaking pitching performance.

Carl Hubbell, who spent many years as director of player development for the New York-San Francisco Giants after concluding his active career, recently recalled that historic 1934 contest:

> Most people forget that I faced Babe Ruth again in the third inning. The Babe tried like hell to hit one of my screwballs out of the park, but he managed only to top the ball and he grounded out to second base. You could really hear the big guy puff as he swung. That made the third out, and I headed for the clubhouse.
>
> Afterwards, the Americans got six runs in the fifth and licked us, but for those three innings I had the greatest day of my life. One of the writers who kept track told me I'd pitched 27 strikes and 21 balls to 13 men, and only five pitches were hit in fair territory.

Arthur Daley, late Pulitzer Prize-winning sportswriter for *The New York Times,* said of Hubbell's achievement: "The greatest pitching feat in the annals of the sport. . . . That exploit will live as long as baseball does."

Carl Hubbell was elected to the Hall of Fame in 1947, with his bronze plaque at Coopertown recounting those five successive strikeouts in the second All-Star Game. This is highly unusual since most plaques are inscribed with a player's lifetime records and not a single game achievement. But on July 10, 1934 at the Polo Grounds, King Carl, the screwball maestro, did something extra special.

John B. Foster, editor of Spalding's annual *Official Base Ball Guide,* commented in the 1935 edition about the 1934 game, particularly in respect to the rule prohibiting a starting pitcher from going beyond the third inning. Foster wrote:

> There is too much stress laid upon the fact that the game establishes one league's supremacy over the other. The American League has won both that have been played, and won them handily, yet there will always remain a doubt as to whether it might have won the second had Hubbell continued in the box. . . .

It does seem indeed likely that the outcome of the game would have been far different if Hubbell had not been yanked in accordance with the rules. And, as for the All-Star Game being a test of the two leagues' strengths, later critics agreed with Foster on general principle—that it's difficult to make judgments on the basis of a single exhibition contest where so many lineup changes are made.

Finally, *Base Ball Guide* editor John B. Foster stressed that the All-Star Game had succeeded in generating enormous fan interest and should be permanently retained as an annual event. Support for the classic was being assured.

Lefty Gomez Talks about Carl Hubbell and His "Screwball"

Lefty Gomez is more than willing to expound at length on the pitching exploits of his opponent in the 1934 All-Star Game, Carl Hubbell. Gomez reports:

> I don't think I ever saw a pitcher with greater mastery on the mound than Carl Hubbell in that 1934 All-Star Game. Everybody knows that I became Hub's sixth and last strikeout victim . . . at least I went down swinging, though I admit I would have had a helluva time hitting that screwball of his with a snow shovel.
>
> Carl was a pitcher's pitcher . . . we all admired him because he had absolute powers of concentration while working, and he had persevered for years to master pinpoint control.
>
> Maybe those big American League sluggers looked so bad against Hubbell on that July day in '34 because they just weren't used to seeing that murderous kind of a screwball. Let me explain what a "screwball" is . . . this is a pitch thrown with a reverse twist of the wrist which makes the ball break in a direction opposite to that of a normally thrown curveball. Since Carl was a southpaw, the pitch broke in toward a left-handed batter instead of away from him—then against a right-handed hitter, the ball broke away from him instead of into him. Hubbell was especially tough against right-handed swingers who would normally expect to murder a southpaw curveballer.
>
> No one had thrown the so-called "fadeaway" pitch, or "reverse curve," so effectively since Christy Mathewson, and he was a right-hander.
>
> Carl ordinarily relied on his screwball in clutch situations only . . . if he threw it all the time, batters would have gotten used to it and belted the ball all over the lot. But the pitch was new to the American Leaguers, and old Hub got them all tied up in knots.

Early in his career, Hubbell was discouraged from using the screwball at all because throwing the pitch required an unnatural motion and placed a great strain on his arm. When Hubbell was with Detroit in spring training in 1928, George Moriarty, the Tigers' manager, warned him, "Young man, if you persist in throwing that pitch, your days in baseball are numbered. It is certain to ruin your arm."

Well, in the end, Hubbell himself confessed, Moriarty was proved correct. He did ruin his arm throwing the screwball—but not before he established himself as one of the greatest left-handers in baseball history.

5

Foxx Bites: 1935

An army of 69,831 fans—the crowd record still stands—jammed Cleveland's huge Municipal Stadium on the shores of Lake Erie on July 8th, 1935 for the third midseason interleague encounter. The stadium, which had been completed midway through the 1932 season at a cost of $2 million (that sum today is barely enough to cover the cost of some of the big league exploding scoreboards now being constructed), was festively decked out for the occasion.

This was the first year in which the big league managers chose the players for the All-Star rosters. The only significant stricture on their choice was that each league club should be represented on its league team.

Player-managers again guided the All-Stars: Mickey Cochrane of Detroit and the A.L., and Frankie Frisch of St. Louis and the N.L. Though Cochrane and Frisch were on the active rosters of their respective squads, neither felt compelled to insert himself into the game.

Frisch started his own left-hander, Bill Walker, on his way to a so-so 13–8 season's record. At the end of the previous season Walker had lost two games in the 1934 World Series against Detroit.

After retiring the Cleveland Indians' hometown hero, Joe Vosmik, Walker passed Charlie Gehringer. Then Lou Gehrig forced Gehringer. That set the stage for Jimmie Foxx who tattooed one of Walker's fastballs and drove it deep into the left field stands for a two-run homer.

The Americans touched the southpaw for another run in the second inning on a triple by Rollie Hemsley and Joe Cronin's long fly to Wally Berger in center. Right-hander Hal Schumacher struck out five in his four-inning tenure for the Nationals, but yielded the Americans' final tally in the fifth. With two down, Joe Vosmik singled and then raced to third on Gehringer's single. After Gehrig walked, loading the bases, Foxx drove a "frozen rope" single, scoring Vosmik.

As Vosmik touched the plate an ear-splitting roar rose from the fans. Vosmik, a native Clevelander, had been a local sandlot star, and in 1935 he enjoyed his finest season in the majors, hitting .348 (just a point below A.L. batting champion Buddy Myer), while rapping out 216 base hits.

The Nationals averted being blanked when Arky Vaughan doubled to right and eventually scored on Bill Terry's solid single.

Restrictions on how long a starting pitcher could remain in the game had been lifted and Manager Cochrane permitted Lefty Gomez to hurl six full innings before throwing Mel Harder into the fray. In those six innings Gomez performed beautifully, giving up only three hits and striking out four. Mel Harder, another Cleveland Indians' star, responded to the cheers of the hometown rooters by blanking the N.L. in the remaining three innings, on only one hit.

Because Harder had worked five innings in the 1934 contest and Gomez six in this one, the National League insisted on a rule change specifying that no pitcher, starter or reliever, could go more than three frames unless the game went into extra innings.

Mel Harder had emerged as an authentic All-Star pitching hero—in eight innings of work against the National League's toughest hitters, he gave up only two hits and no runs.

The Nationals had now dropped three games in a row in what was then called the "Inter-League All Star Series," and some baseball observers began to wonder if the Americans just might be a wee bit stronger. In his account of the 1935 game in the Spalding *Official Base Ball Guide*, John B. Foster even indicated concern about the senior circuit's spirit. He wrote:

> The National League team that took the field probably was representative of the circuit as a body yet did not play with the fire and ardor that the National League teams have shown in the past.

Lefty Gomez, winning pitcher of the 1935 game, recalls:

> All the players from both leagues were really impressed with the size of the crowd. Nearly 70,000 people paid their way into Municipal Stadium, and remember that we were in the midst of the Great Depression. Most of the players had never seen that many people in a ballpark before, and I know everyone got psyched up and went out to play his best. I got into Cleveland the day before the game, and the whole city seemed to have gone baseball mad . . . everywhere I went

there seemed to be a throbbing of excitement. The All-Star Game was still very new then, and for most people it was their first opportunity to see so many great players on the field at one time.

Remember too that baseball was the dominant professional sport of the 1930s—pro football, for example, was small potatoes at the time—and most sports fans confined their interests to baseball.

Why was this Hall of Fame left-hander so effective against the National League? (Gomez had a 6–0 record against the N.L. in five World Series and posted a 3–1 mark in five All-Star appearances.)

"Because I always had great teams behind me!" was the magnanimous and gentlemanly reply.

6

Joe DiMaggio
Wears Goat Horns: 1936

JOE McCarthy, who eventually managed seven All-Star teams, got into his first game on July 7th, 1936—as a pinch-manager for Mickey Cochrane. "Black Mike," Detroit's fiery catcher-manager, was slated to pilot the A.L. in the contest at Boston's Braves Field, but he suffered a nervous collapse early in June and was sent off to a Wyoming ranch to recuperate.

A major sporting news event had preceded the game: a rookie had been chosen for the American League's starting lineup, a New York Yankee freshman named Joe DiMaggio. No one could deny that the 21-year-old DiMaggio had the potential to become a great ballplayer, but never before had a first-year man been selected for the All-Star squad of either circuit.

Even though the selection was made by the eight American League managers, a lot of eyebrows were raised in baseball circles. It was true enough that DiMaggio did plenty to earn the nod—he'd compiled a robust .358 batting average by All-Star Game time, with 60 RBIs and 11 homers, but the critics clamored that he had spent, after all, barely three months in the majors.

And now the youngster would be invited onto the field with the established stars of the game—stars like Luke Appling, Earl Averill, Ben Chapman, Bill Dickey, Rick Ferrell, Jimmie Foxx, Lou Gehrig, Charlie Gehringer, Goose Goslin, Lefty Grove, Mel Harder, and others of the American League; and shining lights like Rip Collins, Dizzy Dean, Leo Durocher, Gabby Hartnett, Billy Herman, Carl Hubbell, Joe Medwick, Mel Ott, Lon Warneke, and others of the National League.

It had been an unwritten rule that anyone picked as an All-Star should have proved himself in the big leagues over a long period. But Joe Di-Maggio was different, for he came to the Yankees as one of the most highly touted rookies in baseball history. In 1933, in his first full year with the San Francisco Seals as an 18-year-old, he electrified the Pacific Coast League by hitting safely in a record 61 consecutive games, while in 1935, still with the Seals, he batted .398, lashing out 270 hits (exactly 100 for extra bases) in 172 games.

Despite these credentials young Joe was human and couldn't suppress his nervousness before the game because he knew that the spotlight would be directed on him. Manager McCarthy set him in right field and did him the honor of placing him third in the batting order.

National League manager Charlie Grimm named Dizzy Dean, a charter member of the zany St. Louis Cardinals' "Gashouse Gang," as his starting pitcher. Dean, considered the top right-hander in the senior circuit, had won 30 and 28 games in the two previous seasons and was on his way to rolling up 24 victories in 1936. He threw a blazing fastball and a curve that took a mean break.

In the top of the first, Luke Appling worked Dean for a walk. Gehringer popped to the infield and that brought up DiMaggio.

If the tall lean Italian-American boy was the least bit jittery, he certainly didn't show it. He took his widespread stance—a stance that would one day be familiar all over America—dug himself a firm toehold, and fixed an intense gaze on the pitcher. Dean cut loose with a hard fastball, and Joe, anxious to make a good showing, swung hard and hit the ball solidly—but it went on the ground straight to third baseman Pinky Whitney, who grabbed it easily and threw to Billy Herman covering second base to force Appling. Herman pivoted and whipped the ball to Rip Collins at first base to complete the double play. Joe, who possessed racehorse speed, was out by a step.

Lefty Grove, making his first All-Star start, blanked the Nationals in the bottom of the first, with DiMaggio making a nice catch of Billy Herman's slicing drive in right field.

Dean threw another goose egg at the Americans in the second.

Frank Demaree, leading off in the bottom of the second, laid the wood to one of Grove's fastballs and drove it to left for a single. Up came Gabby Hartnett, the line-drive-hitting Chicago Cubs' catcher. Grove, trying to work the corners, ran the count to three and one, and then came in with a fastball straight down the pipe.

Hartnett connected and sent a low liner to DiMag in right. The young man who would be known as the "Yankee Clipper" came racing in; he was sure the ball would carry enough so that he could make a knee-high catch. But the horsehide took a sudden dip, and Joe saw that his only chance now would be to make a shoestring grab. He charged in frantically as the ball kept sinking. It finally hit the grass, skipped through his legs, and rolled all the way to the right field fence.

Before the embarrassed rookie could retrieve the ball and fire it back into the infield, Demaree had scored and Hartnett was perched on third with a fluke triple. To make matters worse, Whitney hoisted a long fly to center, and Hartnett scored easily to give the Nationals a 2-0 lead.

Both teams failed to score in the third, and when the A.L. came to bat in the fourth they found Carl Hubbell himself on the mound. Appling, the first man to face the screwball king, fouled out weakly to left field and came back to the bench grumbling that Hubbell was unhittable.

Gehringer, however, proved that Hub was vulnerable by tagging him for a clothesline single to right.

DiMaggio came to the plate finding exactly the same situation he faced in the first inning: man on first, one out. With the count oh-and-two, he hit the ball smack on the nose, and it traveled high and far into the left field stands, but it was foul. Joe grimaced, and on the next pitch he uppercut too much, sending a high popper to shortstop Leo Durocher. This wasn't turning out to be his day at all. Hubbell got out of the inning unscathed.

Schoolboy Rowe of the Tigers went to the hill for the Americans in the bottom of the fourth and held the Nationals at bay. In the top of the fifth Hubbell put another zero on the scoreboard for the A.L.

In the bottom of the inning Rowe retired the first batter, Hubbell, on a pop to the infield. Rowe then threw Augie Galan a fastball down the middle, and Galan smacked a drive down the right field line—the ball struck the flagpole at the foul line and glanced into the bleachers in foul territory. The ruling giving Galan a homer brought strong protests from the American Leaguers until they were assured that it was a standard ground rule in Braves Field.

Rowe, a bit shaken, tried to work the outside corner on the next hitter, Billy Herman, but Herman went with the pitch and sent a shot into right field. DiMaggio started in, but stopped quickly when he knew he had no chance for this one. The ball dropped some 30 feet in front of him and came skipping to him on a series of bounces. Then it happened again.

The ball struck Joe's glove and popped out. He made a grab for the fallen horsehide and bobbled it as if it were a greased pig. By the time Joe got a firm hold on the ball, Herman had raced to second on the error.

This play drew a bit of scattered booing from the stands, but Joe hoped the fumble would not lead to another run. As luck would have it, however, Joe Medwick singled Herman home with the Nationals' fourth run of the game.

In the A.L. half of the sixth, Hubbell got the first two men, but Gehringer walked, giving DiMaggio a chance to redeem himself. With the count one and one, Hub threw the rookie phenom a breaking pitch, but DiMag committed himself too soon, tried to check his swing, and wound up topping the ball weakly back to the box. Joe, an easy out at first, had now gone 0 for 3.

When the Americans came to bat in the seventh, still trailing 4–0, they breathed a sigh of relief since Carl Hubbell, having pitched his three innings, left the scene and was replaced on the mound by the Chicago Cubs' Curt Davis. Lou Gehrig got the inning off to a rousing start when he greeted Davis with a chair-busting homer into the right field bleachers. Earl Averill grounded out and so did Bill Dickey, pinch-hitting for Rick Ferrell.

With two out the A.L. didn't quit; Goose Goslin beat out an infield roller. Jimmie Foxx followed with a single up the middle, Goslin taking second. George Selkirk walked to load the bases. Luke Appling, on his way to a .388 season's average (the highest ever recorded by a big league shortstop in the twentieth century), rapped a single to center, scoring both Goslin and Foxx. Selkirk stopped at second.

The Nationals' lead was cut to 4–3, and the inning wasn't over yet. As the ever-dangerous Gehringer ambled to the plate, Manager Grimm came in to the pitching mound, gave Davis the hook, and brought in Lon Warneke, an All-Star veteran. Warneke missed in trying to hit the corners and proceeded to walk the Tiger star. Now the bases were loaded with the stage set for Joe DiMaggio to break the game wide open.

Seldom, if ever, in big league history had a rookie been placed in such a pressure situation.

DiMaggio, noted for his coolness under pressure, even as a freshman, was certainly no pushover in the clutch at any time. A hush went over the crowd as the tension built. DiMag, not wanting to prolong the tension any longer than necessary, decided to swing at the first decent pitch.

Sure enough, Warneke's first offering came in belt-high, across the heart of the plate, where the Arkansan really didn't want it—a fat pitch.

Joe swung—and baaaam, he hit the ball right on the nose, sending a line shot toward left center. DiMag had raced just a few steps toward first base when he glanced up and saw shortstop Durocher leap and snag the steaming drive in the webbing of his glove. End of inning and the American League rally.

As Joe trotted out to right field, he thought to himself: "That was my chance to pull the game out of the fire . . . if the ball had been a foot higher, or a couple of feet to the right or left of Durocher, I would have had a hit, maybe one for extra bases. I couldn't have hit the ball any harder."

The game wasn't quite over yet. Mel Harder came in to pitch for the A.L. in the seventh and zipped through the inning without incident. Both teams put men on base in the eighth, but no runs came in. Over the last three All-Star Games, Harder had now hurled ten consecutive scoreless inning.

The Americans went into the top of the ninth still trailing by a single run.

Frank Crosetti, pinch-hitting for Harder, went down on strikes. Luke Appling grounded out, but Gehringer, a tough competitor, drove a double into left field. Up came DiMaggio in another clutch situation. In fact, this was the fifth time Joe had runners on base to drive in. All he wanted to do now was to hit a simple single to knock in Gehringer.

Warneke threw the first pitch way wide, and then nipped the inside corner with the second for a called strike. One-and-one. Now the Arkansas Hummingbird reared back and cut loose with a blazing fastball that had more hop to it than a jack rabbit. DiMag took a hard swing, but cut under the ball, and lifted a high infield popper near the second base bag. Billy Herman camped under it, and, as the ball dropped into his glove, the fans broke out into a sustained cheer for the Nationals. The senior circuit had finally come through with its first victory.

DiMaggio was understandably disconsolate after the game. Yet as reporters fired questions at him in the clubhouse, he answered coolly, "I just didn't have any luck out there today."

Joe never let one bad game get him down. He helped lead the Yankees to the pennant and World Series title in 1936, driving in 125 runs during the regular season and batting .346 in the fall classic.

Joe DiMaggio's accomplishments on the diamond are too numerous to recount here, but suffice it to say that a few years ago America's sportswriters voted him as baseball's "Greatest Living Ex-Player."

And the 1936 All-Star Game certainly proved one thing—even the greatest star can have an off day at any time. That's a major reason why baseball has such enormous appeal—the element of unpredictability.

The attendance at the 1936 game, unfortunately, fell to 25,556, a great contrast to the record-breaking crowd of nearly 70,000 at Cleveland the year before. The disappointing turnout was traced to unwise press and radio publicity which made the fans of Boston believe that it would be impossible for them to get tickets if they went to the park. The mix-up resulted in more than 12,000 seats sitting empty.

The Downfall
of Dizzy Dean:
1937

THE 1937 All-Star contest, staged at Griffith Stadium, Washington, D.C., was preceded by elaborate pregame ceremonies which featured President Franklin D. Roosevelt being driven onto the field in an open car. An array of cabinet officers, members of congress, foreign diplomats, and other assorted dignitaries were also in attendance. A delegation of Boy Scouts, attending the first National Jamboree in Washington, assisted in the impressive flag-raising.

This was the year in which the All-Star managers, Joe McCarthy of the Yankees and Bill Terry of the Giants, were given carte blanche to choose their entire All-Star rosters. McCarthy didn't skimp either when it came to his world-champion New York Yankees. He picked five of them as starters: Lou Gehrig, Red Rolfe, Joe DiMaggio, Bill Dickey, and Lefty Gomez. All but Gomez played the full nine innings.

For the first two frames the game was a pitchers' battle as Gomez and Dizzy Dean, making his second consecutive All-Star start for the N.L., traded shutout innings.

Dean retired the first two batters in the third, but then Joe DiMaggio banged out his first All-Star hit, a line single. Facing Lou Gehrig, Dean ran the count to three-and-two and then shook off a call by catcher Gabby Hartnett. Throwing a fastball instead of the sharp breaker, Dean watched Gehrig blast it way over the right field fence, a wallop that measured some 450 feet. Gehrig was no man to fool with. Still at the peak of his career, he had smashed 49 homers the year before and for 1937 was headed for a .351 season average with 159 RBIs.

Obviously miffed with himself, Dizzy tried to fog one past Earl Averill. The "Rock of Snohomish" was expecting a fast one and rifled it back to the box. The ball struck Dean on the left foot and bounded away. Dean chased it down and nipped Averill on a close play, but when he reached the clubhouse he discovered his big toe was broken.

That play proved to be the turning point in Dean's career. He began pitching again long before the injury healed completely, and in doing so he was forced to change his motion. That placed an unnatural strain on his right arm and shoulder and he lost his great speed.

Dean was traded to the Cubs in 1938 and helped them win a pennant with his 7–1 record as a spot pitcher, but he had to depend on his new "dipsey doodle" pitch and sheer cunning. After that he hung on for a while, but by the time he was 30 his big league days were over—he was retired because of his lame arm. His struggle to recover was unavailing, and he never came close to regaining the fastball which had terrified batters.

In the top of the fourth the Nationals picked up a run to bring the score to 2–1. Then Carl Hubbell came in to pitch for the N.L. in the bottom of the frame, and, as he strode to the mound, the crowd gave him a hero's ovation. But this time Hub was to really get roughed up. Cronin led off peacefully enough by fouling out to left field, but then Dickey walked, nearly taking the fourth ball in the head. Then he scampered to third on Sammy West's single to center. Bridges fanned. Then Red Rolfe lashed a triple to the scoreboard in right center, scoring Dickey and West. Gehringer rapped a line single past first baseman Johnny Mize, scoring Rolfe and erasing Hubbell from the game. Three runs had crossed the plate, and the A.L. now led by a more comfortable 5–1.

Manager Terry called in Cy Blanton, and the Pittsburgh right-hander struck out DiMaggio to retire the side.

Hubbell's streak of eight scoreless innings against the Americans over the stretch of three All-Star games had come to a crashing end. Still at his peak in 1937, he went on to win more than 20 games for the fifth year in a row.

The A.L. notched a single run in the fifth against Lee Grissom of the Reds and then concluded the assault with a brace of runs against the Dodgers' Van Mungo in the sixth. The big blow in the sixth was Lou Gehrig's double which brought in both markers. Gehrig easily took batting honors with his four RBIs.

Joe Medwick collected four hits (two doubles and two singles) in a losing cause. "Ducky" was the first player to pound out that many hits in a single All-Star contest and the only one to do it until 1946 when Ted Williams also had four.

Tommy Bridges of Detroit, who pitched the middle three innings for the A.L., got belted for three runs and seven hits, but Mel Harder came in for the final three and held his opponents scoreless. The National

League went down to defeat, 8–3. Master Melvin did give up five scattered hits, but he toughed it out in the pinches and boosted his four-game All-Star pitching performance to 13 straight scoreless innings, a record.

Though Harder enjoyed several good years after 1937, he was never picked for another All-Star squad.

Jim "Doc" Ewell, who had spent 17 years as the Houston Astros' chief trainer before retiring in 1979, was happy to talk about the Dizzy Dean case recently:

Dean, unfortunately, took the old hard-nosed attitude and made the cardinal error of getting back into action long before he was physically ready. We can't really blame Dizzy for the mistake. It just wasn't the fashion in those days to sit out too many games with an injury . . . the idea was to grab a bat or glove and run out onto the field, no matter what.

Don't forget that Dean was only 26 at the time of the accident, and you'd assume that the club management also had a responsibility to keep a close eye on him during the recovery process. However, I doubt we'll see Dizzy Dean-type cases today because we've added a lot of sophistication to our training techniques . . . and within the past several decades intelligent conditioning principles have taken firm hold in the major leagues.

Take the case of Mark Fidrych. There's a million-dollar pitcher who came up with serious arm and shoulder problems. The Detroit Tigers' brass is trying to get him back into the groove, but they keep watching him like a hawk . . . he can't even pick up a ball without getting permission. He always has a coach tailing him. If a pitching coach had really looked closely at Dean trying to throw after that All-Star Game, he would have known something was wrong.

Cesar Cedeno sometimes gets a bad rap from the writers for sitting out a game or two. They think he may be dogging it . . . not true. Cesar plays as hard as anyone I've seen in 40 years of baseball. . . . He runs into walls, slides hard into bases, jams fingers, and all the rest of it. Reporters who charge him with "malingering" don't see the bruises under his uniform.

We never let Cesar Cedeno, or any other player, get into a game unless they're right physically. Why should we take needless chances with a $4-million ballplayer? It's crazy to play hurt and ruin a career.

Sure, Dizzy Dean won 150 games in the majors, but if he had been made to wait awhile longer after getting hit by that batted ball, maybe he could have won 300.

8

Durocher Bunts
a "Homer": 1938

WITH losses in four of the first five All-Star Games, the National League kept hearing it might be "second-class," and so Manager Bill Terry decided to go all out to win the July 6th, 1938 contest played at Cincinnati's Crosley Field. Unlike his course in the 1934 and 1937 match-ups, Terry did not feel obliged to turn the game into an exhibition of National League stars. Save for the pitchers, he stuck with his starting lineup, using only 12 players.

Terry chose John Vander Meer as his starting pitcher; the 23-year-old Reds' left-hander was then the most talked about hurler in all of baseball. Only a few short weeks before the All-Star break, Vander Meer had startled the sports world by throwing two consecutive no-hit, no-run games: on June 11 at Cincinnati, the "Dutch Master" spun his magic against the Boston Braves, and four days later at Brooklyn (in New York City's first night game), he became the first and only pitcher in major league history to fashion back-to-back no-hitters.

Lefty Gomez made his fifth All-Star start for the American League and pitched a strong three innings; the only run he yielded crossed the plate the first inning as a result of a booted ground ball by shortstop Joe Cronin.

Vander Meer didn't disappoint the home fans when he pitched three scoreless innings while giving up a single hit.

Manager Joe McCarthy threw Johnny Allen into the fray for the middle three innings, and the Cleveland Indians' right-hander gave up a legitimate run in the fourth when Mel Ott tripled and rode home on Ernie Lombardi's single.

Lefty Grove, now 38 years old, but still effective and having a good year with the Boston Red Sox, came in to hurl for the Americans in the seventh. The Nationals jumped on him for two quick runs, but both were unearned and resulted from one of the most outlandish plays in All-Star history.

Frank McCormick greeted Grove with a sharp single, and Leo Durocher was ordered to sacrifice. Bill Terry wanted to play for the one run since the N.L. led by only two. Durocher laid down a good bunt along the third base foul line. Jimmie Foxx, playing third (Foxx, normally a first baseman, played third base in several All-Star games so he and Lou Gehrig could both be in the lineup), came charging in, made a nice pickup, and threw accurately to first, but Gehringer failed to cover, and the ball sailed into right field. (Foxx was charged with the error.) Joe DiMaggio retrieved the errant ball, and, in trying to nail McCormick at the plate, he heaved it over Bill Dickey's head and into the National League dugout. Durocher kept pedaling around the bases as the horsehide kept rolling around hither and yon, and crossed the plate on his bunt "home run."

N.L. coach Casey Stengel (he was then employed as manager of the Boston Braves) scooped up the ball from the dugout floor and in almost the same motion threw it into a bucket of ice water, remarking, "This one is just too hot to handle."

The Americans couldn't do a thing with Big Bill Lee, who came in to pitch the middle three innings for the Nationals. Lee, on his way to a 22–9 year, permitted only one hit while on the mound.

Terry called upon Mace Brown, ace Pittsburgh Pirates' reliever, to keep the A.L. bats in check the rest of the way. Brown threw a goose egg in the eighth, but ran into big trouble in the ninth.

DiMaggio opened the inning with a single. Medwick then brought the crowd to its feet with a sensational catch of Dickey's long drive toward the scoreboard in left center. Cronin came through with a long hard double to left, scoring DiMaggio. Gehrig teed off on a Mace Brown fastball and hit a smoking line drive which Ival Goodman reached and snagged near the right field bleachers. Cronin moved to third easily after the catch. Bob Johnson batted for Grove and struck out to end the game.

Final score—Nationals 4, Americans 1.

Brown was pasted around good by the A.L. in the ninth, but he was saved from major embarrassment by the work of his outfielders, and was lucky to escape with only one run scored.

Vander Meer was given credit for the victory, while Gomez took the loss, really a tough one for him. This broke Lefty's All-Star winning streak at three games. No other pitcher in the long history of the dream game has won more than two, consecutive or otherwise.

9

Rapid Robert
Rescues
Damn Yankees:
1939

BECAUSE 1939 was baseball's centennial year, Connie Mack was to manage the American League All-Stars (never mind that Connie's 1938 Philadelphia Athletics had finished dead last), but because of illness he was forced to withdraw at the last minute in favor of Joe McCarthy. After all, Marse Joe's New York Yankees were top dogs in baseball, having clobbered the Chicago Cubs four straight in the 1938 World Series.

Yankee Stadium was specially chosen for the 1939 contest because this was the year of the New York World's Fair. The midsummer classic and the World's Fair made an excellent combination, garnering the paid attendance of 62,892, second highest in All-Star history up to that point. Baseball Commissioner Kenesaw Mountain Landis wanted the largest possible crowd, since a substantial amount of revenue was required to replenish various funds organized for the relief of indigent baseball men.

When the American Leaguers took to the field in the top of the first inning, it seemed almost as if the Nationals had to take on the New York Yankees. Marse Joe had gone and named six of his own boys to the starting lineup: Red Rolfe, Joe DiMaggio, Bill Dickey, George Selkirk, Joe Gordon, and Red Ruffing. Joe had three more Yankees sitting on the bench—shortstop Frank Crosetti and pitchers Lefty Gomez and Johnny Murphy—but for some reason he couldn't work them into the game.

After the public address announcer introduced the six starting Yankees, an inebriated fan with National League sympathies was moved to remark: "That isn't fair. They ought to make Joe McCarthy play an All-Star American League team. We can beat them, but we can't beat the Yankees."

Still, the N.L. broke out on top in the third when it scored a run off Ruffing on singles by Arky Vaughan and Stan Hack plus Lonnie Frey's line double.

The American Leaguers were handcuffed by Paul Derringer, who allowed only two harmless hits in his three-inning stint, but they got to Bill Lee for a couple of tallies in the fourth. With one gone, Dickey walked and Hank Greenberg singled. Another one-baser by Selkirk brought in the first run, and Greenberg subsequently crossed the plate when Vaughan fumbled Gordon's grounder.

Joe DiMaggio closed the scoring for the day in the fifth inning when he poled a mammoth 450-foot home run into the left field stands. That, incidentally, was Joe's only homer in 11 All-Star Games.

The big hero for the American League turned out to be Bob Feller, Cleveland's 20-year-old strikeout king, making his first All-Star appearance. McCarthy called on Feller to take over in a tight spot in the sixth inning. The bases were loaded with one out and the dangerous Arky Vaughan at bat when Bob relieved Tommy Bridges. Vaughan swung at Feller's first pitch and grounded into a fast double play, from Gordon to Cronin to Greenberg. One pitch and the game was saved for the A.L. Rapid Robert remained on the mound for the final three innings and allowed only one hit, a single by Mel Ott in the ninth.

Feller said recently of his confrontation with Vaughan: "That really wasn't a good fastball I threw. . . . I wasn't warmed up properly and felt tight in the shoulders and back, but Vaughan cut at it and rapped the ball straight at Gordon. Luck was with me that day."

Tommy Bridges received credit for the victory, while Bill Lee, who gave up all three of the A.L. runs, was tagged with the loss.

Lou Gehrig, who had played in his last All-Star Game the year before, was named an honorary member of the 1939 team and sat on the American League bench during the game.

10

Two
All-Star Games:
1940

A Winter Game for a Winter War

THERE were two All-Star Games in 1940: one was played during the winter and the other in the summer. The winter affair was staged on March 17 at Tampa's Plant Field for the benefit of the Finnish Relief Fund headed by ex-President Herbert Hoover. (Fund drives to aid Finland in its "Winter War" against Russia were, in fact, conducted throughout the country.) The contest attracted 13,180, the largest crowd that had yet seen a baseball game in Florida, and nearly $20,000 was raised for the relief fund.

The Tampa game was patterned after the midsummer games, and the lineups used were nearly the same as those employed in the 1939 match-up in Yankee Stadium. Players from the 16 major league clubs came to Tampa from eleven spring training sites in Florida and from five in California and Texas. Joe McCarthy piloted the Americans, while Bill McKechnie, manager of the 1939 pennant-winning Cincinnati Reds, took charge of the Nationals.

The game was knotted at 1–1 in the top of the ninth when Brooklyn's Pete Coscarart rapped a single, scoring Boston's Al Lopez from third base. The A.L. couldn't do anything in their half of the ninth and took a 2–1 loss.

The Giants' Harry Gumbert gained credit for the victory, while Bob Feller, who gave up the winning run, was charged with the defeat.

The First Shutout

National League hitters didn't waste any time getting started in the July 9th, 1940 contest played at Sportsman's Park in St. Louis. After Arky Vaughan and Bill Herman opened with sharp singles off Red Ruffing in the first stanza, Max West powered a long homer into the right-center field bleachers.

Johnny Mize flied to Ted Williams in left, Ernie Lombardi singled to center, but Ruffing got Joe Medwick and Cookie Lavagetto to pop out to end the inning.

The hard-throwing New York Yankees' right-hander, winner of 20 or more games the previous four seasons, sailed through the next two innings unscathed, but the damage was already done.

The Nationals wrapped up their scoring with a single run off Bob Feller in the eighth when Mel Ott walked, advanced to second on Frank McCormick's sacrifice, and came home on Harry Danning's line single to right field. In his two innings of work, Feller did strike out three, but he was a bit wild, walking two and hitting a batter.

Buck Newsom, who hurled the middle three innings, kept the National League attack well bottled up, giving up a lone hit, a single by Billy Herman in the fifth.

In the meantime, the American League sluggers were unable to produce a single run, and with a 4–0 verdict went into the record books as the first All-Star team to suffer a shutout. The A.L. could manage only three hits—also a record low—two by Luke Appling, a double and a single, while Newsom tried to help his own cause with a single.

The crafty Bill McKechnie, calling the shots for the N.L., threw five pitchers into the battle to achieve the shutout. He started the game with Paul Derringer and Bucky Walters, his Red aces, and followed with Whitlow Wyatt of the Dodgers, Larry French of the Cubs, and Carl Hubbell of the Giants. The first four twirlers went two innings each, while King Carl mopped up in the ninth. This was Hubbell's fifth and final appearance in All-Star competition, and he bowed out in grand style.

McKechnie's crystal ball seemed to be working when he had a "hunch" and made a last minute switch in his lineup to include Max West in right field in place of Mel Ott. It was West's three-run blow in the first inning, of course, that proved to be the game's decisive factor.

In the following inning, West ran into the wall and crumpled while trying to make a leaping catch of Appling's drive that went for a double. Max had to be assisted to the clubhouse, but the injury was not serious.

Reverting to earlier National League practice, McKechnie tried to trot out all his stars, using exactly 22 players. Terry Moore, familiar with the Sportsman's Park outfield, was the only National Leaguer to play the entire contest.

In a curious move, Joe Cronin was named the 1940 A.L. All-Star pilot because league officials reasoned that Joe McCarthy had held the job too long—this despite the fact that the 1939 New York Yankees were world champions.

Cronin used 18 players and started a lineup that included five Yankees. Jimmie Foxx, playing in his seventh straight All-Star Game, and Joe DiMaggio were the only American Leaguers to go the full route.

Manager Cronin was sharply criticized for not using shortstop Lou Boudreau and second baseman Ray Mack, Cleveland's great double play combination, until the final inning.

11

The Saga of
a Third-Story
Man: 1941

THE 1941 All-Star Game, staged at Briggs Stadium in Detroit, began slowly and gathered steam as it went along.

American League pilot Del Baker had his choice made for him when it came to picking a starting pitcher. The only logical call was for Bob Feller, who was absolutely the hottest hurler in the majors. Winner of 27 games the previous season, the 22-year-old Feller had piled up 16 victories by the All-Star break.

In his three innings work against the National Leaguers, the former Iowa farmboy gave up one harmless hit, walked none, and struck out four as he worked his fastball-curveball combination beautifully.

Wily old Bill McKechnie, who led his Cincinnati Reds to a world championship in 1940, stuck with his procedure of using the N.L. pitchers in two-inning relays—each moundsman was supposed to be at his blazing best for that short stretch.

Starter Whitlow Wyatt didn't disappoint Deacon McKechnie: he didn't allow a hit in his two innings. The only man to get on base was Ted Williams who walked in the second. Williams, the talk of the baseball world in 1941, was hitting well over .400 at the All-Star break (his average was as high as .436 in mid-June) and would finish the season at .406, the last man in the majors to bat .400.

Thornton "Lefty" Lee of the Chicago White Sox blanked the Nationals in the fourth, while the Americans picked up their first run in their half of the inning. Cecil Travis drilled a long double into center field, Joe DiMaggio flied out to Pete Reiser in center, and then Williams lined a double to right, scoring Travis. Right fielder Bob Elliot appeared ready to make the catch on Williams's drive, but he slipped and fell, and the ball bounded by him.

The two teams traded runs in the sixth. Pitcher Bucky Walters, a former infielder, opened the inning by slamming a double down the third base line, and Stan Hack laid down a perfect sacrifice bunt to move Walters to third.

Terry Moore sent a high fly out to Williams in medium-deep left field. Ted camped under the ball, made the catch easily, and rifled a quick throw to the plate in an attempt to catch Walters, who had tagged up at third. But the throw was a little wide, and Walters slid in safely. If the peg had been on the money, the story might have been different.

In the bottom of the sixth, Travis, the leadoff man, lined to Billy Herman at second. DiMaggio worked Walters for a walk—the Reds ace may have been a bit tired after running the bases. Williams, anxious to break the game open, took a mighty cut at Walters's first offering. But he hit under it and lofted a very high soft fly to Reiser in short center. Ted, disgusted with himself, stormed back to the dugout.

Lou Boudreau salvaged the inning for the Americans by drilling a single to center that scored DiMaggio. The A.L. now led 2–1.

In the seventh the Nationals came battling back as Sid Hudson took over the junior circuit's pitching chores. Enos Slaughter led off with a smoking line drive single to left. Williams moved in a few steps, got positioned to pick up the ball, and then booted it. It took a crazy bounce to one side, and before Ted could retrieve it and make the throw back to the infield, Slaughter was standing on second.

At that moment "Timber Ted" wasn't feeling too good about his performance so far in the game: he had made a bad throw to the plate, committed an error on Slaughter's hit, and got his only hit because an outfielder fell down. While Williams was pondering his misfortunes, Arky Vaughan caught hold of one of Hudson's fastballs and bashed it into the upper right field stands. Two runs across and the N.L. now led 3–2.

Williams felt a lot worse now, and so did the American League rooters.

Claude Passeau, the big Chicago Cubs' right-hander, took the mound for the N.L. in the seventh and retired the side without incident.

Edgar Smith, stocky little Chicago White Sox left-hander, arrived on the scene in the top of the eighth and started off with a bang by fanning Pete Reiser. Johnny Mize then lined a wicked double off the right field screen. Smith was supposed to be deadly against left-handed hitters, but no one told Mize about it. Slaughter struck out, and up came Vaughan.

And Vaughan promptly homered again, this shot also landing in the upper deck of the right field stands. The Nationals with their 5–2 lead appeared to have the game in the bag. Vaughan, who became the first man in All-Star history to hit two homers in one game, looked like he had emerged as the day's big hero with his four RBIs. Oddly enough, Vaughan was not noted as a home run slugger—during the entire 1941 regular season he hit only six times for the circuit.

In the last of the eighth Joe DiMaggio kept American League hopes glimmering when he doubled with one away. It was now up to Ted Williams to do something.

Passeau, a control artist who knew how to mix up his offerings, bent a curve over the inside corner for a called strike. Ted stepped out of the box, stepped back in, and waited for what seemed like an eternity before the slow-working Passeau threw again. The Cubs' ace finally released the ball—another curve that cut the inside corner of the plate as Williams watched without making a move.

"Steee-rike two!" boomed plate umpire Bill Summers.

Ted grimaced, waved his bat several times, and made up his mind to swing at the next pitch if it came anywhere near the plate. Passeau went into a full windup and threw a blazing fastball right down the middle. Williams took a long powerful swing—and missed. The mighty Boston slugger had struck out.

All was not lost, though, for Dom DiMaggio, rising young Red Sox star, came up and singled to drive in older brother Joe with the A.L.'s third run. This marked the first time two brothers appeared in the same All-Star Game.

Edgar Smith got all his best pitches together and blanked the Nationals in the ninth.

The Americans definitely had their "backs up against the wall" in the bottom of the ninth, and the situation grew worse as leadoff man Frank Hayes popped up to second. But Kenny Keltner, batting for pitcher Smith, bounced a scratch single off shortstop Eddie Miller's glove. Joe Gordon kept things going by lining a single to right, Keltner stopping at second. Travis walked, filling the bases. Joe DiMaggio stepped into the batter's box as Williams moved to the on-deck circle. Passeau was getting himself into big trouble.

Passeau's first pitch, a fastball, nipped the outside corner for a called strike. He followed with a sharp-breaking curve that Joe swung at and missed. The pressure was now on the Yankee Clipper with a zero and two count.

The next pitch came in, and DiMag swung, and this time he got some wood on it. But the ball, a hot grounder, headed straight for shortstop Eddie Miller, one of the best infielders in the business. It looked like a sure double play ball.

Miller picked up the routine grounder easily and tossed it to Herman to force Travis at second. Then the Americans got their break of the day. Herman pivoted, and in hurrying his relay, when he really didn't have to, he threw to the inside of first base. Frank McCormick, the first sacker, lunged desperately for the ball, but succeeded only in knocking it down. DiMaggio made it to first, Keltner scored, and Gordon advanced to third. The stage was now set for Williams, who had been handed the extra turn at bat because of the bad play.

With runners on base, Passeau took a short stretch and threw the first ball inside. Ted, irritated because he saw spectators inching toward the exits, fouled off the next one, and then took the third pitch for another ball. With the count two and one the veteran right-hander sent a blistering fastball right down the pipe, just above the knees—on a similar pitch the previous inning, Ted had struck out.

This time the "Splendid Splinter" made direct contact, and, as the sharp crack of the bat resounded through Briggs Stadium, those spectators heading for the exits stopped dead in their tracks and watched the ball zoom like a rocket. It kept climbing and climbing and didn't stop until it crashed against the facade atop the stadium's third tier. Gordon and DiMaggio scored ahead of Williams to give the American League its dramatic come-from-behind 7–5 victory.

Manager Del Baker, ordinarily a reserved man, couldn't contain his excitement and gave the grinning Williams both a bear hug and a kiss. Wild jubilation also reigned in the A.L. clubhouse—and never before or since has an All-Star Game been concluded in such a spectacular fashion.

A sportswriter working in the Briggs Stadium press box that historic day commented: "Williams's ball traveled a good 450 feet before it hit the third tier, but unobstructed I'm sure it would have gone over 500 feet. I've never seen a baseball hit harder—not even by Babe Ruth.

"When it comes to hitting, Ted has the most perfect coordination of any batter in baseball. He puts absolutely his whole body into the swing, including his ass."

The entire proceeds of the 1941 game went to the United Service Organizations (U.S.O.), a privately funded group devoted to the needs of American servicemen and servicewomen.

12

Baseball
Goes to
War

WHEN the United States entered World War II in December 1941, many high-ranking baseball officials felt that the major leagues would have to suspend operations for the duration of the hostilities. Shortly after the devastating loss of capital ships at Pearl Harbor, Baseball Commissioner K. M. Landis wrote to President Franklin Roosevelt asking if the government wanted the ball parks to remain open.

On January 15, 1942, the President replied, stating in part: "I honestly feel it would be best for the country to keep baseball going. . . . These players are a definite recreational asset to their fellow citizens—and that, in my judgment, is thoroughly worthwhile."

President Roosevelt's answer was accepted as a "green light" for baseball to carry on and provide diversion and relaxation from the strains and pressures of world conflict for millions contributing to the war effort in plants turning out munitions, ships, planes, tanks, and other materiel. It was made clear that Roosevelt, an ardent fan himself, approved the continuation only so long as baseball was able to keep operating with the player personnel that remained—no player was to be given any kind of exemption from the national draft.

The All-Star series was also allowed to continue, and games were played in 1942, 1943, and 1944. However, because of severe wartime travel restrictions, the 1945 game was cancelled.

The overall quality of major league baseball during the 1942 season wasn't seriously affected because the pool of player talent remained large. But by 1943 the draft had siphoned off substantial numbers of the top stars, and for the rest of the war the caliber of big league play was decidedly subpar.

Rosters of all teams from 1943 through 1945 consisted in large part of physically disqualified 4Fs, veterans past the draft age, and 17- to 18-year-old recruits. But baseball kept going, and games in both circuits were well attended despite the inferior quality of the product. War workers had plenty of money to spend, and they generously patronized all professional sports.

Bombed in the First: 1942

The 1942 All-Star Game, a twilight affair, was originally scheduled for Brooklyn's Ebbets Field, but since the net proceeds were earmarked for various war charities, Dodger president Larry MacPhail permitted the contest to be switched to the Polo Grounds because of its larger crowd capacity. The Polo Grounds thus became the first park in the big leagues to accommodate a second All-Star match-up.

The paid attendance of 34,178 fell well below expectations, but there were extenuating circumstances. Afternoon showers fell in New York, and shortly before the scheduled 6 P.M. game time a sudden cloudburst hit the Polo Grounds. The downpour all but wrecked the sale of unreserved seats.

The game finally started at 7:22 P.M., and N.L. starting pitcher Mort Cooper, who had been warming up nearly two hours before, needed to loosen up all over again. The long delay obviously had an adverse effect on the St. Louis Cardinals' ace, because he got belted in the first inning.

Leadoff man Lou Boudreau picked on Cooper's second pitch and whacked it into the upper left field stands for a homer. Tommy Henrich followed with a double, and then Cooper managed to retire Ted Williams and Joe DiMaggio. But Rudy York caught hold of a curveball and sliced a drive into the lower right field bleachers about five feet inside the foul pole. York scored behind Henrich, giving the A.L. a quick 3–0 lead.

Cooper settled down and blanked the Americans in the second and third innings, while his three successors (Johnny Vander Meer, Claude Passeau, and Bucky Walters) also pitched scoreless ball.

The A.L. actually didn't need any more than those three first-inning runs, for the N.L. managed to dent the plate only once, with that tally coming in the eighth inning on a pinch homer by Mickey Owen. Ironically, Owen didn't hit a single homer in 133 league games that year, nor did he get any in 1943 (106 games), though he finally hit for the circuit once in 1944. There's something about an All-Star Game that can inspire a ballplayer!

Because the winning team was scheduled to play Mickey Cochrane's Service All-Stars in Cleveland the following evening, the three-inning rule for pitchers was waived. Manager Joe McCarthy took advantage of the rule, allowing Spurgeon Chandler to pitch the first four innings and Al Benton the last five. Chandler was particularly effective, giving up only two singles in his stint.

N.L. Manager Leo Durocher didn't work any of his pitchers more than the traditional three innings. Durocher wound up using twice as many players as McCarthy, 22 to 11.

The game was finished barely two minutes before the metropolitan New York area "blackout" began at 9:30. During World War II blackouts were held periodically throughout the country as a civil defense procedure.

Danny Litwhiler, a member of the 1942 National League team, recently recalled the game at the Polo Grounds. (Litwhiler has been head baseball coach at Michigan State University for many years, and one of his prize pupils there was Steve Garvey.) He said:

Durocher called on me to pinch-hit for Johnny Vander Meer in the sixth inning. As I walked to the plate, I was determined to hit the ball some place off Benton. Al threw a high inside fastball, and I swung a little late but connected pretty good and hit a drive over the second baseman's head for a single. That happened nearly 40 years ago, but it seems like yesterday.

Danny ranks his 1942 All-Star hit as one of the highlights of his 15-year professional career, along with his homer in the 1944 World Series for the St. Louis Cardinals.

At Cleveland on July 7, the American League All-Stars defeated Mickey Cochrane's Service All-Stars 5–0. Cochrane's team consisted mostly of top-notch big leaguers who were serving in the army and navy. Jim Bagby, Jr. received credit for the victory, while Bob Feller, in the midst of a three-and-a-half year tour of duty with the navy at the time, took the loss.

The game attracted a paid crowd of 62,094 besides several thousand servicemen who were admitted free. Well over $100,000 was raised for the Army-Navy Relief Fund and for the Ball and Bat Fund, which provided recreational equipment for U.S. military personnel serving throughout the world.

The First All-Star Night Game: 1943

The 1943 match, played on July 13 at Philadelphia's Shibe Park, made history as the first All-Star contest played entirely at night. Many years later it would become standard procedure for All-Star Games to be played exclusively at night in order to attract the largest possible television audiences, and even weekday World Series games eventually became nocturnal affairs for the same reason.

Irked by constant criticism that he favored his own players, A.L. skipper Joe McCarthy elected not to use any of his five Yankees who qualified for the squad—Ernie Bonham, Spud Chandler, Bill Dickey, Joe Gordon, and Johnny Lindell all sat on the bench for the entire game. Yankee Charlie Keller also qualified for the team, but because of an injury he was replaced at the last minute by Detroit's Dick Wakefield. No matter, even if Charlie had suited up, he wouldn't have played anyway.

McCarthy proved that the Americans minus the Yankees were no patsies as he directed his forces to victory, the A.L.'s eighth triumph in eleven games.

The Nationals touched Dutch Leonard, Washington's star knuckleballer, for a run in the top of the first. Stan Hack singled over second, and Billy Herman singled to left, sending Hack to third. Stan Musial (appearing in the first of his 24 All-Star Games) flied deep to Chet Laabs in center, Hack scoring after the catch.

Mort Cooper, starting his second straight game for the N.L., went through the first inning without mishap, but blew his slim one-run lead and got belted around in the second and third stanzas.

With one out in the second, Cooper walked Laabs and Jake Early. Bobby Doerr, batting eighth, caught hold of a fastball and drove it into the lower left field stands for a three-run homer, setting up an A.L. lead that held through the remainder of the game. Leonard followed with a single to right, but George Case grounded into a double play, Hack to Herman to Elbie Fletcher.

Cooper still was shaky in the third as Ken Keltner and Wakefield, the first two batters, both doubled. Keltner scored on Wakefield's blow. After Vern Stephens sacrificed Wakefield to third, Manager Billy Southworth derricked Cooper in favor of Johnny Vander Meer. The Reds' lefthander fanned both Rudy York and Chet Laabs to end the inning.

Vander Meer, pitching two and two-thirds innings, struck out six (that tied Carl Hubbell's All-Star record for most strikeouts in one game), but was on the mound when the Americans scored their fifth run in the fifth inning. Case, the leadoff man, walked, and then Vandy got Keltner and Wakefield on strikes. Stephens singled, sending Case to third. With York up, a double steal was tried, and Case scored when Herman uncorked a wild return throw to the plate. The inning ended when York became Vander Meer's sixth strikeout victim.

Vince DiMaggio, who came into the game in the fourth inning as a pinch hitter, turned out to be the Nationals' batting hero as he singled, tripled, and homered in three attempts. After nicking Hal Newhouser for a single in the fourth, Vince, the eldest of the DiMaggio brothers to make the big leagues, led off the seventh by tripling against the left field wall off a delivery by Tex Hughson. He scored on Dixie Walker's long fly to left field. Leading off against Hughson again in the ninth, DiMaggio blasted a towering homer into the upper left field seats.

That made the final tally 5–3, since the Americans failed to score against Rip Sewell or Al Javery, who worked the final three innings for the Nationals.

In going three for three, Vince established the DiMaggio family record for most hits in a single All-Star Game—Joe and Dom never had more than two.

Just over $65,000 from net gate receipts was donated to the Ball and Bat Fund, and the fund was enriched by another $50,000 from the following sources: $25,000 from the Gillette Company for the radio rights, $20,000 from Commissioner Landis's office, and $2,500 from each of the two major leagues.

American fighting men throughout the world had the opportunity to hear the game via shortwave radio.

Cavarretta's Big Day: 1944

The American League started well enough for the 1944 laurels contested on July 11 at Forbes Field in Pittsburgh. The boys from the junior circuit put the game's first run up on the scoreboard in the top of the second inning against the pitching of Bucky Walters.

Leadoff man Ken Keltner singled to left, and when Bobby Doerr grounded out to Connie Ryan at second, Keltner moved up a notch. Keltner took third on Rollie Hemsley's grounder to Marty Marion at shortstop, and then scored on pitcher Hank Borowy's single to center. A classic way of scoring a run!

Borowy fared extremely well on the mound during his three-inning stint as he blanked the Nationals on three hits. Phil Cavarretta did give Borowy a bit of trouble, however—the Chicago Cubs' veteran tripled and walked against the Yankees' right-hander.

Tex Hughson, Borowy's successor, zipped through the fourth inning, but blew sky high in the fifth as the game quickly unraveled for the Americans.

Ryan opened with a single to center, and stole second as Marion struck out. Bill Nicholson doubled down the right field line, scoring Ryan. Augie Galan bounced a single off shortstop Vern Stephens' glove as Nicholson raced across the plate. Cavarretta walked. First baseman

George McQuinn dropped Doerr's throw on Musial's grounder, and that filled the bases. Walker Cooper singled to left, scoring Galan, but Cavarretta was nailed at the plate trying to score, Johnson to Hayes, Musial taking third on the play. Musial scored on Dixie Walker's single to right. At this point Bob Muncrief relieved Hughson and got Elliott to foul out to Johnson. Four runs, five hits, and two errors.

As the game progressed, the Americans' bats were stymied by the Nationals' pitching, while in the seventh the N.L. picked up two more runs against the slants of Hal Newhouser. Cavarretta led off with a single to center, and advanced to second on Musial's sacrifice. Cooper beat out a slow grounder to second, Cavarretta going to third. Walker popped to Stephens. With two out Whitey Kurowski ripped a long double to left center scoring Cavarretta and Cooper.

The Nationals' final run in the eighth came without the benefit of a hit. Marion, leading off, struck out but reached first safely when catcher Hayes missed the third strike. Medwick advanced Marion to second on a sacrifice, and Galan and Cavarretta both walked to fill the bases. Musial flied to Johnson, Marion scoring.

Ken Raffensberger, Rip Sewell, and Jim Tobin, who combined to pitch the final six innings for the Nationals, succeeded in blanking the Americans during that stretch on one hit. The final score read 7–1.

Phil Cavarretta was clearly the senior circuit's offensive hero as he set an All-Star record by reaching base safely five straight times on a triple, single, and three walks. Each of the passes came from a different pitcher: Borowy, Hughson, and Newhouser.

Connie Ryan, who went 2 for 4 and handled eight chances at second base, said recently after recalling the game: "The victory was a sweet one for the National League since we hadn't done too well in All-Star competition up to that point, and the writers kept saying that the Americans had a big edge over us. But we won this one decisively and looked good doing it."

With approximately $76,000 from net gate receipts, including a contribution by Sportservice from concessions, plus $25,000 from the Gillette Company for broadcasting rights, the game produced a hefty $101,000 for the Ball and Bat Fund.

Arch Ward, sports editor of *The Chicago Tribune* originated the idea of the major league All-Star Game. *(The National Baseball Hall of Fame and Museum, Cooperstown, N.Y.)*

(below) Lefty Gomez, high-kicking Yankee left-hander, won baseball's first All-Star Game in 1933. Gomez started and hurled three scoreless innings. He also knocked in the first run of the game.

Connie Mack, veteran Philadelphia Athletics manager, piloted the 1933 American League All-Stars. Lefty Grove, his fireballing ace, shut out the Nationals in the final three innings. *(The National Baseball Hall of Fame and Museum, Cooperstown, N.Y.)*

(right) Babe Ruth, the "Sultan of Swat," smashed the first homer in the All-Star series. His two-run blast in the third inning of the 1933 game at Chicago's Comiskey Park proved to be the winning margin in the American League's 4–2 triumph.

Al Simmons, then with the Chicago White Sox, started in center field for the American League in the first three All-Star contests (1933–34–35). The future Hall of Famer batted .462 in those three games (6 for 13).

(below) Pittsburgh Pirate Hall of Famer Paul Waner batted .333 for his twenty years in the National League, but went 0 for 8 in four All-Star Games. *(The National Baseball Hall of Fame and Museum, Cooperstown, N.Y.)*

(right) Earl Averill of the Indians was the A.L. batting hero in the 1934 game. He lashed a run-scoring triple in the fourth inning and then doubled across two runs more in the fifth. Averill, a .318 hitter in thirteen big league seasons (1929–1941), was embittered because he had to wait until 1975 before he was elected to the Hall of Fame.

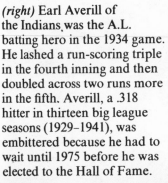

(above) "King Carl" Hubbell, Hall of Fame pitcher with 253 big league victories, is probably best remembered for his performance in the 1934 All-Star Game when he struck out five of the American League's mightiest sluggers in succession: Babe Ruth, Lou Gehrig, Jimmie Foxx, Al Simmons, and Joe Cronin. *(Topps Chewing Gum Co.)*

(right) Jimmie Foxx paced the American League to its 4–1 win in the 1935 game. Then with Philadelphia, Foxx was traded to Boston at the end of the season.

Charlie Gehringer holds the All-Star record for the highest batting average for those players who performed in at least five games. The Hall of Fame second baseman hit an even .500 (10 for 20) in six games, 1933–1938.

(center) Joe Medwick, star outfielder for the St. Louis Cardinals' "Gas House Gang" smacked a three-run homer in the 1934 contest, but it wasn't enough as the N.L. lost 9–7. Medwick spent the later years of his career with the Brooklyn Dodgers. In ten All-Star contests he batted .259 (7 for 27).

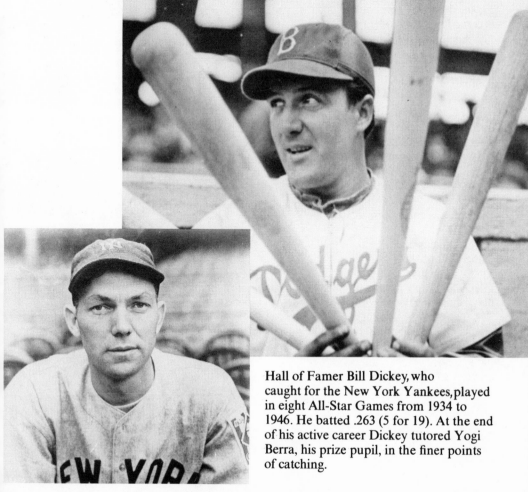

Hall of Famer Bill Dickey, who caught for the New York Yankees, played in eight All-Star Games from 1934 to 1946. He batted .263 (5 for 19). At the end of his active career Dickey tutored Yogi Berra, his prize pupil, in the finer points of catching.

Joe Cronin was the starting American League shortstop in seven games: 1933–35, 1937–39, and 1941. He went on to become league president for 12 years. No ex-player ever held such a high executive position in major league baseball.

(right) Dizzy Dean's career turned sharply downward after his appearance in the 1937 All-Star Game. Earl Averill broke the fastballer's big toe with a hard line drive back to the box. After that, Diz was never the same again.

Nine Yankees were named to the 1939 All-Star squad, a record for one team. Even shortstop Frankie Crosetti, a good fielder but a .233 hitter for the season, was named, though he didn't get into the game. Six Yankees did appear, however, all as starters, and they played a key role in the 3–1 victory.

Although five New York Yankees qualified for the 1943 game, manager Joe McCarthy didn't use a single one of them because he'd been severely criticized for favoring his own players in previous midsummer classics. McCarthy's Americans still beat the Nationals 5–3, with his Yankees riding the bench. "Marse Joe" is seen here in his earlier days as manager of the Chicago Cubs. *(The National Baseball Hall of Fame and Museum, Cooperstown, N.Y.)*

(below right) Paul Derringer, Cincinnati Reds' right-hander, pitched in four All-Star Games and won his only decision in the 1940 contest.

(below left) Lou Boudreau, Cleveland's playing manager, led off the 1942 game at the Polo Grounds with a homer off Mort Cooper. The Americans went on to score two more runs in the opening stanza and that was all they needed for a 3–1 win.

Ted Williams, Boston Red Sox slugger, provided the All-Star Game with some of its greatest moments. His three-run ninth inning homer gave the A.L. its 7-5 win in the 1941 encounter, and his 4 for 4 performance helped destroy the senior circuit 12–0 in 1946. In 18 All-Star Games Williams batted .304 and posted a record 12 RBIs.

(below right) Bobby Doerr led the A.L. to a 5–3 victory in the 1943 game at Philadelphia's Shibe Park by slamming a three-run, second inning homer off Mort Cooper. Doerr, still active in a professional career that began in 1934, is now a coach with the Toronto Blue Jays.

(below left) Johnny Pesky, starting shortstop in the 1946 All-Star Game, calls Ted Williams's performance in that historic Fenway Park encounter, "The greatest one-man exhibition I've ever seen in forty years in baseball."

Johnny Mize became one of the first players to perform in the All-Star Game for both leagues. He saw action with nine N.L. squads from 1937 to 1949 as a member of the St. Louis Cardinals and New York Giants and played for the A.L. in 1953 as a New York Yankee.

In five All-Star Games Ralph Kiner, of the Pittsburgh Pirates and later of the Chicago Cubs, had four hits—one double and three homers. Now a broadcaster for the Mets, Kiner's motto used to be "Home run hitters drive Cadillacs; singles hitters drive Fords."

(above) Jackie Robinson, major league baseball's first black player, appeared in six games from 1949 through 1954. He batted .333 and played well in the field.

(left) Pee Wee Reese, durable Brooklyn Dodger shortstop, went through his first seven All-Star Games without a base hit. In his eighth and final game in 1953 he finally broke the ice and went 2 for 4, helping the N.L. triumph 5–1.

(right) Stan Musial's six home runs in All-Star competition is a record.

Dominic DiMaggio, Joe's younger brother, was a great outfielder in his own right in his decade with the Boston Red Sox. Dom played alongside Joe in several All-Star contests and batted a healthy .353 in six games.

(right) Yogi Berra batted an anemic .195 in fifteen All-Star Games (8 for 41), but he holds most of the fielding records for catchers, including most chances accepted, 68, and most games played.

(below) In four All-Star Games Cincinnati's Ted Kluszewski batted a fat .500 (7 for 14). Yes, "Big Klu" is fully dressed for a game—the 6′ 2″, 240-pound slugger liked to wear no sleeves and frighten opposing pitchers with his massive arms.

Detroit outfielder Al Kaline batted .324 in sixteen All-Star Games and handled 22 chances in the field without an error.

(above right) Al Lopez played in two All-Star Games as a National Leaguer (1934 and 1941) and led the Americans in the midsummer classic three times as a manager (1955 and twice in 1960). As an All-Star manager Lopez was 0 and 3.

(right) Casey Stengel managed in ten All-Star Games between 1950 and 1959, a record. His six losses are also a record. As Yankee manager in ten World Series Stengel did much better, winning seven.

13

The Americans Own
the Postwar
Diamond

Terrible Ted Rips Rip's Eephus: 1946

MAJOR league baseball enjoyed a banner year in 1946 since the big stars were all back from military service, and attendance figures reached record highs as the public's appetite for the diamond sport seemed to be insatiable.

Attendance at big league games in 1946, the first full postwar season, was, in fact, 63 percent greater than in 1945. The American League had just over 9.6 million paid admissions and the National had nearly 9 million. Ten teams had a paid attendance of more than one million, as compared with five in 1945 and none in 1944. No fewer than 12 of the 16 clubs in the two leagues broke their previous attendance records.

In Boston, with stars like Ted Williams, Dom DiMaggio, Bobby Doerr, Johnny Pesky, and Tex Hughson back from the wars, the town went baseball mad. The Red Sox went on to win their first pennant in 28 years, and attendance for the year skyrocketed to just over 1.4 million, or nearly two and one-half times the 1945 level. With a season's record of 104–50, the Bosox, in fact, made a runaway of the 1946 pennant race, finishing 12 full games ahead of the second place Detroit Tigers.

This was clearly Boston's year, with four Red Sox crashing the All-Star starting lineup: Williams, DiMaggio, Doerr, and Pesky. Rudy York and Hal Wagner eventually got into the game, and Dave Ferriss and Mickey Harris were also named to the team. Eight members of the Red Sox on the American League squad!

As luck would have it, Boston was chosen as the locale for the first postwar All-Star Game, and a standing-room-only crowd of nearly

35,000 jammed their way into picturesque old Fenway Park on that hot July 9th afternoon.

Claude Passeau, so well remembered from the 1941 contest at Briggs Stadium, aged 37 and in his fifteenth year of professional baseball, was Manager Charlie Grimm's choice to start on the mound for the N.L.

Passeau got leadoff man Dom DiMaggio to bounce to Mize at first, then Schoendienst tossed out Pesky. Williams walked on a 3–2 pitch, and then Charlie Keller unloaded a homer into the right field stands. Two quick runs for the Americans.

Bob Feller, the A.L. starter, pitched a strong three innings giving up two harmless singles (to Johnny Hopp and Walker Cooper) and striking out three. Passeau settled down in his next two innings and blanked the Americans.

Kirby Higbe went to the box for the Nationals in the fourth, but he ran into a bundle of trouble. Ted Williams, with a count of two-and-one, homed in on one of Higbe's fastballs and bashed a tremendous 425-foot home run into the center field bleachers.

After Higbe got Snuffy Stirnweiss on strikes to start the fifth inning, the roof really caved in on him. Buddy Rosar slashed a single into left and advanced to third on Hal Newhouser's pop fly single into right center. Newhouser took second on Hopp's throw to Whitey Kurowski at third. Stan Spence walked, loading the bases. Vern Stephens drilled a double down the right field line, scoring Rosar and Newhouser. Williams lined a single to left, scoring Spence and sending Stephens to third. At this point Ewell "The Whip" Blackwell relieved Higbe and got the side out without further damage.

With those three runs across the plate in the fifth, the A.L. extended its lead to a fat 6–0.

Blackwell stopped the Americans' offense in the sixth—and in the meantime Newhouser was brilliant in his three innings on the hill, giving up only one hit (a pinch single by Peanuts Lowrey in the sixth), while striking out four.

Ewell "The Whip" continued his magic into the seventh as he retired the first two batters: Sam Chapman flied out to center and Stephens hit a sizzling grounder straight at shortstop Marty Marion. Williams, who obviously carried his rabbit's foot with him this day, scratched a single off Cavarretta's glove at first base. Keller worked the count to three-and-two and walked. Joe Gordon laid into one of Blackwell's crossfire pitches and lashed a double high off the left field wall, scoring Williams and Keller. York popped to Marion on the outfield grass.

The Americans now had an 8–0 bulge.

Rip Sewell took the mound for the Nationals in the eighth and was greeted with a single by Stirnweiss to left. Wagner flied out to Lowrey in deep center, but pitcher Jack Kramer rifled a single off the close left field wall, sending Stirnweiss to third. Chapman flied to Lowrey, Stirnweiss coming home. Stephens scratched a single to second. With two men on, Williams strode up to the plate.

Sewell, a 38-year-old veteran whose professional career dated back to 1931 (he was a two-time 20-game winner for the Pirates), had developed an array of trick pitches, including his celebrated blooper pitch he called an "eephus" ball. The eephus, with its 20- to 25-foot-high arc, came up to the plate like a pop fly. Sewell had the count at one-and-one on Williams when he threw him an eephus ball out of the strike zone. Ted lunged at it and missed by at least a foot. Then Rip challenged Williams with another eephus, and as the ball dropped tantalizingly, Ted ran a couple of steps toward it and blasted the horsehide into the right field bull pen some 400 feet away. He scored behind Stephens and Kramer.

Keller mercifully fouled to catcher Phil Masi to end the inning. Four hits and four runs off Rip Sewell.

Kramer set down the Nationals in order in the ninth. In his three innings on the hill, "Gentleman Jack" allowed no hits, walked one, and struck out three.

The final score read: Americans 12, Nationals 0. This was the soundest thrashing ever administered to either team in the long history of the All-Star classic. The Nationals managed only three singles, and not a man reached third base against Feller, Newhouser, and Kramer, who struck out ten batters between them.

Ted Williams stole the show, of course, in going four for four, and, with his walk, he tied Phil Cavarretta's All-Star record of reaching base safely five consecutive times. His four runs scored has never been equaled, while his record of five RBIs was tied by Al Rosen in 1954. Ted's one-game mark of ten total bases has also never been equaled.

In answering a reporter's question about Williams's homer off his eephus ball, Sewell said: "That was the first homer ever hit off that pitch. And I still don't believe it. What got me most, though, is that he laughed all the way around the bases."

Ted Williams himself later recalled the drama of his long homer off Sewell: "Before that 1946 game I watched Sewell throw some of those bloopers while he was warming up. I remember I was standing in the dugout with Bill Dickey, and I said to Bill, 'Gee, I don't think anyone could ever generate enough power to hit that pitch out of the park.' Nobody ever had. Dickey said the way to do it was to advance a step or two as the ball came toward you. Kind of run at it. That's about what I did. . . ."

After the game Charlie Grimm said of Williams: "That boy is the best hitter I've seen in more than 30 years of baseball." And American League manager Steve O'Neill testified with awe: "This guy doesn't miss one swing in ten. He seldom offers at a bad pitch inside. He has a great natural gift for coordinating mind and muscle. I told Grimm and McKechnie yesterday that they'd be up against the greatest hitter I ever saw. And I've seen Ruth, Cobb, and Jackson."

Pitchers' Battle: 1947

The 1947 game, played at Chicago's Wrigley Field on July 8th before a packed house of more than 41,000, proved to be one of the tightest and most dramatic clashes in All-Star history. Baseball observers were expecting a slugging match. The fact that Wrigley Field had long been known as a hitter's park added to that expectation. The pundits would have to wait for another time for fireworks, though.

The two starting pitchers, Hal Newhouser of the A.L., and Ewell Blackwell of the N.L., were extremely sharp as they matched goose eggs on the scoreboard. Each gave up a single hit—Newhouser fanned two, while Blackwell whiffed four. Those first three innings flew by quickly.

N.L. manager Eddie Dyer called on Harry Brecheen to take over the pitching in the fourth, and "The Cat" responded by throwing another blank at the Americans.

Rookie Frank "Spec" Shea followed Newhouser and retired the first two men to face him, but Johnny Mize got hold of a 1–1 pitch and drove it halfway up into the right field bleachers.

The Americans finally got to Brecheen for a run in the sixth. Luke Appling, batting for Buddy Lewis, singled to left and raced to third when Ted Williams singled to right. Joe DiMaggio picked on Brecheen's first pitch and sent a hot grounder down to shortstop Pee Wee Reese, who turned it into a 6–4–3 double play. Appling scored from third to knot the score at 1–1.

Johnny Sain came in to pitch for the Nationals in the seventh and got leadoff man George McQuinn to ground out to short. Bobby Doerr then singled to left. Taking a long lead off first, Doerr broke for second and had it practically stolen when Sain whirled and threw the ball. It struck Doerr on the back, and, before Reese could retrieve the ball on the outfield grass, Doerr had reached third on the error. Buddy Rosar fanned for the second out.

Stan Spence, batting for pitcher Shea, fell behind in the count at no balls and two strikes, and then drilled a high fastball into center field for a single, Doerr scoring easily with the lead run. That ended the day's scoring with the Americans taking the 2–1 squeaker.

Credit for the victory went to Spec Shea, the first rookie to gain this distinction in All-Star competition.

Lou Boudreau, the Americans' brilliant shortstop, easily emerged as the game's fielding hero as he handled eight chances, four assists, and four putouts, with several of them being classic plays.

In the eighth inning, with Walt Masterson pitching, the Nationals mounted a serious scoring threat, but Boudreau's fielding stopped them. Leadoff man Andy Pafko drove a ground ball deep into the hole at short, with Boudreau making a neat pickup and rifling off the long peg to first, just nailing the runner. Willard Marshall walked. Phil Cavarretta struck out. As the dangerous Johnny Mize strolled to the plate, manager Joe Cronin replaced Masterson with Joe Page, the left-handed New York Yankees' relief ace. Mize promptly singled for his second hit of the game, advancing Marshall to third.

The Nationals now had the tying run on third and the winning run on first with Enos Slaughter, one of baseball's most feared clutch hitters, at bat. He rifled a grounder to the right of second base. Doerr made a heroic but futile effort to reach the ball. Then seemingly out of nowhere the catlike Boudreau appeared. He had crossed to the opposite side of second base, made a diving snag of the ball, whipped it to first, and nipped Slaughter by the proverbial eyelash, ending the inning and snuffing out the Nationals' last challenge.

In a postgame interview, Eddie Dyer, in effect, blamed Johnny Sain for the defeat for allowing Stan Spence to hit the game-winning single. Sain got the two strikes on Spence by keeping the ball low. . . . Dyer, in fact, told him several times, "Don't give him a high one." Sain took a chance anyway with the high pitch that Spence liked, and there went the ball game.

The Americans now led the All-Star series ten games to four and National League executives, especially president Ford Frick, were distraught over the situation. Frick hadn't forgotten about the 12–0 drubbing in 1946, and went so far as to tell the managers and players of his league that unless they took the game more seriously and put forth their best efforts the series would be abandoned.

Walking Wounded Win: 1948

The American League went into the 1948 game, played at Sportsman's Park, St. Louis on July 13, with four of its premier performers hampered by a variety of injuries. Three of the A.L. wounded, who really should have been in the infirmary, made token appearances.

Joe DiMaggio, hobbled by a battered left knee, and Williams, hurting with torn rib cartilage, came in as pinch hitters, while Hal Newhouser, wracked by the pain from bursitis in his left shoulder, saw service as a pinch runner. George Kell, who had a severely sprained ankle, mercifully did not get the call to action.

Manager Bucky Harris surprised everyone when he chose Walt Masterson to start the game. Masterson, the "ace" of the Washington Senators' pitching staff, was on his way toward fashioning an 8–15 season's record. After the first inning, Harris's decision did not look good at all.

Leadoff man Richie Ashburn beat out an infield bounder and promptly stole second. Red Schoendienst grounded out to McQuinn, Ashburn going to third. Hometown hero Stan Musial teed off on a Masterson fastball and belted a homer to the right field pavilion roof at the 360-foot mark. Two runs across.

The Senators' right-hander wasn't quite off the hook yet. Johnny Mize singled to center, and advanced to second on a wild pitch. Enos Slaughter walked. Andy Pafko grounded to Ken Keltner at third, forcing Mize. Walker Cooper bounced to Keltner, who threw to second forcing Pafko.

Masterson settled down in the next two innings, however, and permitted no further scoring. In the meantime, the American Leaguers unlimbered their bats.

Walter "Hoot" Evers made it a 2–1 game in the second inning when he cracked a Ralph Branca fastball into the left field bleachers for a homer.

In the third, Mickey Vernon, batting for Masterson, walked. Pat Mullin also walked. Vernon and Mullin executed the double steal as Tommy Henrich fanned. Lou Boudreau flied to Slaughter, Vernon scoring the tying run.

Evers opened the fourth against Johnny Schmitz, the new N.L. pitcher, by popping out to Pee Wee Reese in short left. Kenny Keltner singled over the third base bag and George McQuinn followed with a single to center, Keltner stopping at second. Birdie Tebbetts walked, filling the bases. Pitcher Vic Raschi then came through with a single to left, scoring Keltner and McQuinn, Tebbetts racing to third.

Manager Leo Durocher trotted out to the mound and replaced Schmitz with Johnny Sain. DiMaggio batted for Mullin and lined to Musial in left, Tebbetts scoring the third run of the inning. Henrich popped to Reese for the third out.

That ended the scoring for the day, as the Americans won by a 5–2 count.

Raschi, who pitched the middle three innings, received credit for the victory, while Joe Coleman completed the task of holding the Nationals in check for the final three frames.

The End of the All-Star Color Bar: 1949

The 1949 game, played on July 12 at Brooklyn's Ebbets Field, was historic; for the first time black players appeared in All-Star competition. Jackie Robinson, Roy Campanella, and Don Newcombe of the host Dodgers were selected for the N.L. squad, and Larry Doby of the Indians for the A.L.

Jackie Robinson broke the "color line" when he joined the Dodgers in

1946, but it took black players another three years before they made the All-Star teams.

Warren Spahn, N.L. starting pitcher, struck out leadoff man Dom DiMaggio, but from then on he had nothing but trouble and woe. George Kell reached first safely when Johnny Mize dropped Eddie Kazak's low throw from third base. (After first calling it an error on Mize, the official scorers charged it to Kazak, but several days later the error was officially given back to Mize.) Williams fanned as Kell swiped second. Joe DiMaggio singled to left, scoring Kell. Eddie Joost walked. Eddie Robinson singled to right, scoring DiMaggio and sending Joost to third. Pee Wee Reese fumbled Cass Michaels's bounder, Joost scoring on the error and Robinson moving to second. Tebbetts singled to left scoring Robinson, and Michaels scampered to third when the bag was left unprotected. Mel Parnell struck out.

That made it four runs, three hits, one walk, two errors, and two left.

The Nationals, in their half of the first, didn't waste much time in getting to Mel Parnell. Pee Wee Reese bounced back to the box, but then Robinson ripped a double to left. Musial followed with a homer over the right field screen, scoring behind Robinson. Musial, in fact, earned the nickname "The Man" for his extraordinary hitting in Ebbets Field.

In the second, after Dom DiMaggio fouled out to Mize, Kell singled to center and Williams walked. At this point, manager Billy Southworth lifted Spahn and replaced him with Newcombe. The big Dodger right-hander stopped the trouble quickly by retiring Joe DiMaggio and Joost.

Parnell ran into another jam in the bottom of the second. After he walked Willard Marshall, Kazak followed with a single to left, Marshall stopping at second. The Boston southpaw then unleashed a wild curve which hit Andy Seminick. Manager Lou Boudreau thought Parnell obviously didn't have his stuff and yanked him in favor of Virgil "Fire" Trucks.

Newcombe, a good hitting pitcher, lashed a long drive headed for the left field bleachers. At first it looked like a homer, but the wind caught the ball, giving Ted Williams just enough time to race over and spear it with one hand. This turned out to be the top defensive play of the day, since Williams deprived Newcombe of what would have been a certain base-clearing three-bagger. Marshall did tag up and score after Williams's catch, but Reese grounded into a double play to end the threat.

Newcombe blanked the Americans in the third, and the Nationals forged ahead in their half of the inning when they pushed two runs across. Robinson worked Trucks for a walk and rambled to third on Musial's single to left. Ralph Kiner grounded into a 6–4–3 double play, Robinson scoring. Mize singled to right. Marshall walked. Hodges ran for Mize and scored on Kazak's single to left. Andy Seminick grounded to Kell ending the inning.

Tough luck dogged Newcombe again in the fourth inning as the A.L.

chased across two runs on a fluke hit and went back into the lead at 6–5. After Dom DiMaggio grounded out to Sid Gordon at third, Kell singled to left and Williams walked. Joe DiMaggio, who must have been watching his younger brother, also grounded out to Gordon, the two runners advancing.

Newcombe then jammed Joost, who managed to send a slow roller toward Gil Hodges at first base. The ball, which danced along near the line like a miscued billiard shot with plenty of English on it, hit Hodges on the wrist and rolled away as the two runners scored. Joost received credit for a single.

The two teams took a breather from all their scoring in the fifth inning, but they started going at it again in the sixth. The two DiMaggio brothers played key roles in this latest A.L. offensive thrust; the victim was Vern Bickford who had just taken the mound. Dom led off with a double down the left field line. Kell walked. Williams flied to Pafko in deep right center, Dom taking third after the catch. Bob Dillinger ran for Kell. Joe D smashed a long double to left center, scoring both runners. Bickford got out of the inning without further damage, but the A.L. now led 8–5.

Lou Brissie, who assumed pitching duties for the A.L. in the fourth, had thrown two scoreless innings, and then ran out of gas in the sixth. Leadoff man Reese walked. Robinson forced Reese at second. Musial tapped in front of the plate and was thrown out by Berra, as Robinson took second. Kiner, on his way to hitting 54 homers for the season, belted a drive into the lower left field bleachers, and scored behind Robinson. The Nationals now trailed only by one run.

Left-hander Howie Pollet tried unsuccessfully to stem the Americans attack in the seventh, as three more runs came across before the dust settled. Gordon led off with a double to right. Berra grounded out Reese to Hodges, with Gordon holding second. Vic Wertz, batting for Brissie, flied to Pafko, who made a beautiful diving catch in center. Dom DiMaggio singled to left, scoring Gordon, and took second on the throw to the plate. Dillinger singled to left, scoring DiMaggio. Dale Mitchell lined a double to left, scoring Dillinger. The inning ended as Doby grounded to Hodges, who tossed to Pollet covering first.

This three-run outburst concluded the day's scoring with the Americans coming out on top by a comfortable 11–7 margin.

Virgil Trucks received credit for the victory, though Vic Raschi did the best pitching of the afternoon. The Yankee right-hander, on his way to a 21–10 season's record, hurled the final three innings and blanked the Nationals with just one hit. Don Newcombe got tagged with the loss.

The game was actually a loosely played affair marred by six errors (the All-Star high for a nine-inning game), five of them committed by the Nationals.

The two teams pounded out a total of 25 hits, with the A.L. taking only a slight 13–12 edge in this department. Manager Billy Southworth used seven of the eight pitchers on the N.L. squad; only Brooklyn's Ralph Branca did not receive a call.

After the game, Southworth absorbed a lot of barbs for choosing southpaw Boston Braves' ace Warren Spahn to face an American League starting lineup loaded with six right-handed hitters.

A number of sportswriters also criticized both teams, especially the Nationals, for general lack of competitive attitude, but that type of criticism is frequently off base. Even the greatest of players can have their off days, whether they come in a regular season game, All-Star Game, or any other kind of game.

The American League now held a commanding lead in the All-Star series, twelve games to four.

At the 1978 New York Mets' "Old-Timers Day" Lou Boudreau told which of his All-Star games he remembered best:

It would have to be the 1949 game, of course. . . . Really, one of my pleasant experiences in baseball came when I was chosen to manage the American League All-Stars. The glow hadn't worn off yet from Cleveland's world's championship of 1948.

Then I got a lot of flak when I picked Joe DiMaggio to start in center field and hit in the cleanup spot. Remember that this was the year that Joe didn't start playing for the Yankees until nearly midseason because of his Achilles' heel injury . . . in fact, he had played in only a handful of games before the All-Star break. But Joe came through for us with those two key hits and three RBIs, and he made the difference in the game.

A lot of people thought I picked DiMaggio for sentimental reasons—that just wasn't the case. I wanted him in the starting lineup because I had a feeling he was back in the groove all the way and could help us win the ball game. Joe always played his best when the chips were down.

14

The Tables Turn

Five Extra Innings: 1950

THE 1950 All-Star Game, played on July 11, returned to Chicago's Comiskey Park where the interleague series began back in 1933.

A long and lively pregame rhubarb was stirred up when National League manager Burt Shotton sought to change his league's starting lineup that had been named by the fans. Since none of the three fly-chasers chosen—Ralph Kiner, Enos Slaughter, or Hank Sauer—was a center fielder, Shotton wanted to start his own Brooklyn Dodger center fielder, Duke Snider, in place of Sauer.

Following a spirited outburst of complaints from both players and fans, Commissioner A. B. "Happy" Chandler ordered Shotton to play the outfield trio as originally selected, and Slaughter, who opened in center, fielded the position as if to the manner born. The controversy, however, resulted in a decision to have fans in the future vote for the outfielders by position instead of as a group.

In the first inning, Kiner caught hold of a Vic Raschi fastball and lined a drive to deep left-center field. Ted Williams raced back and made a spectacular one-handed catch, but in doing so he banged into the wall and hurt his left elbow in the crash. Despite considerable pain, he remained in the game until the ninth inning. X rays taken the next day showed a fracture, an operation was necessary, and Ted was sidelined until early September. No runs came across in this inning.

Robin Roberts, the great Philadelphia Phillies' right-hander, making the first of his five All-Star starts, blanked the Americans in the first two frames, but the Nationals picked up two markers against Raschi in the second.

Jackie Robinson singled and scored easily from first as Slaughter slammed a triple off the right-center field wall. Hank Sauer followed with a fly to right field, scoring Slaughter.

The Americans nicked Roberts for a run in the third when Cass Michaels, batting for Raschi, led off by bouncing a ground-rule double into the center field bull pen. Phil Rizzuto bunted safely down the third base line, Michaels advancing to third. Rizzuto took second on a wild pitch, which Roy Campanella knocked down to hold Michaels at third. Larry Doby struck out. George Kell flied to Slaughter in deep center, Michaels scoring. Williams, bad elbow and all, rapped a hard line drive to left, and Kiner had to make a fine running catch to prevent further scoring.

Bob Lemon, the Cleveland ace, took over the pitching in the top of the fourth and held the N.L. scoreless, while Don Newcombe of Brooklyn did the same thing to the A.L.

In the fifth, however, the Americans tore into Newcombe for two runs and took the lead, 3–2. Lemon led off with a walk, but Newcombe got Rizzuto on strikes. Doby doubled on a wicked grounder behind second which Robinson barely managed to knock down in a heroic attempt to snag the ball. Lemon stopped at third. Kell hoisted a long fly to Andy Pafko, who had gone to center at the start of the fifth, Lemon scoring and Doby advancing to third. Williams, the man with the broken elbow and a super athlete with a high threshold of pain, smacked a sharp single to right, scoring Doby.

The game sailed along at 3–2 until the top of the ninth, when Ralph Kiner, leading off against Art Houtteman, unloaded a homer deep into the left field stands. That blow made it 3–3.

The Americans failed to score in the bottom of the inning against the offerings of Larry Jansen, who had been doing a nifty relief job. So the 1950 game went into the record books as the first extra-inning affair in All-Star history.

Allie Reynolds stymied the Nationals in the top of the tenth, while Jansen zapped the Americans in the bottom half.

In the eleventh, the Nationals threatened with one out as Kiner picked on a Reynolds fastball and doubled to right center. Manager Casey Stengel then ordered Stan Musial to be purposely passed to set up a double play situation. Jackie Robinson was scheduled to bat, but Shotton surprised everyone in the park when he lifted him in favor of left-handed pinch hitter Johnny Wyrostek, a man headed for a season's batting average of .249. Wyrostek flied to center, ruining Shotton's strategy. Slaughter reached first safely as Jerry Coleman booted his grounder at second, filling the bases. Pafko flied to Dom DiMaggio in deep left to end the inning.

Shotton sent Red Schoendienst in to play second base.

The game began taking on the appearance of a marathon as it moved into the fourteenth inning, still knotted at 3–3.

Left-hander Ted Gray's first pitch to leadoff man Schoendienst was a fastball, and Red socked it into the left field seats for a homer, giving the N.L. a margin for the first time since the third inning. Schoendienst, a switch-hitter, batted left-handed against Gray.

Ewell Blackwell, who pitched the final three innings for the Nationals, received credit for the victory. The game ended as Joe DiMaggio rapped into a 5–4–3 double play.

Larry Jansen was another of the National League heroes as he threw five shutout innings striking out six and allowing only a single hit. His six whiffs tied a record set by Carl Hubbell in 1934 and matched by Johnny Vander Meer in 1943 and Ferguson Jenkins in 1967.

This was a sweet victory for the Nationals since it broke their four-game losing streak, and it also marked the senior circuit's first triumph in nine All-Star Games played in American League parks.

Home Run Derby: 1951

The custom of having the two circuits alternate as host was broken when the 1951 game was played in Detroit. Originally, the match was scheduled for Philadelphia under the auspices of the Phillies, but the baseball magnates decided to transfer it to Detroit for July 10th as part of the Motor City's 250th anniversary celebrations.

Briggs Stadium, always known as a hitters' park, lived up to its reputation that day.

The Nationals pushed across a run in the first inning against Ned Garver when Richie Ashburn doubled, advanced to third on Alvin Dark's short fly to right field, and scored when Stan Musial, who had walked, attempted to steal second. Nelson Fox dropped Yogi Berra's perfect throw to second, permitting Ashburn to cross the plate.

The Americans tied the game in the second when Berra singled and came home on Ferris Fain's triple off the right field screen. Fain's poor baserunning cost the A.L. a second run. Standing on third with one out, he held up on Chico Carrasquel's Texas league single to center, thinking it was going to be caught. Fain started for home too late and was thrown out by Ashburn.

N.L. manager Eddie Sawyer showed his anxiety for victory when he pulled starting pitcher Robin Roberts for a pinch hitter after the Phillies' ace had worked only two innings.

The Nationals bombed Eddie Lopat for three runs in the fourth. Musial started the inning off by homering into the second deck of the right field stands. After Jackie Robinson lined to Dom DiMaggio in deep left center, Gil Hodges scratched a single off the third base bag. Bob Elliott followed with a towering homer over the left field screen, scoring behind Hodges.

In the Americans' half of the fourth, Vic Wertz made it a 4–2 game when he belted a Sal Maglie pitch into the second deck in right.

Fred Hutchinson checked the Nationals in the fifth, while the Americans in their half moved one notch closer as George Kell homered over the left field screen.

From that point the National Leaguers got busy and proceeded to put the game out of reach by tallying a pair of runs in the sixth and one in both the seventh and eighth.

After Robinson opened the sixth with a walk, Hodges followed with a two-run smash over the left field screen. The one run in the seventh came as a result of a walk to Ashburn, a single through the middle by Dark, and an RBI squeeze bunt single by Robinson. Hutchinson was victimized for the three runs in these two innings.

The N.L. concluded its scoring in the eighth when Kiner walloped a long homer into the second deck in left center. The final score read 8–3, as the senior circuit achieved its first back-to-back victories in All-Star competition.

Sal Maglie received credit for the win, but the real pitching hero for the N.L. was Don Newcombe, who gave up only two hits in his three innings of work (the sixth through the eighth) while striking out three. Eddie Lopat took the loss.

The Nationals' four home runs marked a one-game All-Star record as did the two-team total of six.

Richie Ashburn emerged as the N.L.'s outstanding player with his single, double, two runs scored, stolen base, and great work in the field. He pulled off the game's most spectacular fielding play in the sixth inning when he raced to the right-center field fence and hauled down Vic Wertz's long drive.

Joe DiMaggio, who announced his retirement at the close of the season, was a member of the A.L. squad, but a nagging leg injury prevented him from seeing action. He was picked for the All-Star team in every one of the thirteen years he played for the Yankees.

Gate receipts totaled $124,000, less than $2,000 short of the record set by the 1950 contest at Chicago's Comiskey Park. The proceeds went into the players' pension fund.

Short and Wet: 1952

Lady Luck was with the National Leaguers in the 1952 game played at Philadelphia's Shibe Park on July 8, because they were leading 3–2 at the end of the fifth inning when the rains came down and cut short the proceedings. This marked the first time in All-Star history that a contest had to be abbreviated.

Once again the senior circuit utilized the home run ball as its most lethal weapon. Jackie Robinson opened the scoring in the first stanza when he deposited a Vic Raschi pitch into the upper left field seats.

Big Hank Sauer teed off on a Bob Lemon fastball in the fourth and drilled the horsehide onto the roof in left center for a two-run homer that proved to be the margin of victory. Musial, who was hit by a pitch, scored ahead of Sauer.

Curt Simmons, ace left-hander of the hometown Phillies who started for the Nationals, did a masterful job for three innings as he blanked the junior circuit on one hit and struck out three.

The Americans did rough up Bob Rush for two runs in the fourth. Pinch hitter Minnie Minoso led with a double down the right field line, and Al Rosen walked. Eddie Robinson singled sharply off Jackie Robinson's glove into right field, Minoso scoring from second and Rosen racing to third. Bobby Avila singled over second base, scoring Rosen. The A.L.'s 2–1 lead was to be short-lived because of Sauer's two-run blast.

Bobby Shantz, the gutsy little Philadelphia Athletics' southpaw, took the mound in the fifth and whiffed Whitey Lockman, Robinson, and Musial in succession. The rain robbed wee Bobby (he stood 5′6½″) of a chance to try to equal Carl Hubbell's record five strikeouts in a row.

Shantz's 1952 record was a shining 24–7 as he captured the American League's MVP award.

Rain, which fell sporadically during the morning and almost steadily during the game, made the field soggy and the footing insecure, but the crowd viewed a particularly well-played game. There were no errors and good fielding plays abounded.

Because of the weather, both teams had to omit the usual pregame drills, and the start of the game was delayed 20 minutes in the expectation there might be a letup in the showers.

E. Slaughter = A Slaughter: 1953

Enos Slaughter stole the show as the National League notched its fourth straight All-Star victory over the Americans with a 5–1 decision at

Cincinnati's Crosley Field on July 14. The 37-year-old St. Louis Cardinals' flychaser rapped out two hits, drew a base on balls, scored two runs, knocked in another, and made a spectacular catch in right field.

The game began as a pitchers' battle as both starters, Robin Roberts of the N.L. and Billy Pierce of the A.L., sailed through the first three innings without allowing a run. Warren Spahn and Allie Reynolds continued to match the goose eggs in the fourth, but the Nationals broke through Reynolds's armor in the fifth by scoring twice.

With one out, Eddie Mathews was hit on the left foot by a pitched ball. After Gus Bell popped out, Slaughter walked, moving Mathews to second. Richie Ashburn, batting for Spahn, singled to center, scoring Mathews, with Slaughter stopping at second. Pee Wee Reese, hitless in 15 plate apearances in eight previous All-Star contests, lined a single to right, scoring Slaughter.

In the top of the sixth, with Curt Simmons pitching for the N.L., leadoff man Harvey Kuenn smashed a drive into right field that looked like a sure hit. Slaughter, off at the crack of the bat, raced in and speared the ball with his gloved hand just a few inches above the grass. He held on to the horsehide as he turned a complete somersault. Veteran sportswriters all agreed that this was one of the finest outfield plays in any All-Star Game.

The Nationals picked up another marker in the seventh against the slants of Mike Garcia. With one out, Slaughter smashed a sizzling grounder off Chico Carrasquel's glove at short that went for a single. With pinch hitter Jackie Robinson at the plate, Slaughter dashed to second and completed the steal by making a headlong slide to evade Carrasquel's tag. Robinson popped out, but Reese doubled through the gap in left center, scoring Slaughter.

The Nationals concluded their scoring for the day in the eighth with two runs off Satchel Paige, who at the age of 47 became the oldest player ever to perform in an All-Star Game. Leadoff man Gil Hodges lined out to Larry Doby in deep center. Roy Campanella, hitless in 13 times at bat in All-Star competition, singled through the box. Paige then got Mathews to pop out, but walked pinch hitter Duke Snider. Slaughter singled over second base, scoring Campanella and sending Snider to third. Murry Dickson lofted a single into short left center, Snider scoring easily, but Dickson was thrown out trying to take second.

The American Leaguers, held to only two hits in the first eight innings, finally broke into the scoring column in the ninth against the pitching of Murry Dickson. Singles by Ferris Fain, Johnny Mize, and Minnie Minoso produced the run.

Spahn received credit for the victory, while Reynolds was charged with the loss.

For the first time since the 1944 game, there were no home runs, though old Crosley Field had convenient dimensions for power hitters.

With four straight victories, the N.L. narrowed the A.L. advantage to 12–8 in the All-Star series.

Captain Ted Williams, just returned from U.S. Marine Corps flying duty in Korea, threw out the first ball and then sat on the bench as an honorary member of the American League squad. The A.L. could have used his big bat.

Blasts and a Bloop: 1954

Cleveland caught baseball fever early in the 1954 season when it began to look as if the hometown Indians were going to run away with the pennant the New York Yankees had monopolized for the last five years. The Indians grabbed the league lead early in May and kept rolling in high gear. The men in pinstripes were destined to finish the year with a fantastic record of 103 wins and 51 losses, but still wound up eight full games behind Cleveland. The Indians' 111 and 43 record, an amazing .721 percentage, is still the American League record. The Yankees' imperium was broken.

With that record in the making, it was appropriate that at the July 13th All-Star Game in Cleveland's Municipal Stadium, a coterie of Indians led by infielder Al "The Hebrew Hammer" Rosen played starring roles in the slugfest that immortalized the 1954 contest as one of the most exciting in the history of the classic.

A hollering horde of 68,751 fans, the second highest attendance in All-Star annals, paid $292,678 to see the show, topping any previous gate by more than $100,000. Did they get their money's worth? You be the judge.

The wide-open game produced six home runs, four by the American League, and set records for the most runs by both teams, 20; most hits by both teams, 31; and most hits by one team, with 17 for the winners. And if the high spots of the game seemed to be the long distance smashes, the final hit was a blooper over second base by the White Sox' Nellie Fox; it proved to be the decisive safety.

With the bases loaded and the score knotted at 9 to 9 in the eighth inning, Fox lofted a "dying quail" just beyond the desperately outstretched hands of shortstop Alvin Dark. Now, as the ball fell safely, Mickey Mantle and Yogi Berra of the Yankees raced home with the two runs that gave the A.L. its first All-Star victory since 1949.

Casey Stengel had won five straight pennants and world's championships as manager of the Yankees, but he'd lost in his last four attempts in the midseason contest. Nellie's little hit snapped Casey's jinx. Succeeding Chuck Dressen as the Dodger manager, Walt Alston was at the helm of the National League forces. No first-timer's luck for him—he went down to defeat in the first All-Star Game he'd ever witnessed.

Indian fans had plenty to cheer about. Bobby Avila lined three singles, scored once, and drove in two runs; Larry Doby smashed a pinch home run in the eighth inning; and Al Rosen took the day's slugging honors by connecting for two successive homers and a single. The pair of homers and five RBIs tied All-Star Game records. Together the three Indians drove in eight of the A.L.'s eleven runs, virtually dominating the game. The home town earned some additional luster when Bob Lemon came in as a relief pitcher in the fourth and helped snuff out an N.L. rally.

Rosen had been a doubtful starter at first base because a month before he had fractured his right index finger on a fielding play and the healing process was a slow one. He had been in and out of the Cleveland lineup, but still led the nationwide voting for the A.L. All-Star team. To further complicate the situation, Rosen spent a sleepless night because he had lain on the finger and it was sorer than ever.

Rosen, lately president of the New York Yankees, recalls the details of that historic game played more than a quarter-century ago:

> I felt obliged to play because the fans had given me more votes than any other member of the American League team. On the other hand, I felt that because of my sore finger and the fact I had been in a bad slump, I wouldn't do the team any good.
>
> I went to Casey Stengel before the game and told him how I felt about it. There's a rule that says players voted to the starting team must play at least three innings. Casey said he wouldn't break the rule without consulting with Commissioner Ford Frick.
>
> It was decided that I should take one turn at bat. Casey said he would leave it up to me after that point. If I still thought the finger injury would handicap me, I was to tell him to lift me.
>
> When I struck out in the first inning, I guess pride took over. I just couldn't make myself go over to Stengel and ask him to relieve me. Maybe if I had done anything else but strike out—even a groundout—I would have asked to be removed.
>
> When I was scheduled to come up in the third, I saw Mickey Vernon picking up a bat. There were two men on, and Casey had him ready to hit for me, but I let Casey know that I wanted to stay in. Robin Roberts threw me a good fastball, and as soon as I made contact, I knew the ball was going to clear the fence in left center. The ball must have cleared the wire fence by maybe 15–20 feet and traveled 380–385 feet.

Rosen's second homer of the day, a two-run shot off left-hander Johnny Antonelli in the fifth inning was an even longer blast than the first one—the ball sailed some 400 feet, deep into the lower left field stands. Rosen had no trouble remembering that Antonelli's home run pitch was a low curveball.

The slugger still wasn't through for the day—he singled in the sixth off Warren Spahn, and in the eighth he was walked by Carl Erskine. The walk helped set the stage for Nellie Fox's game winning single.

"Flip" Rosen played the entire nine innings in the field. He handled seven putouts at first base and then was switched to third base in the ninth inning.

Says Rosen:

If you were to ask me why I was able to have that kind of day at the bat when I was injured, I just couldn't tell you exactly—maybe that was just my day on earth. Playing before a huge hometown crowd clearly gave me a psychological lift and the adrenalin simply started flowing. And when anyone asks me about this game, I always want to mention my teammates Bobby Avila and Larry Doby because they also rose to the occasion in a pressure situation.

You know that right index finger of mine never came around to normal. I got off to a real good start in '54 and was lucky to finish the year batting at an even .300. Then in 1955 and 1956, I felt I was hitting below my usual standard and decided to retire. I was only 32, but pride wouldn't permit me to play when I knew I couldn't go a hundred percent. When Frank Lane was general manager of the Indians in 1958, he tried to get me out of retirement—he thought a year's rest might have helped, but I told him my playing days were over.

Before his injury, Al Rosen was headed toward a career that might well have qualified him for the Hall of Fame. He was voted the American League's Most Valuable Player in 1953 when he batted .336, hit 43 homers, and drove in 145 runs. In seven full and three partial seasons he belted 192 homers. He was a gritty and excellent fielding third baseman during the first part of his career, and then in 1954 he began dividing his time between third and first. Maybe Al Rosen won't ever be elected to an honored place in Cooperstown, but his performance in the 1954 All-Star Game won't be the reason why.

One of the most heated arguments in All-Star history broke out in the eighth inning when the National League was batting. After Gus Bell slammed a two-out, two-run pinch homer, Red Schoendienst reached second when Minnie Minoso dropped his long fly ball near the right field foul line. Al Dark's infield single moved Schoendienst to third, and it was at this point that Dean Stone, rookie Washington southpaw, was called in to relieve Chicago's Bob Keegan and face the dangerous Duke Snider.

As Stone started his third pitch, Schoendienst made a surprise move to steal home. The A.L. moundsman hurried his motion and threw to catcher Yogi Berra just in time to nail the runner at the plate. The National Leaguers, led by coaches Leo Durocher and Charlie Grimm, protested vehemently that Stone had balked, but plate umpire Bill Stewart turned a deaf ear.

A number of sportswriters, including Franklin Lewis, then sports editor of *The Cleveland Press,* editorialized that Durocher in particular protested too loudly and too long, sullying the dignity of the All-Star Game.

The Nationals were still leading 9–8 after the Schoendienst brouhaha, but then the Americans scored those three big runs in their half of the eighth and held the senior circuit scoreless in the ninth to snatch the victory in this cliffhanger. Oddly, credit for the victory went to Stone, who threw only three balls and did not retire a single batter.

15

The Mid-Fifties

Messiah at the Bat: 1955

MILWAUKEE'S County Stadium on July 12, 1955 was the site of another All-Star Game that can be described as a standout.

The Americans gave Robin Roberts, the Nationals' starter, his second roughing up in a row in All-Star competition, blasting him for four runs in the first inning. (The A.L. hit Roberts for a four-run inning in the 1954 game, but on that occasion had the courtesy to wait until the third inning before they laid into him.)

Harvey Kuenn led off with a single to left field, and Nellie Fox followed with a single to right center, sending Kuenn to third. With Ted Williams up, Roberts, normally a control artist, uncorked a wild pitch, permitting Kuenn to score and Fox to take second. Williams then walked.

Mickey Mantle, the powerful switch-hitter, batting left-handed against Roberts, laid the wood to a fastball and drove a 430-foot homer over the center field wall. Mantle scored behind Fox and Williams.

Roberts went on to retire Yogi Berra, Al Kaline, and Mickey Vernon, but the Americans had a quick 4–0 lead, and it appeared as if they had already done in the Nationals. However, the game was far from over.

Roberts settled down during his final two innings on the mound, allowing no further scoring, while Billy Pierce, the A.L. starter, pitched superbly in his three-inning stint, giving up only one hit and fanning three.

Harvey Haddix, the St. Louis Cardinals' left-handed curveball specialist, continued to keep the Americans' offense in check in the fourth and

fifth frames, but yielded a tally in the sixth. With one out, Berra singled
to right field, and Kaline got a double when his smash bounced off Eddie
Mathews's knee into left field. Berra went to third. The Yankee catcher
raced across the plate when Vernon bounced out to Ted Kluszewski at
first base.

Early Wynn, who followed Pierce to the mound, also pitched three
scoreless innings, but the Nationals finally broke into the scoring column
in the seventh when they tagged Whitey Ford for two runs.

Willie Mays led off with a single to left, but both Kluszewski and
Ransom Jackson lined out to Mantle. Hank Aaron, appearing in the first
of his 24 All-Star games, walked, and then Johnny Logan rifled a single
to right, scoring Mays and sending Aaron to third. Pinch hitter Stan
Lopata grounded to shortstop Chico Carrasquel, who fumbled the ball
and then threw wildly to second in an attempt to force Logan. Aaron
scored on the error.

When the inning ended, the A.L.'s lead had been cut to 5–2.

The Nationals hammered away again at Ford in the eighth. After the
Yankees' premier lefty retired Schoendienst and Musial on infield
grounders, Mays, Kluszewski, and Jackson all singled to right field. With
Mays having scored, and runners on first and second, manager Al Lopez
yanked Ford and replaced him with Frank Sullivan.

Aaron greeted Sullivan with a resounding single to right field, scoring
Kluszewski and sending Jackson to third, When Kaline's long throw to
third got through Al Rosen, Jackson also scored. Logan ended the inning
by grounding out to short, but not before three runs had scored.

The game was now deadlocked at 5–5.

Joe Nuxhall blanked the Americans in the ninth, and in the bottom
half of the inning Sullivan started out by retiring Lopata and Nuxhall
before he ran into a bit of trouble. Schoendienst singled to center and
Musial walked, bringing the ever-dangerous Willie Mays to the plate.
Sullivan rose to the occasion, however, and caught Mays looking at a
fastball for a called third strike.

Now, for the second time in All-Star history, the game was sent reeling
into extra innings.

Tension ran high in the tenth and eleventh frames, but both Nuxhall
and Sullivan continued to match goose eggs. Nuxhall had a close call in
the eleventh, when, with two out and runners on first and second, he
faced Yogi Berra. Yogi rapped a hot grounder past Nuxhall, but Schoendienst raced far to his right, grabbed the ball, and made a quick throw to
first to nip Berra for the best infield play of the game.

Manager Leo Durocher called on Gene Conley, the 6'8" Milwaukee
Braves right-hander, to take over the mound duties from Nuxhall in the
twelfth, and as Conley completed his work for the inning he received a
standing ovation from the nearly 46,000 fans. He struck out in succession

Kaline, Vernon, and Rosen, three of the American League's most dangerous hitters.

The applause for Conley had hardly subsided when Stan Musial, leading off in the bottom of the twelfth, stepped into Sullivan's first pitch, a hopping fastball, and bashed it over the right field screen for a homer to win the game for the Nationals, 6–5. The National Leaguers had fought their way back from a fat five-run deficit to take the match in extra innings.

The game was particularly sweet for Musial. For the first time since 1947 he had not been selected for his league's first team, and he got into action only as a replacement for Del Ennis in the fourth inning. Then he went 0 for 3 before hitting his dramatic homer.

Musial called the All-Star homer his personal high spot for the entire 1955 season, a year in which the Cardinals finished a disappointing seventh. He recalled that circuit blast in his autobiography, *Stan Musial: "The Man's" Own Story,* "Even before the ball fell among leaping spectators for a homer, I knew it was gone. So, like Babe Ruth, I didn't bother to sprint. I jogged joyfully around the bases, listening to the roaring crowd. . . ."

Ballot Stuffing for Foggy Bottom Honors: 1956

The 1956 All-Star Game, played at Washington's Griffith Stadium on July 10th, made it crystal clear that the Nationals no longer had to play second fiddle to the junior league. The senior circuit won decisively by a 7–3 count, continued to show long-ball power, and whittled the A.L.'s once overwhelming All-Star game edge to 13–10.

Ken Boyer, sophomore St. Louis Cardinals' star third sacker, emerged as the game's real hero as he went 3 for 5 at the plate and made several outstanding plays in the field. In the very first inning Harvey Kuenn hit a sizzling drive down the third base line, but the acrobatic Boyer lunged to his left and snared the ball while sprawled on the ground to rob Kuenn of a certain hit. Boyer went on to harass the American Leaguers throughout the entire game.

The Nationals broke the scoring ice in the third on Roy McMillan's walk, a sacrifice by pitcher Bob Friend, and Johnny Temple's RBI single.

Whitey Ford, the prize New York Yankee southpaw, started the fourth inning auspiciously enough by getting Stan Musial to look at a third called strike. But then Boyer singled to left, and pinch hitter Willie Mays rocketed a 425-foot homer into the distant left-center field bleachers, making it a 3–0 game.

The N.L. picked up another tally in the fifth when Boyer's single to center scored Temple from second base. In the bottom of the inning,

Boyer robbed Kuenn of another hit when he speared his hot smash down the line and made the long throw to first just in time to get his man.

The senior circuit kept pecking away as it scored run number five in the sixth when Ted Kluszewski rumbled home from third on Tom Brewer's wild pitch.

In the sixth, the Americans finally came to life when they chased Warren Spahn, who had hung zeros on the scoreboard in the two previous frames. Nellie Fox opened with a single to left center, and Ted Williams followed with a shot into the right-center field bull pen for a two-run homer. Mickey Mantle came through with a poke into the left field breachers, making it a 5–3 game. At this point Johnny Antonelli came in to relieve Spahn and retired the Americans without further damage.

Mantle's homer was actually the result of an act of courage. He'd gone into the game with a pulled hamstring in the back of his right knee which handicapped him considerably. It was apparent to everyone that he couldn't pivot properly on the knee, and he was an easy strikeout victim in his three other times at bat.

The Nationals added their final two runs in the seventh when Musial pounded a long homer into the left-center field bleachers—and Mays, who got on with a walk, scampered home on Kluszewski's double into the right field corner.

In the bottom of the seventh, Boyer made yet another great play when he leaped into the air and stabbed pinch hitter Ray Boone's drive that appeared to be a sure double. Veteran sportswriters agreed that Boyer's combination batting and fielding performance was one of the best ever in All-Star play.

Both starting pitchers figured in the decision: Bob Friend was credited with the victory; Billy Pierce took the loss.

N.L. manager Walt Alston was criticized for a possible rule violation when he permitted Antonelli to pitch four innings and finish the game. Alston pointed out that according to All-Star rules, however, a pitcher is allowed to go three innings *after* the one into which he has come as a reliever.

Eyebrows were raised before the game because the fans had named five Cincinnati players to starting berths in the N.L. lineup, while three other Reds were runners-up at their positions. The Reds did have an excellent team, and were in first place at the time of the game, but Cincinnati radio stations and newspapers had spurred a tremendous All-Star voting spree in the area. Cries of "ballot box stuffing!" echoed in towns where fans thought their own favorites had been cheated out of a share of All-Star glory. It was not the first time the nation's capital had heard charges of electioneering irregularities.

Minnie's Squeaker: 1957

All-Star voting from the Cincinnati area for the 1957 game (played at St. Louis's Busch Stadium on July 9) got so far out of hand that Commissioner Ford Frick had to intervene.

A veritable Niagara of more than 500,000 late votes from Cincinnati resulted in all of the Reds' regulars, except first baseman George Crowe, winning the fan balloting for their respective positions. This time Commissioner Frick felt that the Cincinnati madness needed to be bridled. Because of the "overbalance" of Cincinnati votes, he ordered Reds' outfielders Gus Bell and Wally Post dropped. Manager Walt Alston later added Bell to the squad as a reserve, but Post, on his way to batting a rousing .244 for the season, was expected to buy a ticket if he cared to attend the game.

In order to prevent such a fiasco from reoccurring, Frick, with the acquiescence of the club owners, "disenfranchised" the fans and delegated the All-Star voting responsibilities to the players, managers, and coaches. It wasn't until 1970 that All-Star voting was returned to the public.

The Americans jumped off to a 2–0 lead in the second against the combined efforts of Curt Simmons and Lou Burdette. Mickey Mantle singled, Ted Williams walked, and Vic Wertz followed with a single through short, scoring Mantle and moving Williams to second. After Yogi Berra walked, filling the bases, Burdette replaced Simmons on the mound. Burdette retired George Kell on a foul and Jim Bunning on a fly to short center, but he walked Harvey Kuenn, forcing Williams across the plate.

The A.L. touched Jack Sanford for a run in the sixth when Bill Skowron doubled off the right field screen, took third on a wild pitch, and scored on Berra's single to left.

The Nationals finally broke into the scoring column with two markers in the seventh when they pinned back Early Wynn's ears for three straight hits. After leadoff man Stan Musial lined out, Willie Mays and Ed Bailey singled, and pinch hitter Gus Bell drove them both across with a double into the left field corner. Manager Casey Stengel gave Wynn the hook then and replaced him with Billy Pierce, who averted further trouble in the inning.

In the ninth, the A.L. expanded its lead to 6–2, with Clem Labine on the mound as the N.L.'s fifth pitcher. Pierce led off with an infield hit, and Gil McDougald reached first when Red Schoendienst bobbled his slow grounder to second base. After Nelson Fox's sacrifice advanced the runners, Al Kaline drove them both in with a single to left center. Mantle struck out, but Minnie Minoso, who had just replaced Williams in the lineup, doubled to deep right center, scoring Kaline.

Musial opened the Nationals' half of the ninth with a walk, and then scored on Mays's triple to the right field corner. With pinch hitter Hank Foiles at the plate, Pierce threw a wild pitch, permitting Mays to score. Foiles proceeded to single over second base, and Bell walked. That was all for Pierce, as Stengel called for Don Mossi, the ace Cleveland reliever.

Mossi fooled Eddie Mathews with a called third strike, but Ernie Banks singled off Frank Malzone's glove, scoring Foiles. When Bell attempted to advance to third on the play, however, he was cut down by a perfect throw from left fielder Minoso to Malzone. Banks went to second on the throw.

With pinch hitter Gil Hodges coming to the plate, Stengel called in right-hander Bob Grim to face him. Hodges caught hold of Grim's second pitch and sent a cannon shot to deep left center, but Minoso raced over and hauled it down to save the game for the Americans.

During his single inning in the game, Minnie Minoso provided the bat, glove, and the arm that enabled the Americans to take the 6–5 squeaker from the Nationals.

Minoso, then 35, was still around the midpoint of his active career. After he left the majors in 1964, he continued playing in the Mexican League through the 1973 season—and then in 1976, while coaching for the Chicago White Sox, club owner Bill Veeck allowed him to appear in several late season games as a designated hitter. Minoso, nearly 54 at the time, was still in top physical shape.

Silver Anniversary Singles: 1958

For the first and only time in All-Star history, in the 1958 game (played at Baltimore's Memorial Stadium on July 8) neither team produced an extra-base hit. The pitchers stole the show as the Americans nipped the Nationals 4–3, with the A.L.'s attack consisting of nine singles. The N.L. had only four hits, all singles. This was also the second successive game in which no homers were hit.

An unusual amount of pageantry preceded the game, because the midsummer classic's Silver Jubilee was celebrated in 1958, and Vice-President Richard M. Nixon came over from Washington to throw out the ceremonial first ball.

The Nationals worked starter Bob Turley over for two runs in the first. Singles by Willie Mays and Stan Musial, followed by Hank Aaron's sacrifice fly, produced the first marker. Ernie Banks was then hit with a pitched ball and Frank Thomas walked, filling the bases. With Bill Mazeroski batting, Musial scored on a wild pitch.

The Americans got one run back in their half of the first. Nellie Fox reached first when Banks's throw from shortstop pulled Musial off the bag. Mantle's single to left center—the longest hit of the game—sent Fox going to third. Fox scored when Jackie Jensen hit into a 5-4-3 double play.

Turley went to the showers when the nationals tagged him for another run in the second. Mays, after forcing Warren Spahn, stole second, continued to third on catcher Gus Triandos's throwing error, and scored when Bob Skinner singled. Ray Narleski replaced Turley on the mound after Skinner's blow.

The Americans countered again for a run in their half, and then knotted the game at three-all in the fifth. They tallied the winning run in the sixth. Frank Malzone singled, Yogi Berra popped out, but Ted Williams reached first when Thomas booted his grounder, and Gil McDougald's single drove in Malzone.

Bob Friend, who gave up the A.L.'s final two runs, took the loss, while Early Wynn, who pitched only one inning, the sixth, received credit for the victory. However, the real mound hero for the Americans was Billy O'Dell. The Baltimore left-hander retired nine successive batters over the final three innings to protect the thin one-run lead.

16

Let's Play Two!

ALL-STAR tradition was broken in 1959 when owners and players agreed to expand the midsummer classic into a double feature. The regularly scheduled All-Star game was played at Pittsburgh's Forbes Field on July 7, while the encore was contested at Los Angeles's Memorial Coliseum on August 3.

The idea of staging a second All-Star match received much unfavorable reaction from the press when it was first announced early in 1959. The sportswriters booed that a repeat performance would cheapen the whole event and transform it into a kind of traveling circus. The arrangement proved so successful, however, that it was decided to play two games again in 1960. The two-game plan held through 1962.

The central idea behind expanding the All-Star attraction was to raise additional money for the players' pension fund, for aiding youth baseball, and for helping needy old-timers. As in the case of the regular game, the club owners agreed to turn over 60 percent of the net gate receipts from the second contest to the players' pension fund.

The two-game system was abandoned after 1962 for two basic reasons: First, it was becoming more difficult than ever to shoehorn into the schedule two interleague matches because of the new 162-game regular season—the A.L. went from 154 games to 162 in 1961, and the N.L. followed in 1962. Second, the club owners agreed to turn over 95 percent of the net revenue from the first game to the players' pension fund, instead of the previous 60 percent. The pension fund would lose little overall, then, making only one contest sufficient.

Willie Whips Whitey: 1959 (I)

Vice-President Richard Nixon, whose appetite for baseball was insatiable, threw out the ceremonial first ball for the second All-Star Game in succession.

Home runs by Eddie Mathews in the first frame and Al Kaline in the fourth accounted for the only runs as Don Drysdale and Lou Burdette, hurling for the Nationals, and Early Wynn and Ryne Duren for the Americans, dueled on even terms for the first six innings. Between them the four pitchers struck out a total of 13 batters.

The remarkable Early Wynn, then 39, was enjoying his finest season in his long career in the majors as he rolled up a 22–10 record, helped lead the Chicago White Sox to the pennant, and took the Cy Young award. The big burly right-hander, who looked as mean as a junkyard dog on the mound, had a way of intimidating the hitters.

In the seventh, the N.L. ripped into Jim Bunning for two runs on a long double by Ernie Banks and singles by Del Crandall and Bill Mazeroski.

Roy Face, the forkballing Pittsburgh relief ace who was 12–0 at the time (his season's record was 18–1), had retired the side in order in the seventh and got the first two men in the eighth before he suddenly fell apart and allowed three runs. Two singles, a walk, and Gus Triandos's double did the damage as the A.L. pulled out to a 4–3 lead. Manager Fred Haney had to call on Johnny Antonelli to get the third out.

With Whitey Ford on the mound for the Americans in the eighth, the Nationals battled right back. Ken Boyer, batting for Antonelli, singled to left center, and Dick Groat, batting for Mathews, moved Boyer to second with a sacrifice. Hank Aaron singled to center, scoring Boyer. Willie Mays, with the count one-and-two, drove a triple over center fielder Harvey Kuenn's head, scoring Aaron. That was the ball game, as the N.L. walked off with a 5–4 decision.

This marked the fourth time Willie had hit against Ford in All-Star competition. He rapped him for two singles in the 1955 game and hammered him for a homer in 1956.

After the game Ford told reporters: "Willie has batted against me four times, and I still haven't gotten him out. He hits me like he owns me. In this game I threw him a sinker that just didn't sink."

Don Drysdale, now an ABC sportscaster, recently recalled the first 1959 game as the most memorable of his eight All-Star appearances: "... and not only because it was my first All-Star appearance when I had the luck to retire nine men in a row. Just three days before the game, my wife gave birth to our first child, our daughter Kelly. . . . However, with the Pittsburgh game and the Dodgers being on the road at the time, I didn't see Kelly for the first time until she was more than three weeks old. Now she's almost ready to graduate from college!"

Transcontinental Doubleheader: 1959 (II)

For the second game of the All-Star "doubleheader," the managers were allowed to pick their own starting lineups, and Casey Stengel took advantage of the ruling by placing six left-handed swingers at the head of his batting order to face right-hander Don Drysdale. The strategy paid off as the Americans roughed up Drysdale for four hits and three runs in the second and third innings.

In the second, Frank Malzone popped a homer over the convenient left field screen for the first run. The damage to Drysdale would have been worse except that leadoff man Mickey Mantle, who singled, was thrown out stealing. Yogi Berra's line-drive homer over the right field fence with Nellie Fox on base accounted for two more runs in the third.

The Nationals in the meantime had nicked A.L. starter Jerry Walker for a run in the first. Johnny Temple led off with a double and eventually scored on Hank Aaron's sacrifice fly. Frank Robinson narrowed the gap to 3–2 when he slammed Early Wynn's first pitch in the fifth inning deep into the left-center field bleachers.

After going hitless for three innings, the Americans touched "Toothpick Sam" Jones for a run in the seventh on a walk, two infield errors, and Nelson Fox's single through the middle.

The Nationals got the run back in their half of the seventh when Jim Gilliam skied a Billy O'Dell fastball over the screen in left center.

In the eighth, leadoff man Rocky Colavito concluded the day's scoring when he caught hold of Roy Face's first pitch and rocketed a 430-foot homer halfway up into the distant left field stands.

With their 5–3 victory, the Americans succeeded in splitting the "twin bill." Home runs accounted for six of the game's eight runs. Jerry Walker received credit for the victory, while Don Drysdale was charged with the loss.

A Day in the Furnace: 1960 (I)

Kansas City hosted its first-ever All-Star Game in 1960, and the local fans were so anxious to see the big league stars that the 101-degree afternoon heat didn't stop them from turning out en masse. Municipal Stadium was packed to capacity with a paid attendance of nearly 31,000.

It was so hot that the TV cameras had to be wrapped in ice to prevent them from overheating.

The National League bats were as hot as the weather in the first as starter Bill Monbouquette was raked for three runs. Willie Mays led off with a triple into the right field corner, and Bob Skinner promptly drove him home with a sharp single to left center. Monbouquette retired Mathews and Aaron, but Ernie Banks homered over the left field screen to give the N.L. a 3–0 lead.

With one out in the second, the Nationals struck again as Del Crandall picked on a Monbouquette fastball and lined it over the left field screen. Bob Friend struck out, Mays singled to left, and Skinner ended the inning as another strikeout victim.

"When Monbouquette came back into the dugout, we thought he was going to pass out from the heat," recalled Jim Ewell, one of the American League trainers who was then with the Kansas City Athletics. "We had to give him a strong whiff of oxygen and a few splashes of ammonia water on the back of his neck to get him back to normal. The official temperature may have been 101, but it was even hotter on the playing field surface," Ewell remembered.

Chuck Estrada took over the A.L. pitching duties in the third and yielded the N.L.'s fifth and final run on a double by Banks and singles by Joe Adcock and Bill Mazeroski.

Held in check for five innings by Bob Friend and Mike McCormick, the Americans nicked the Giant southpaw for a run in the sixth when Nelson Fox singled with the bases loaded. With one out and the bases still filled, Roy Face relieved McCormick and induced Luis Aparicio to ground into a double play to snuff out the rally.

Bob Buhl gave up the A.L.'s other runs in the eighth. Harvey Kuenn reached first as second baseman Charlie Neal booted his grounder, and Kaline followed with a homer over the left field screen.

The Americans threatened in the ninth when they had runners on first and second with only one out. But Vern Law, who replaced Buhl at this point, quickly disposed of Brooks Robinson and Kuenn to end the game with the Nationals on top at 5–3.

Trainer Jim Ewell also recalls: "I've never seen so many players bushed at the end of nine innings. Despite the fact that the park was almost like a furnace, they all played hard, and we were lucky that no one suffered heatstroke. Willie Mays, who had three hits and did plenty of running on the bases and in the field, especially needed the trainers' attention at the end of the game."

"Twin Bill" Sweep: 1960 (II)

The two All-Star squads flew in from Kansas City to New York for the second half of the "twin bill," but the fans in Gotham took a blasé attitude about this game, as only 38,362 of them showed up, filling little more than half of Yankee Stadium's capacity.

Led by Willie Mays, the Nationals hammered out an easy 6–0 win over the Americans and cut the junior circuit's edge in the series to 16–13.

The game marked a triumphant return to New York for Mays who banged out three hits, including a homer, and sparkled in the field. Mays, an idol of the New York fans in the 1950s, moved to San Francisco when the Giants' franchise was shifted in 1958. Willie's six-hit performance in the two 1960 games stands as one of the finest individual offensive efforts in All-Star history.

Eddie Mathews got the Nationals rolling in the second when he powered a homer into the lower left field stands, scoring behind Joe Adcock, who had singled. This was the first of four senior circuit four-baggers. Mays hit his homer in the third, a drive into the lower left field stands. Willie's first inning single and the homer both came off Whitey Ford, giving him six straight All-Star hits against the Yankee southpaw. Nowhere in All-Star annals is there a comparable hitting streak.

Stan Musial earned a standing ovation in the seventh when he appeared in a pinch-hitting role and slammed a titanic homer into the third deck of the right field stands, his sixth in All-Star competition, a record. Ted Williams, with four circuit blasts, ranks second in the All-Star home run derby.

In the ninth, with Norm Larker on base, Ken Boyer teed off on a Gary Bell pitch and lined it for a four-baser into the left field stands to cap off the Nationals scoring. All six runs came across as a result of the home run shots.

Manager Walt Alston threw six pitchers against the American Leaguers, who collected eight hits but couldn't make any of them count. Vern Law, Johnny Podres, and Stan Williams hurled two innings each, while Larry Jackson, Bill Henry, and Lindy McDaniel worked one apiece.

The great Ted Williams, making his final All-Star appearance, singled as a pinch hitter in the seventh.

The Cave of the Winds: 1961 (I)

The 1961 All-Star contest at San Francisco's Candlestick Park has gone down as perhaps the weirdest game ever played in the long inter-league series.

Candlestick Park is situated on Candlestick Point, a sliver of lowland that sticks out into San Francisco Bay. The location is spectacular enough, but questionable because the ballpark is continually subjected to freakish winds coming in off the bay. Most of them blow in from left field to home plate, much to the chagrin of right-handed hitters . . . once those winds drop down into the bowl of the cavernous stadium, they can become very tricky. They can play havoc with high flies, transform perfect throws into bad ones, and even blow ground balls off their course. Candlestick Park didn't get its nickname "Cave of the Winds" for nothing.

The winds certainly blew on July 11th, 1961 at Candlestick, especially in the later innings when they reached galelike velocities.

Since the pennant-winning Yankees had given Casey Stengel the boot following the 1960 season, Paul Richards, manager of the runner-up Orioles was named to pilot the Americans. Danny Murtaugh of the world champion Pittsburgh Pirates led the N.L. squad.

The Nationals struck first in the second when Roberto Clemente tripled to deep right center off a Whitey Ford pitch and scored on Bill White's sacrifice fly. The N.L. picked up another marker in the fourth. Willie Mays started the inning by rapping a hot grounder off shortstop Tony Kubek's knee and proceeded to second on the error as the ball rolled into left field.

Dick Donovan gave up three singles in the fifth (to Smoky Burgess, Maury Wills, and Willie Mays), but the Nationals failed to capitalize and did not score.

The Americans finally posted a run on the board in the sixth when pinch hitter Harmon Killebrew caught hold of a Mike McCormick fastball and lofted it over the left field fence for a homer.

George Altman made it a 3–1 game in the eighth when he came in as a pinch hitter and lined a homer over the right field fence.

As the A.L. came to bat in the ninth, with Roy Face on the mound, the winds really began to blow. The game was transformed into an almost unbelievable spectacle. Pinch hitter Jim Gentile fanned, but Norman Cash doubled to right center for only the second A.L. hit. Nelson Fox ran for Cash and scored on Al Kaline's single to center. At this point, Murtaugh lifted Face and replaced him with Sandy Koufax. Roger Maris greeted Koufax with a line single to right, Kaline stopping at second.

Murtaugh, playing percentage baseball to the hilt, yanked Koufax in favor of right-hander Stu Miller to face right-handed-hitting Rocky Colavito. As Miller, a control artist, was getting ready to pitch to Colavito, the howling wind threw him off stride, nearly blew him off the mound, and caused him to commit the only balk in his career. The two runners advanced. Colavito then hit a windblown grounder that twisted like a serpent down to Ken Boyer at third. Boyer couldn't find the handle and was charged with an error, Kaline scoring. That made the score 3–3.

Miller eventually got out of the inning without further damage, but not before two more N.L. errors that tied his stomach in knots. Burgess dropped Tony Kubek's foul pop that wiggled on the way down (Kubek struck out anyway), and second baseman Don Zimmer's throw to first on Yogi Berra's grounder developed a life of its own in the wind and pulled Bill White off the bag.

Hoyt Wilhelm held the Nationals in the bottom of the ninth. In the top of the tenth, Fox walked with two out. Kaline then bounced to Boyer, but the bedeviled third baseman's throw took off like a jet plane, went way past White and sailed into right field. Fox raced around the bases and scored to give the Americans a 4–3 lead.

However, the Nationals came roaring back in their half of the tenth and tallied two runs against Wilhelm, who had difficulty throwing his knuckleball in the wind. Pinch hitter Hank Aaron opened with a single, and Mays bounced a double down the left field line, scoring Aaron. Frank Robinson was hit by a pitched ball. Clemente came through with a clutch single to right, driving in Mays with the winning run.

The seven errors in the game, five of them by the winning team, set an All-Star record. Five of the miscues were committed in the last two innings, and all five were directly attributable to the wind.

The N.L.'s 5–4 victory marked the first time that either circuit had salvaged a game from the fire in overtime. It also gave the Nationals a 3–0 record in extra-inning encounters.

Deadlock: 1961 (II)

On July 31st in Boston's Fenway Park, the second half of the 1961 "doubleheader" went down in the All-Star record books as the only game to end in a tie. A heavy downpour that fell just as the ninth inning ended forced the two teams to settle for a 1–1 deadlock. Mother Nature had a starring role, then, in both 1961 contests.

Pitching was the name of the game as both teams could manage only nine hits between them. Jim Bunning and Camilio Pascual each tossed three innings of hitless ball, and Art Mahaffey hurled a pair. Stu Miller gave up a lone single in his three innings of work and struck out five.

Rocky Colavito's first inning homer over the left field wall off Bob Purkey accounted for the A.L.'s only score. No other American Leaguer advanced past second.

The N.L.'s single run came in the sixth inning as the result of a mental lapse by shortstop Luis Aparicio. With one out, Eddie Mathews walked. Willie Mays flied out to Al Kaline in short right, but Orlando Cepeda got on when he was nicked by a Don Schwall pitch. Then on Eddie Kasko's dribbler toward short that should have ended the inning, Aparicio waited for the ball instead of moving in for it. The last bounce was a peculiar one, and by the time Luis got the ball, it was too late for a play. The infield hit loaded the bases.

Only a moment later a great play by Aparicio proved to be the game-saver for the Americans. Bill White slammed a sizzling grounder toward the box, which Schwall barely deflected. Racing behind second, Aparicio made a spectacular stop to prevent the ball from rolling to the outfield. Mathews scored on the hit, but Aparicio's play forced Cepeda to stop at third. The inning ended as Frank Bolling flied out to Colavito in left.

With the skies turning dark, the Fenway Park lights were switched on at the start of the seventh inning. When the rains began falling, play was immediately halted, and after a 30-minute wait, the umpires called the game.

Maury Wills Steals the Show: 1962 (I)

A capacity crowd of more than 45,000, including President John F. Kennedy and Vice-President Lyndon B. Johnson, saw the Nationals nip the Americans 3–1 in a sharply pitched game on July 10th, 1962 at Washington's D.C. Stadium. President Kennedy tossed out the ceremonial first ball.

With this victory, the senior circuit cut its deficit in the interleague series to 16–15.

Jim Bunning and Camilio Pascual blanked the N.L. for the first five innings, while Don Drysdale and Juan Marichal did the same to the A.L.

In the sixth, N.L. manager Fred Hutchinson called on 41-year-old Stan Musial to bat for Marichal. Stan, appearing in his 22nd All-Star Game, looked at two strikes and then lined a single into right. Maury Wills went in to run for Musial and promptly stole second, getting such a good jump on Pascual that catcher Earl Battey didn't even bother to throw.

Dick Groat followed with a single through the middle which scored the Dodger speed merchant. Groat advanced to second when Roberto Clemente grounded a single into left, the Pirate outfielder's third successive hit. A long fly to center by Willie Mays moved both runners up a base, and Groat tallied the second run of the inning on Orlando Cepeda's groundout to third.

The Americans came back in their half of the sixth to post their lone run on singles by Rich Rollins and Billy Moran plus a long fly ball by Roger Maris which Mays caught against the right-center field fence.

Mays bumped his back hard against the wire fence, but he held onto the ball and helped to kill a budding rally.

Wills gave the crowd a spectacular baserunning exhibition in the eighth after he led off with a single. Jim Davenport followed with a short single to left. Wills rounded second, stopped momentarily, and then made a mad dash to third when Rocky Colavito threw behind him to second. Second baseman Moran rifled the ball to Brooks Robinson at third, but Maury just beat the throw with a beautiful slide. Felipe Alou fouled out to Leon Wagner in medium deep right field, and Wills scored after the catch, sliding in ahead of Wagner's peg.

As Wills, a Washington native and a product of the city's high schools, brushed himself off, the crowd gave him a rousing ovation. Maury's greatest season in the majors came in 1962 as he stole 104 bases—then a record—and copped the National League's MVP award.

The Americans made a strong bid to tie the score in the ninth. With Bob Shaw on the hill, Colavito walked to open the frame. After Shaw disposed of the next two batters, John Romano singled, and Luis Aparicio belted a drive to deep right center. For a moment it looked like a sure triple, but Mays, running like a man possessed, flagged the ball down to end the game.

Homers Make the Difference: 1962 (II)

On July 30, 1962, at Chicago's Wrigley Field, the American League prevented the Nationals from tying up the All-Star series by hauling out the most lethal weapon in its arsenal, the home run, to hammer out an easy 9–4 victory.

Both teams posted ten hits, but three A.L. circuit blasts made the difference. The first came from an unlikely source, Pete Runnels, who whacked the ball into the left-center field bleachers as a pinch hitter in the third against Art Mahaffey. The Boston infielder had averaged less than four homers per season in his dozen years in the majors.

That made the score 1–1 since the Nationals had picked up a run in the second when Johnny Podres doubled and Dick Groat singled.

Leon Wagner also picked on a fat pitch from Mahaffey when he clubbed a two-run homer over the right field wall in the fourth, scoring behind Earl Battey who had walked. The A.L. now led 3–1.

After the A.L. picked up another run in the sixth off Bob Gibson (Tommy Tresh drove Al Kaline in from first with a long double), Rocky Colavito put the game out of reach, smashing a long three-run homer off Dick Farrell in the seventh. Brooks Robinson and Roger Maris were on base when Rocky connected to make the score 7–1.

The Nationals nicked Hank Aguirre for single runs in the seventh and eighth, but the Americans added two insurance runs in the ninth off Juan Marichal. Pinch hitter Yogi Berra reached second when Eddie Mathews booted the Yankee catcher's ground ball and then threw wildly to first. Mathews was charged with two errors on the play. Bobby Richardson, running for Berra, took third on a wild pitch and scored on Maris's double to right. Maris went to third on another wild pitch and trotted home on Colavito's long fly to center. For Rocky it was his fourth RBI of the day.

John Roseboro concluded the afternoon's scoring by socking the Nationals' only homer over the right field wall—off Milt Pappas—in the ninth.

Ray Herbert, the second of four A.L. twirlers, received credit for the win. Despite giving up three hits, he faced only ten batters in his three-inning tenure. Two quick double plays helped the White Sox pitcher out of trouble. Mahaffey took the loss.

Vengeance

17

THE Nationals began their real dominance of the All-Star series in 1963 when they whipped the Americans 5–3 at Cleveland. Including that game, they rolled up eight successive victories, lost in 1971 at Detroit, and then went on to win eight more in a row. That gave the N.L. 16 of 17 games, and pulled them way ahead in the series, 31 to 18.

This phenomenon will be discussed later in a special chapter entitled, "National League Supremacy: What Does It Mean?"

The Nationals' All-Star dominion notwithstanding, however, the Americans have never taken a back seat in the World Series. In the 76 World Series played from 1903 through 1979 (there was no postseason play in 1904), the Americans have won 45 championships to 31 for the Nationals. In total World Series games, the Junior Circuit has won 245, lost 202, and tied three. The National League may, of course, catch up to its adversary in this phase of the game, but it is unlikely to do so until sometime in the 21st century.

Those American League fans (including me) who may be distressed at reading a long litany of losses will take some comfort from Earl Weaver. He reminds American League aficionados that they shouldn't feel too badly since many of the losses came in close games and that the All-Star match-ups are basically exhibitions. But let's face it, Earl, a loss is a loss is a loss. Maybe we've just been outplayed.

Wonderful Willie (I): 1963

Major league magnates decided to hold the 1963 game in Cleveland to help revive baseball interest in that city. Few fans went to see the 1962

Indians' games and the 1963 edition of the club was to draw fewer than 600,000 paid admissions; the club owners found themselves awash in red ink. Though the All-Star crowd of 44,160 on July 9th was by far the season's largest gathering in Municipal Stadium, it was still 30,000 under capacity. Nevertheless, this attendance produced a healthy net of just over $250,000, with 95 percent of the revenue going into the major league players' pension fund.

The A.L. outhit the N.L. 11 to 6, but nearly everything else went wrong for the Americans when the chips were down. And then the Nationals had Willie Mays, who was easily the game's standout performer. Willie rapped only one hit, but he drove in two runs, walked once, swiped two bases, scored twice, and made the game's most spectacular fielding play.

Mays started his team on the victory road when he walked in the second inning, stole second, and raced home on Dick Groat's single. After the Americans tied the score in their half of the inning, the senior circuit came up with two more markers in the third on a single by Tommy Davis, an infield out, a run-scoring single by Mays, another theft by Willie, and Ed Bailey's single.

The Americans fought back in their turn against Larry Jackson and again managed to tie the score. Albie Pearson doubled off the fence in left center (that was the game's only extra-base hit) and scored on Frank Malzone's single. An infield out and Earl Battey's single brought Malzone home.

The Nationals broke the stalemate against Jim Bunning in the fifth on a walk to Davis, an error by Bobby Richardson, and Mays's infield out. They picked up an insurance run off Dick Radatz in the eighth when Bill White singled, stole second, and rode home on Ron Santo's single.

Mays, the "Say Hey Kid," electrified the crowd in the eighth when he raced back to the center field fence, near the 410-foot marker, and hauled down Joe Pepitone's drive. Willie caught his right foot under the wire barrier and hopped around in pain for a few moments, but then trotted to the dugout. Luckily he was not injured.

The Americans threatened to score several times after the third inning, including in the sixth and ninth, but Bobby Richardson killed both rallies by grounding out into inning-ending double plays.

Stan Musial, who retired at the end of the season, set a record by playing in his 24th All-Star Game, a record later tied by Willie Mays and Hank Aaron.

A tribute was paid to Mickey Mantle as the managers, coaches, and players named him the A.L.'s starting center fielder even though he was unable to play because of a broken foot. Albie Pearson of the Los Angeles Angels, runner-up for center field in the league's balloting, moved into the starting spot.

Two Strikes, Two Outs, in the Bottom of the Ninth: 1964

The 1964 All-Star Game, played on July 7th before a capacity crowd of more than 50,000 at New York's spanking new Shea Stadium, was almost a carbon copy of the 1941 thriller staged in Detroit, when Ted Williams belted a three-run homer with two out in the ninth to give the Americans a dramatic come-from-behind 7–5 victory. This time, however, it was the National Leagues' turn to put on a Frank Merriwell finish.

At the end of five innings, the N.L. led 3–1, but in the sixth the A.L. tied the score on Brooks Robinson's two-run triple. Willie Mays, who performed sensationally on defense in center field, handling seven putouts, barely missed a diving try for Robinson's liner.

The Americans took the lead in the seventh when big Elston Howard rumbled in from third on Jim Fregosi's sacrifice fly to center. Mays thrilled the crowd again when his long bulletlike throw almost nailed Howard.

The N.L. came to bat in the bottom of the ninth trailing 4–3. Dick Radatz, the big Boston relief ace, had already hurled two hitless innings while striking out four and appeared to be almost untouchable.

Leadoff man Willie Mays managed to wheedle a walk out of Radatz, fouling off five pitches on the three-and-two count before getting the fourth ball. Then in an unusual move, Willie stole second, just beating Elston Howard's throw to Bobby Richardson. When you're one run behind in the ninth, you don't try to steal bases—that is, unless your name is Willie Mays.

Orlando Cepeda followed with a bloop single to short right field. Mays, running like Whirlaway, tore around third, stopped momentarily, and then went on to score when first baseman Joe Pepitone, who had retrieved the ball, made a bad throw to the plate. Cepeda reached second on the error.

Curt Flood came in to run for Cepeda, and, after Ken Boyer popped out to third base, Johnny Edwards was purposely passed. Pinch hitter Hank Aaron struck out on three blazing fastballs.

That brought up Johnny Callison, the Philadelphia Phillies' young left-handed-swinging power hitter. With a count of one ball and two strikes, Radatz reared back and tried to blow a fastball by the hitter, but Callison, expecting to see the hard one, whipped his bat around and met the ball squarely. He sent the white pellet far over the right field fence for a three-run homer, as the crowd came to its feet. The Nationals won the game, 7–4 with this one swipe of the bat, and evened the All-Star series at 17–17.

League president Warren Giles rushed into the Nationals' clubhouse and personally congratulated Callison for his game-ending blast. Callison was awarded the first Arch Ward Memorial Trophy as the classic's most valuable player. (Baseball writers covering the game do the voting for the MVP.)

Juan Marichal, who pitched the final inning for the N.L., received credit for the victory, while Radatz, of course, was charged with the loss.

The Americans again outhit the Nationals, this time 9 to 8, but the senior circuit mustered its long ball power with three homers. In addition to Callison's smash, Billy Williams and Ken Boyer hit for the circuit, both those blows coming in the fourth inning.

Walt Alston managed the Nationals while Al Lopez piloted the Americans. Lopez inherited the A.L. helm because Ralph Houk of the 1963 flag-winning New York Yankees had moved up from manager to general manager of the club. Lopez's Chicago White Sox had finished second in 1963.

Wonderful Willie (II): 1965

Willie Mays made a habit of bedeviling the American League in All-Star competition and he did it again in the 1965 game played under a bright, cloudless sky at Metropolitan Stadium in Bloomington, Minnesota.

Mays didn't waste any time. He led off in the top of the first and whacked Milt Pappas's second pitch into the left-center bleachers for a 420-foot homer. It just wasn't Pappas's day, for he gave up a single to Willie Stargell and then Joe Torre followed with the inning's second homer, a shot into the lower left field seats just inside the foul pole. Ernie Banks singled and Pete Rose walked, but Pappas got Maury Wills to bounce back to the box to end the inning, mercifully enough.

The Nationals kept hammering away in the second inning against Jim "Mudcat" Grant, who came in to replace Pappas. Juan Marichal singled through the box, and Mays walked on four pitches. Hank Aaron bounced into a 5–4–3 double play, erasing Mays with Marichal taking third. Stargell then lashed a Grant fastball into the right-center field bull pen, giving the Nationals a fat 5–0 lead.

Marichal blanked the Americans for the first three innings, but the junior circuit came to life in the fourth and fifth when they worked Jim Maloney over for five runs to tie the game. The A.L. nicked Maloney for one run in the fourth on a single by Dick McAuliffe, a walk to Harmon Killebrew, and a single by Rocky Colavito.

The deluge hit Maloney in the fourth as the Americans belted him for

four runs on two two-run homers. After the Cincinnati speedball specialist retired Vic Davalillo and Earl Battey, he walked Jimmy Hall, and
McAuliffe followed with a drive that traveled over the center field fence
in the deepest part of the park, 410 feet from home plate. Brooks Robinson beat out a slow grounder to Ron Santo at third. Killebrew, with a
2–2 count, laid all of his 220 pounds into a Maloney fastball and sent a
415-foot rocket shot into the left field pavilion to tie the score at 5–5. The
roar of the crowd could be heard all over Minneapolis and St. Paul . . .
after all "Killer" Killebrew was the Minnesota Twins home run king.

For a brief while it appeared as if the American League might snatch
victory from the jaws of defeat—but the Nationals had Willie Mays on
their side.

In the seventh, with Sam McDowell on the mound, Mays led off with
a walk. The big Cleveland southpaw made the mistake of pitching too
finely to him. Aaron stroked a single to right center, sending Mays to
third. Pinch hitter Roberto Clemente forced Aaron on a grounder to
third, as Mays held up. Ron Santo dribbled a single through the middle;
shortstop Zoilo Versalles knocked the ball down but had no chance for a
play, as Mays scored the go-ahead run. Torre grounded into a double
play to end the inning.

The Americans threatened in both the eighth and ninth innings, as the
game turned out to be a real cliff-hanger. In the eighth, with two out and
men on second and third, Hall lined a drive to deep center field. Mays
slipped as he started back for the ball, but the brilliant outfielder recovered almost instantaneously and made a leaping backhanded catch to
prevent two runs from scoring.

Tony Oliva led off the ninth with a ringing double to left center. Max
Alvis, attempting to sacrifice, popped to pitcher Bob Gibson, and then
the Cardinals' flamethrower struck out both Killebrew and pinch hitter
Joe Pepitone to sew up the 6–5 victory.

For the first time since the All-Star Game was launched, the senior
circuit gained the lead in the series. With this victory, their seventh in the
last eight decisions, the Nationals took an 18–17 edge.

Despite Mays's heroics in the 1965 game, Willie ran second to Juan
Marichal in the press box voting for the Arch Ward Memorial Trophy.

A Hot Time in St. Louis: 1966

The 1966 All-Star Game was played out of turn in St. Louis to help
commemorate the city's bicentennial and to celebrate the opening, earlier in the season, of the new Busch Memorial Stadium on the Missis-
sippi river front.

Most of the nearly 50,000 fans who attended the game will remember the affair for the searing 106-degree heat, but many will also recall the shimmering 2–1 National League victory in 10 innings.

Just how hot was it in St. Louis during that scorching July afternoon? Brooks Robinson recalled recently: "Busch Stadium was a real hotbox that day. Early on, our batboy passed out in the dugout, and I saw fans in the stands pass out during the course of the game." The shriveling heat was so bad that nearly 150 persons required first aid at the stadium.

Jim Ewell, then the Houston Astros' chief trainer, who served the National League that day, says: "It was sure hotter 'n hell in St. Louis for that game. We had our cold packs, smelling salts, and oxygen ready for players who began to feel woozy. I remember working on Hank Aaron and Willie Mays a little toward the middle of the game. Those two guys hung in there for the whole ten innings. Remember what I said about that 1960 game in Kansas City, when it was also over 100 degrees. The true stars give it all they've got for every play no matter what the weather is."

The Americans scored their lone run in the second off Sandy Koufax when, with one out, Brooks Robinson smacked a liner to left field and wound up with a triple when Hank Aaron momentarily lost sight of the ball in the background of white shirts. Starting in late, he slipped, and the ball skipped past him to the wall. Koufax induced George Scott to foul out to the first baseman, but while facing Bill Freehan, he uncorked a wild pitch, permitting Robinson to cross the plate.

The Nationals got the equalizer in the fourth as Willie Mays and Roberto Clemente led off with singles. Willie McCovey forced Clemente, Mays going to third, and Ron Santo's slow roller single down the third base line brought Willie in.

The game continued as a pitchers' battle until the bottom of the tenth. With Pete Richert on the mound, Tim McCarver grounded a single to right, and then moved to second on Ron Hunt's sacrifice. Maury Wills brought McCarver home with another single to right field.

Gaylord Perry, who pitched the final two innings for the N.L., received credit for the victory.

Brooks Robinson won the Arch Ward Memorial Trophy as the game's outstanding player. Brooks rapped out three of the A.L.'s six hits, scored his team's only run, and established the All-Star record for third basemen by handling eight chances.

Ted Williams and Casey Stengel, both about to be inducted later in the summer into the Hall of Fame at Cooperstown, N.Y., served as honorary coaches. Williams, a veteran of eighteen All-Star Games, sat in the A.L. dugout, while Casey Stengel, who retired the year before as manager of the New York Mets, had a place on the N.L. bench.

Thirty, Count 'Em, Thirty Strikeouts: 1967

The California Angels' Anaheim Stadium was chosen as the site for the 1967 All-Star Game in keeping with the major leagues' policy of giving new parks priority in playing host for the midsummer classic. The Angels' new home was opened in 1966.

The Nationals extended their winning streak in the interleague series to five games by edging the Americans 2–1 in 15 innings, making this contest the longest in All-Star annals. The 1967 game was the fifth to go extra innings, with the N.L. taking all five.

Twelve pitchers combined to register an incredible total of 30 strikeouts, an All-Star record: 17 American Leaguers whiffed, while 13 National Leaguers hit the breeze. Ferguson Jenkins led the strikeout parade as he fanned six A.L. batsmen to equal the All-Star standard for one game.

Many players blamed the late-afternoon start (4:15 P.M. California time) for the strikeout epidemic. The 4:15 starting time was chosen so the game could occupy prime evening hours for television in the Eastern and Midwestern time zones. A survey estimated that a TV audience of at least 55 million saw the contest, then a record for a video baseball attraction aside from the World Series.

Roberto Clemente, on his way to winning a fourth National League batting title in 1967, voiced what many players were thinking. "Those late-afternoon and early twilight shadows made breaking pitches especially tough to follow. No wonder everybody was swinging at the wind."

Willie Mays, on the other hand, refused to go along with Clemente's theory. Said Willie: "It was the pitching, not the light conditions."

Oddly, all the runs in the game resulted from solo homers. Richie Allen put the Nationals one up in the second inning when he blasted a Dean Chance fastball over the center field fence. Brooks Robinson tied the score in the sixth when he walloped a four-bagger off Jenkins.

Finally, in the top of the 15th inning when it was nearly eight o'clock in Anaheim, Tony Perez caught hold of Jim "Catfish" Hunter's one-strike fastball and drove it over the left field fence.

Don Drysdale, who pitched the 13th and 14th innings for the N.L., received credit for the victory, while Tom Seaver got the save retiring the Americans in the bottom of the 15th.

Tony Perez, appearing in his first All-Star Game, won the Arch Ward Trophy as the MVP.

A few jaded baseball writers were heard to say that this was the dullest of the midseason classics. But if you love mound mastery, you would have loved the 1967 game at Anaheim.

Wonderful Willie (III): 1968

The 1968 All-Star Game, staged at Houston's famed Astrodome, attracted a capacity crowd of more than 48,000 fans—and then NBC-TV estimated that the contest, played in prime evening televison time, was watched by a television audience of at least 60 million.

What did those multitudes see? They saw the American League lose, of course, this time 1–0, making this the first and only one-zip decision in the history of the event.

The game also featured a number of other All-Star firsts: the first played in the South, the first played indoors, and the first played on artificial turf.

Willie Mays, now 37 and in his 17th year in the National League, was not slated to be in the starting lineup, but got the call because of an injury to Pete Rose of Cincinnati.

Willie Mays in the All-Star lineup usually means bad news for the American League. Sure enough, Willie opened the bottom half of the first inning with a ground single past Brooks Robinson into left field. Cleveland's Luis Tiant, the A.L.'s starting pitcher, watched Willie carefully, and then threw to Harmon Killebrew at first on an attempted pickoff. Killebrew let the ball get past him for an error, and Willie scrambled to second.

Tiant, a little unnerved, walked Curt Flood, and when the fourth ball was a wild pitch, Mays took third. Mays then crossed the plate when Willie McCovey, his San Francisco Giants' teammate, grounded into a double play, Rod Carew to Jim Fregosi to Killebrew.

The run may have been a bit tainted, but it was enough to do the American League in, as the Nationals' pitching and defense were superb.

In fact, pitchers from both teams dominated the game as the N.L. collected only five hits and the A.L. just three. The eight hit total tied the previous low set in the five-inning, rain-shortened game at Philadelphia in 1952. The game was perfectly tailored to "Year-of-the-Pitcher" dimensions—it was in 1968 that Carl Yastrzemski led the American League in hitting with a puny .301 average.

Don Drysdale, who received credit for the victory, tied All-Star records when he started his fifth game and pitched in his eighth. His three-inning sting gave him a total of nineteen and a third frames, the All-Star high for a hurler from either league. Tom Seaver pitched two exceptionally strong innings, striking out five.

Mays walked off with the Arch Ward Memorial Trophy as the game's MVP.

The Washington Massacre: 1969

After nosing out the Americans by single run margins in the previous four All-Star games, the Nationals hauled out the lumber and really battered the junior circuit, winning by a lopsided 9–3 score in the 1969 match-up at Washington, D.C. This was the N.L.'s seventh straight All-Star victory, and by this time the American Leaguers were getting a bit punchy.

The game had been scheduled for the night of Tuesday, July 22, but torrential rains forced postponement until the following day. This was the first and only rain postponement in All-Star history.

Major league baseball celebrated its centennial in 1969 with a gala pregame All-Star extravaganza that included a black-tie dinner on the evening of July 21, honoring the "Greatest Team Ever," and a White House reception for the game's "400."

The National League then did some celebrating of its own as it piled up eight runs in the first three innings: one in the first, two in the second, and five in the third. The run in the first off Mel Stottlemyre was unearned. Matty Alou, who had singled and advanced to third, scored easily when big Frank Howard muffed Hank Aaron's soft fly to left for a two-base error.

Cleon Jones led off the second with an infield single and scored ahead of Johnny Bench, who homered into the left field mezzanine.

John "Blue Moon" Odom replaced Stottlemyre in the third and really got his ears pinned back as the Nationals tagged him for five hits and five runs before Manager Mayo Smith gave him the hook with only one man out.

Aaron greeted Odom with a single to left, and Willie McCovey followed with a titanic homer off the scoreboard in right center. Ron Santo grounded out to Rico Petrocelli at short, but then Petrocelli fumbled Jones's grounder for an error. Bench sliced a single to right, Jones racing to third. Felix Millan bounced a double over Sal Bando's head at third scoring both Jones and Bench. Pitcher Steve Carlton drilled a double to left center, Millan scoring. At this point Darold Knowles relieved the beleaguered Odom and retired the next two men to end the inning.

The Nationals scored their ninth and final run off Denny McClain in the fourth when Willie McCovey homered again, this time over the fence in right. McCovey became the fourth player to homer twice in one All-Star Game.

As for the Americans' offense, Frank Howard and Bill Freehan smashed solo homers in the second and third innings, respectively, while Freehan singled Reggie Smith across in the fourth.

Pitchers for both teams tightened the screws for the final five innings, which were scoreless.

Denny McClain caused a flap when he reported to the park a bit late— he ambled into the dugout during the second inning. Mayo Smith had planned to start McClain, who compiled an amazing 31–6 record the year before, but with the postponement Denny had returned to Detroit to keep a dental appointment, and encountered problems making connections back to Washington. McClain did pitch a token inning, however.

A Thorny Rose: 1970

For the first time since 1957 when Cincinnati's superenthusiastic baseball nuts had stuffed the ballot boxes to elect their favorite Reds, selection of the starting lineups for the midsummer classic was placed back in the hands of the country's baseball fans. Commissioner Bowie Kuhn's office maintained that proper safeguards were in force to prevent outrages of the type that had been committed 13 years earlier.

Appropriately, Cincinnati's spanking new Riverfront Stadium was host for the 1970 game, which attracted a capacity crowd of nearly 52,000 fans, including President Nixon. At least another 60 million sat in at this night game via television.

The game started out as an intense pitchers' duel, as neither side scored through the first five innings, but in the top of the sixth the A.L. broke through for a run against Gaylord Perry when Carl Yastrzemski singled home Ray Fosse. The Americans nicked Perry for another run in the seventh when Fosse's sacrifice fly with the bases loaded brought Brooks Robinson in.

The Nationals got one run back in the seventh when Bud Harrelson crossed the plate as Willie McCovey was grounding into a double play. Pitcher Jim Perry, Gaylord's older brother, was lucky to escape the inning with limited damage.

Brooks Robinson extended the junior circuit's lead to 4–1 in the eighth when he tripled over center fielder Cito Gaston's head to drive in Yastrzemski and Willie Horton. Robinson had picked on a Bob Gibson fastball to his liking.

Going into the bottom of the ninth, the Americans were only three outs away from victory, as some of the fans in the predominantly N.L. crowd began heading for the exits. But catcher Dick Dietz stopped them in their tracks when he led off the inning with a homer over the 404-foot mark in center field off new A.L. pitcher Jim "Catfish" Hunter. Harrelson singled, Gaston flied out, and when Joe Morgan singled, Manager Earl Weaver lifted Hunter in favor of Fritz Peterson. McCovey promptly singled to center, Harrelson scoring from second and Morgan going to third. Mel Stottlemyre replaced Peterson, and Roberto Clemente brought in the tying run when his sacrifice liner to Amos Otis in right center brought in Morgan.

The crowd went back to their seats as the match went into extra innings.

The Americans mounted scoring threats in the 10th, 11th, and 12th innings against Claude Osteen, but were unable to dent home plate.

After Clyde Wright retired pinch hitter Joe Torre and Clemente in the bottom of the 12th, Pete Rose singled to center, and Billy Grabarkewitz followed with a line hit to left, Rose stopping at second. Jim Hickman lined a single to center. Rose raced home and just beat Amos Otis's strong throw to score the winning run, bowling over catcher Fosse in a violent collision that left both players bruised and battered for more than a week.

The final score: N.L. 5, A.L. 4. In the six overtime struggles that have been played, the Nationals have made a clean sweep.

The Americans gained a little satisfaction when Carl Yastrzemski was given the Arch Ward Memorial Trophy as the game's MVP on the strength of his four hits and fine fielding.

"Did you have to knock down Ray Fosse like that?" I asked Pete Rose recently. Rose, who plays hard every minute he's on the field, replied:

"You know, Ray Fosse is a friend of mine. On the evening before the game, Ray visited at our house in Cincinnati, but when I saw that the play at home was going to be close, with Ray trying to block the plate, I had no choice except to knock him over. I collided with Fosse just a split second before the ball arrived, and he never even had a chance to catch it. If I'd tried to slide, I might have been tagged out."

18

Every Dog Has His Day: 1971

SOMETHING extraordinary happened at Detroit's Tiger Stadium on the night of July 13, 1971—the American League actually won an All-Star game, snapping the National League's winning streak at eight. The A.L. triumphed 6–4 in a battle of homers, each side hitting three, and, oddly enough, the circuit blasts accounted for all of the scoring.

For a while it looked as if the Nationals would make it nine in a row as homers by Johnny Bench and Hank Aaron off starter Vida Blue gave them an early 3–0 lead. In the second inning, with Willie Stargell on base, Bench's wind-aided blast landed in the upper deck in right center. The wind, in fact, helped the long ball hitters throughout the game, and Aaron next took advantage of the forces of nature in the third frame when he poled a towering drive into the upper stands in right field. That was Bad Henry's first homer in All-Star competition.

Then in the bottom of the third the Americans got Blue off the hook quickly when they went to work on Dock Ellis, who had blanked them in the two opening frames. Luis Aparicio, the fans' choice as A.L. shortstop despite his meager .209 batting average, led off with a line single to center. Manager Earl Weaver then went to his bench and called on Reggie Jackson to bat for Blue, and Reggie responded by hitting one of the longest homers in All-Star history, a 520-foot blow that would have gone clear out of Briggs Stadium had it not struck a light tower projecting above the stands in right center field.

Ellis, a bit shaken up, walked Rod Carew, but settled down and retired Bobby Murcer and Carl Yastrzemski. Frank Robinson, hitless in his last 14 All-Star at-bats, sliced a line home run into the right field seats, scoring behind Carew. The A.L. now had a 4–3 edge.

Robinson's smash off Ellis gave him the distinction of being the first player in All-Star annals with a homer to his credit in each league. Frank's only other four-bagger in the interleague series came in the second 1959 game while he was a member of the Cincinnati Reds.

Harmon Killebrew clinched the Americans' victory in the sixth when he lined a homer into the left field stands after leadoff man Al Kaline had singled. Ferguson Jenkins, the Chicago Cubs' fireballing right-hander, was the victim of the two-run outburst.

Roberto Clemente concluded the day's scoring in the eighth when he jumped on a Mickey Lolich fastball and powered a drive into the bleachers in deep right center.

The game's six homers tied a record established in the same park in 1951 and equaled in 1954 at Cleveland. Frank Robinson won the Arch Ward Trophy as the game's MVP for his two-run homer that gave the A.L. its lead.

The capacity crowd of 53,559 at Tiger Stadium produced record gate receipts of $435,134.

19

Business as Usual

AFTER its 1971 victory, the American League slid right back into its routine. They kept on losing through the 1970s for a number of reasons: the big hitters didn't come through in the clutch; relief pitchers got bombed; the defenses came unglued; key players found assorted excuses to skip the game—one could go on and on. And then it just may be that the National League takes the All-Star Game more seriously than its opponent.

Little Big Man: 1972

The American League went into the eighth inning of the 1972 game, played in the bandbox Atlanta Stadium, on the short end of a 2–1 score. Then they suddenly went one up when Cookie Rojas, pinch-hitting for Rod Carew, homered off Bill Stoneman with Carlton Fisk on base. For a moment it appeared that the long-abused A.L. might take two All-Star games in a row for the first time since 1957–58.

Rojas's blast over the left field fence, together with another A.L. run scored in the third frame, had offset Hank Aaron's four-bagger with Cesar Cedeno aboard in the sixth. Aaron, playing before more than 50,000 screaming hometown fans, picked on one of Gaylord Perry's "wet" sliders and drove it far over the left field fence.

However, the Nationals nicked Wilbur Wood for a run in the bottom of the ninth to knot the score at 3–3. Back-to-back singles by Billy Williams and Manny Sanguillen put runners on first and third with none out, and as Lee May forced Sanguillen at second, Williams raced across the plate. But the N.L. lost a chance to win it when Ron Santo grounded into a fast 5-4-3 double play to end the frame and send the game into extra innings.

Tug McGraw, who took the hill for the senior loop in the ninth, retired the Americans in order in the tenth. McGraw struck out four men in his two-inning tenure.

Dave McNally, who replaced Wilbur Wood on the mound in the bottom of the tenth, walked leadoff man Nate Colbert on a 3-2 pitch. Chris Speier sacrificed successfully, and Joe Morgan followed with a line single to right center to score Colbert with the winning run.

The Nationals had now triumphed in all seven affairs. The long ball belters from both leagues were supposed to have a field day in Atlanta Stadium, known as a hitters' park, but the game turned out to be a relatively low-scoring affair at 4-3.

For his winning blow and outstanding defensive play at second base, Morgan took the Arch Ward MVP Trophy. Morgan's only hit of the day was the decisive "gamer," but he also handled eight chances in the field flawlessly. After the game, little Joe—he stands only 5'7" and weighs 160 pounds—told reporters: "The longer you play, the better your chances are to do something good." He and first baseman Lee May were the only National Leaguers to go the full route.

Even now, when asked which of his more than 2,000 big league games he remembers most, Joe Morgan beams, "Hey man, it's got to be that 1972 All-Star Game when I knocked in the winning run."

The Kansas City Stomp: 1973

"To be perfectly honest, I'd have to say that we really beat the piss out of the American League in the 1973 Kansas City game," declared Sparky Anderson recently. "This was *the* game in which the National League displayed its dominance in every phase of the sport: batting power, running, pitching, and fielding."

The A.L. actually broke into the scoring column first when Reggie Jackson led off the second inning with a double off the center field wall and came home on Amos Otis's single.

From then on, however, the N.L. got its offensive machine rolling and posted runs in the next four successive innings, the third through the sixth. In the third a pair of runs materialized from two walks and RBI singles by Cesar Cedeno and Hank Aaron. Johnny Bench led off the fourth by homering into the left field seats.

The butchery really started when Manager Anderson inserted Bobby Bonds into right field in the fourth inning. Bonds failed to get the fans' vote for the N.L. starting team, but Sparky had announced before the game: "Bobby Bonds is the best player in the National League, and I want to get him in my lineup just as soon as possible."

Bonds immediately justifed Anderson's faith in him. In his first time at bat in the fifth, he picked on a fastball thrown by Bill Singer and bashed a two-run homer over the left-center field fence. Joe Morgan, who had doubled, scored ahead of Bonds. Singer had a rough night: he threw the gopher ball to Johnny Bench, too.

The N.L. concluded its scoring in the sixth when pinch hitter Willie Davis tied into one of Nolan Ryan's blazers and slammed a home run over the right field fence following a walk to Ron Santo.

Bonds electrified the sellout crowd of more than 40,000 with an extraordinary display of hustle in the seventh. After he stroked an ordinary-appearing single to left field, he raced on to second and slid in safely for a double, beating Bobby Murcer's throw by an eyelash. Even the partisan American League Kansas City fans gave Bonds an ovation for his daring.

In the end, the Royals' brand new $2-million scoreboard had to light up another humiliating thrashing of the Americans, 7–1 this time.

Bobby Bonds easily placed first in the press box balloting for the game's MVP.

The contest was marked by the appearance of a record 54 players, 28 for the National League. Of the 58 selected for the two squads, only 4 were not called upon.

Special ceremonies were held before the game to celebrate the 40th anniversary of the first All-Star classic played at Chicago's Comiskey Park. Over 20 participants from that 1933 game were present at the ceremonies, including such Hall of Famers as Earl Averill, Joe Cronin, Bill Dickey, Charlie Gehringer, Lefty Grove, Lefty Gomez, and Carl Hubbell.

The Write-In Hero: 1974

Steve Garvey, the Los Angeles first baseman whose name did not even appear on the official All-Star ballot, made the National League's starting lineup as a write-in candidate and justified the fans' confidence in him by emerging as the star of the evening at Pittsburgh's Three Rivers Stadium on July 23. Garvey was awarded the Arch Ward Trophy for leading the N.L. to a decisive 7–2 win over the A.L. by delivering two key base hits and playing flawlessly in the field.

The senior circuit drew first blood in the second inning off the pitching of Gaylord Perry. With two outs, Garvey grounded a single to center and then raced home on Ron Cey's line double to left center.

The Americans got their two runs in the third off Andy Messersmith, taking a 2–1 lead, and threatened to make it a really big inning. However, with runners on first and second and two out, Garvey went far to his right to make a sensational grab of Bobby Murcer's smash and threw to Messersmith covering first to kill the rally.

In the bottom of the fourth, with Luis Tiant pitching, Johnny Bench and Jim Wynn opened the inning with singles. Garvey then drilled a double down the left field line, scoring Bench from third, with Wynn going to third. Cey's infield groundout scored Wynn to give the N.L. a 3–2 edge.

The Nationals padded their lead by picking up single runs in the fifth and seventh and two more in the eighth. Reggie Smith produced the tally in the seventh with a homer into the right field bleachers.

The American League threw four pitchers in to stop the onslaught, but each was roughed up for at least one run.

Lee MacPhail, the new American League president, had done everything in his power to get his circuit back on the winning track in '74. McPhail issued a blizzard of memos to all of his teams' managers telling them that starting pitchers should be rested before the big game and urged All-Star pilot Dick Williams to use the best talent available, regardless of the feelings of players who did not see action. Alas, the memoranda did no good. Baseball games are won on the field, not in the executive suite.

Madlock and Matlack: 1975

The Nationals jumped out to an early 3–0 lead in the 1975 encounter. Milwaukee's County Stadium admitted 51,480 fans that night of July 15, the largest crowd that had yet seen a ballgame in the nation's "Beer Capital."

Oakland's Vida Blue gave up first inning singles to Pete Rose and Joe Morgan, but got through that canto without anyone crossing the plate. In the second, however, the first two men to face him, Steve Garvey and Jim Wynn, lined homers into the left field stands.

With Steve Busby pitching in the third, Lou Brock singled, moved to second on a balk, stole third, and then trotted home on Johnny Bench's single to left.

The score remained 3–0 going into the sixth, and it appeared as if the Nationals were on another cakewalk as Tom Seaver strode to the mound. Even though "Tom Terrific" owned a formidable All-Star record, he was not at his brilliant best that night. He gave up a single to Joe Rudi and walked Gene Tenace. With two on and two out, Carl Yastrzemski, pinch-hitting for Jim Kaat, picked on Seaver's first pitch and lined it into the right-center field bull pen for a three-run homer. One swipe of the bat, and the game was knotted at 3–3.

The score stayed tied going into the top of the ninth, when Jim "Catfish" Hunter, who had blanked the N.L. in the seventh and eighth, ran into big trouble. Leadoff man Reggie Smith dumped a soft fly into short left field, but Claudell Washington, after a late start, caught up with the ball only to let it plop out of his glove for a single. The official scorer was charitable. Al Oliver then sliced a drive to left which Washington misjudged and failed to overhaul. Oliver got a double out of it, and Smith stopped at third.

Manager Alvin Dark came out to replace the unfortunate Hunter with Rich "Goose" Gossage, the right-handed flamethrower. Gossage promptly hit Larry Bowa with a pitch to load the bases. With the infield drawn in, Bill Madlock singled past third base to score Smith and Oliver, as Bowa raced to third. Bowa scored on Rose's long sacrifice fly to left center to make the final tally 6–3.

The Sporting News's Joe Marcin yawned later that Claudell Washington's fielding was "somewhat short of All-Star caliber."

For the first time there were cowinners of the game's Most Valuable Player trophy: Bill Madlock for his game-winning hit, and Jon Matlack for hurling two scoreless innings (the seventh and eighth) and striking out four.

The junior circuit had at least put up a good fight in the 1975 game, but baseball writers everywhere began to write that the series had turned into an increasing embarrassment to the American League.

The Juniors Saw Red: 1976

To help commemorate the nation's bicentennial, the 1976 All-Star Game was played in Philadelphia, with 63,974 spectators, including President Gerald Ford, jamming their way into Veterans Stadium.

The Nationals demolished the Americans 7–1 as five N.L. pitchers throttled the junior circuit's top batsmen, allowing five measly hits. The A.L.'s lone tally came in the fourth inning on Fred Lynn's homer into the right field bleachers off Tom Seaver.

Five members of the Cincinnati Reds were chosen by the fans to the N.L.'s starting lineup: third baseman Pete Rose, second baseman Joe Morgan, center fielder George Foster, catcher Johnny Bench, and shortstop Dave Concepcion. Then Manager Sparky Anderson picked two more of his own Reds as reserves: first baseman Tony Perez and right fielder Ken Griffey. Among them, they accounted for four runs scored, four runs batted in, and seven of their team's base hits.

The Nationals went right to work on starter Mark Fidrych for two runs in the bottom of the first. Rose lined a single to center, and Steve Garvey followed with a humpback liner to right field that fell in front of Rusty Staub and then bounced past him for a triple, Rose scoring. Garvey scored on Foster's groundout.

Fidrych was tagged for singles by Bench and Concepcion in the second, but managed to struggle through the inning allowing a run.

"Catfish" Hunter gave up another brace of runs in the third. After Garvey fouled out, Morgan singled to center and Foster hammered a long homer far over the wall in left center.

The Nationals went scoreless for the next four frames and then erupted for three more tallies against Frank Tanana in the eighth. Tanana gave up a walk, two singles, and a homer, the latter a two-run blow by Cesar Cedeno.

George Foster, making his first All-Star appearance, won the Arch Ward MVP Trophy for his three RBIs.

Hard-boiled baseball writers now began to use stronger words to describe the junior circuit's dismal performances in the interleague series. Headlines like "American League Humiliated Again" began to creep over the country's sports pages.

On a more telling note, an estimated 60 million people watched the Veterans Stadium proceedings on ABC television. Commenting on this phenomenon, *The Sporting News* observed dryly: "The competition on NBC and CBS was the Democratic National Convention, and the Nielsen ratings proved what everybody knew all along—even a bad baseball game is preferred viewing to a conclave of politicians spouting windy oratory."

Right Where It Hurts: 1977

Sparky Anderson was both brief and refreshingly candid when he addressed his National League troops before the 1977 All-Star Game at the newly refurbished Yankee Stadium. "The only reason we're here," intoned Sparky, "is to kick living hell out of those guys."

The Nationals took him at his word and unloaded right off in the top of the first. Leadoff man Joe Morgan worked the count to three-and-two and then lined a Jim Palmer fastball into the right field seats. Morgan thus became the fourth player to club a leadoff All-Star four-bagger.

During Palmer's unfortunate first frame, Dave Parker singled and scored on George Foster's long double to left center. Foster crossed the plate after Greg Luzinski sliced a homer into the right field seats. The shell-shocked Palmer had barely worked up a sweat before the Nationals had laid a four-spot on him.

Palmer sailed through the second inning unscathed, but got the heave-ho from Manager Billy Martin after Steve Garvey led off the third with a long homer into the left-center bleachers.

Palmer, a three-time Cy Young Award winner, had actually been pressed into service as a starter on an emergency basis bacause the A.L. corps of starting pitchers was decimated for various reasons. Frank Tanana of the California Angels and Mark Fidrych of the Detroit Tigers remained out of uniform because of arm problems, while California's Nolan Ryan, irked at not being originally named to the squad, refused to accept the role as a substitute for Tanana. Despite Martin's pleas for him to join the team, Ryan remained at home at Laguna Beach where he sulked for three days.

The American League attack was bottled up by Don Sutton and Gary Lavelle for five innings, but signs of life appeared in the sixth when Tom Seaver took the mound. With two out and Fred Lynn and Rod Carew on first and second respectively, Richie Zisk knocked both men in with a long double to right center.

Willie Randolph's single scored Butch Wynegar in the seventh to make it a 5–3 game.

The N.L.'s offense began rolling again in the eighth when Sparky Lyle came in to pitch. Leadoff man Garry Templeton bounced a double over Graig Nettles's head, and Jerry Morales was hit by a pitch. Both men moved up on a wild pitch, and Dave Winfield drove them in with a ground single to left to run the score to 7–3. Said Sparky Lyle of his pitching performance that day, "I got my ass kicked."

George Scott homered off Rich Gossage with Bert Campaneris on base in the bottom of the ninth to make the final score 7–5.

Winning pitcher Don Sutton took home the game's MVP trophy.

Disappearing Act: 1978

"This might be only an exhibition, but it's still a game we want to win very badly," Billy Martin testified at a press conference the day before the 1978 game at San Diego. "The American League has been getting racked up in this game too often, and we want to give the other league the same medicine we gave Los Angeles in the 1977 World Series."

The cocky Martin took American League All-Star managing honors for the second year in a row because of the Yankees' back-to-back pennants.

Tom Lasorda, the National League pilot, threw back to Martin "I'm managing one of the finest teams you'll every see on a ball field."

"Did Reggie Jackson get here yet?" asked one of the West Coast reporters as the press conference moved along.

"We just got a call from Reggie saying he can't make it because he's got a temperature of 104," explained Billy Martin, as a slight crinkle creased his face.

"A likely story," muttered one of the reporters in the back of the room. No matter that the fans had chosen Reggie for a starting spot in the A.L. outfield.

Thus, one of the sluggers the Nationals feared most was missing from the competition. Never mind that by the night of the game Jackson had recovered sufficiently from his malady so that he was involved in an altercation at a New York movie house, an episode that rated a banner headline on the front page of *The New York Post*.

After Billy Martin's sad news, Bob Fishel, the A.L. public relations chief, brought in more ill tidings: Carl Yastrzemski, a reserve AL outfielder who ranked very high in the fan vote, couldn't make it either. Dick Young, *New York Daily News* sports editor, wondered out loud why Yaz was "begging off," but the best answer he could get from anybody in the room (including Don Zimmer, Red Sox manager and an All-Star coach) was that the veteran slugger was "tired." Yastrzemski, though pushing 39, was still regarded by the Nationals as one of the opposition's main offensive threats. Two of their big guns gone, but some folks still wonder about the American League's "bad luck" in All-Star play.

Rod Carew, the perennial batting champion, got the Americans off to a roaring start when he caught hold of one of Vida Blue's offerings and banged a line drive triple to the left-center field wall. Center fielder George Foster of Cincinnati, normally a left fielder, hesitated a bit in tracking down the drive that appeared to be catchable. George Brett then slammed a double to left center, Carew scoring easily.

Jim Rice grounded to second, Brett taking third, and Richie Zisk kept the rally alive by drawing a base on balls. Carlton Fisk lofted a pop-up into shallow right, where second baseman Joe Morgan caught it, racing away from the plate. Brett broke for the plate and had an easy time making it as Morgan bounced his off-balance throw to relay man Steve Garvey. Zisk was thrown out trying to steal second, but the A.L. had succeeded in scoring two quick runs.

Jim Palmer held the N.L. at bay for the first two innings, and his chances for a pitching victory looked bright as the Americans picked up another marker in the third.

Carew opened the inning with his second triple off Blue to even deeper left center, and again Brett got him home—with a sacrifice fly. Carew thus earned the distinction of becoming the first batter to ever slam two triples in the same All-Star Game.

The A.L. lead went right down the chute, however, as Palmer ran into big trouble in the third. Leadoff man Larry Bowa popped a single to short right center, but pinch hitter Reggie Smith, batting for Blue, became Palmer's fourth strikeout victim as Bowa stole second. When Pete Rose grounded out to first, Bowa moved to third, where he remained as Joe Morgan and George Foster drew walks, filling the bases. A third base on balls, to Greg Luzinski, forced in the first N.L. run, and Steve Garvey's ground single to left (just out of the reach of 5' 4" shortstop Fred Patek), scoring Morgan and Foster, knotted the score at 3-3.

At this point Billy Martin hustled out to the mound and excused Palmer in favor of Oakland right-hander Matt Keough, who got out of the inning without doing further damage.

Palmer said the pitch to Garvey was the only bad one of the inning, a slider that didn't break. Of his control lapse, he said he had trouble gripping the ball, a result of his inability to get the pine tar off his hand after batting in the second. Curiously, this was the first time Palmer had batted in championship competition in five years, and that emphasizes just how sticky these annual affairs were getting for the American League.

The game remained deadlocked until the last half of the eighth when Steve Garvey stroked a line drive triple high against the right-center field wall off fastballer Rich Gossage, who had just taken the mound. Garvey promptly scored when Gossage uncorked a wild pitch. This was only the beginning of the disaster, however, as things went from bad to horrible for Gossage and the American League.

Dave Concepcion walked. Dave Winfield lined a hard single to left, Concepcion taking third and Winfield second when Chet Lemon booted the ball. Bob Boone singled to center, Concepcion and Winfield scoring. Ron Cey grounded to third, Boone taking second—and when Davey Lopes singled to right, Boone scored. Jack Clark struck out, and Lopes was caught stealing to end the inning, but not before the Nationals had pushed four runs across.

The Americans went down meekly 1-2-3 in the ninth, blowing another All-Star Game, this time 7-3.

The N.L. outhit the A.L. only 10-8—the Americans, however, managed only one infield hit over the last four innings and a measly three hits over the last six, as Steve Rogers, Rollie Fingers, Bruce Sutter, and Phil Niekro strung a row of zeros on the scoreboard.

The Nationals four-run outburst made an All-Star winner out of Bruce Sutter, whose blinding split-finger fastball retired five batters in order until with two down in the ninth, the Cubs' ace reliever glanced up from the mound to see Lasorda waddling over from the dugout.

Sutter was as mystified as the 51,000-plus spectators until Lasorda explained his unexpected mission and motioned for Phil Niekro, the 39-year-old Atlanta knuckleball specialist.

"Niekro had never pitched in an All-Star Game," Lasorda said, "and I wanted to make sure he got in. He's been a super pitcher, a credit to the game," concluded Lasorda, who, as a rookie All-Star manager, had accorded Pete Rose the honor of taking the lineup to home plate.

It was a nice touch but not exactly accurate. Niekro had worked a perfect inning in the 1969 game at Washington.

Billy Martin was asked why he had replaced his Yankees ace, Ron Guidry, with Gossage after the brilliant left-hander (13-1 at the midseason break) had retired the only batter he faced (Guidry induced pinch hitter Willie Stargell to fly out to end the seventh inning). This move was apparently the A.L. manager's fatal mistake. Martin replied:

"I have just as much faith in Gossage as Guidry, and the National League was sending up a bunch of right-handed hitters in the eighth," he explained. "Gossage is right-handed, I thought he'd get 'em out."

He did, but only eventually.

Gossage himself expounded on the evening's disaster:

I feel like I let a lot of people down. The reason our league has been losing All-Star games is pitching, and I guess it was my turn now. What can I say? They just kicked my butt.

It's tough to lose this thing, a lot tougher than a regular season game. During the season, if you know you have an outing like this, you know there's always tomorrow. This team won't get another crack at it until next year.

It was ironic, somehow, that Gossage should wind up wearing the goat horns. In the preceding year, after all, he played with—not against—the National League. Gossage then represented the Pittsburgh Pirates, and he hurled the ninth inning for a team that took a 7-5 decision in Yankee Stadium. Some folks began to believe that the American League teams wore a curse.

Then what did Rich Gossage do against the Los Angeles Dodgers in relief appearances in the 1978 World Series? He was almost unhittable and became one of the major factors in helping the Yankees dominate the Series. Figure that one out.

For his key role in helping the National League win its seventh straight midsummer classic, Steve Garvey won his second All-Star Game Most Valuable Player trophy (his first came in 1974). The two-run third-inning single and the eighth inning triple were enough to earn the award for the Los Angeles first baseman, who also fielded his position flawlessly.

The two hits gave Garvey an All-Star batting average of .500 (8 for 16) for four All-Star Games.

Garvey thought for a while he might miss the San Diego encounter altogether. He had been forced out of the second game of a double-header in Houston the previous Saturday when a pickoff throw by Dodger right-hander Bob Welch sailed and struck him under the chin, creating a gash that required 22 stitches. Garvey did come back Sunday to drive in his team's only run in a losing effort against the Astros.

He still looked like a medical case at San Diego because he needed to wear a large protective bandage on his chin.

Asked by reporters after the game if the injury interfered with his play, Garvey replied, "I don't hit with my chin." Then he confessed, "When I went into third on the triple, I think I popped a stick, though. But I'll take a popped stitch for a triple anytime."

With Steve in the lineup it was the American League that wound up taking it on the chin, however.

During the postgame interview Garvey also took a backhand slap at the several players who skipped the San Diego event, claiming "injury" or "illness."

"If anybody ever wants three days off and doesn't want to play in this [All-Star] game, I hope they'll give me a call," Garvey said.

How did Garvey fare in the Dodgers' losing effort against the Yankees in the 1978 World Series? Batting in the cleanup spot, he failed to drive in a single run in six games.

San Francisco Giants' ace Vida Blue, who won the starting assignment for the N.L., gained the distinction of being the first pitcher to start an All-Star Game for both leagues. The hard throwing left-hander started the 1971 and 1975 contests for the A.L. while a member of the Oakland Athletics.

In his report on the '78 game at San Diego, Lowell Reidenbaugh, managing editor of *The Sporting News,* was moved to comment: "The American League's annual disappearance act, which may some day rank with Judge Crater and the Roanoke Colony as major unsolved mysteries, has reached the embarrassment stage."

It's 11:30 P.M.—Do You Know Where Your Children Are?
Don't Worry, Mom, They're With George Brett!

It's 11:30 P.M. on the evening immediately following the All-Star Game, and the scene is the main lobby of San Diego's Sheraton Harbor Island Hotel, headquarters for both teams. George Brett, Kansas City Royals' third baseman, emerges from one of the elevators and heads for the registration desk to check out. Tommy Lasorda, winning manager for the National League, spots Brett, goes over to him, pats him on the back, and congratulates him for the excellent game he played. The two men talk baseball for fifteen minutes or so—and Brett is obviously well taken with Lasorda's outgoing and amiable manner.

It's now 11:45 and Brett asks a bellman to call him a cab so he can get to the airport to catch a plane to a distant city where he will rejoin his Royals teammates to begin the season's second half of play. For George Brett it's been a long hard day, and he's clearly a tired young man.

At this point six or seven boys, ranging in age from about 10 to 12, all wearing Little League baseball uniforms and carrying boxes of baseball bubblegum cards, sidle up to the weary All-Star and plead almost in unison: "Mr. Brett, may we have your autograph?" as they thrust at him cards inscribed with his color photo.

What will Brett do . . . sign or not sign?

Without a moment's hesitation the Royal's young star puts down his suitcase and heavy equipment bag, smiles broadly, signs autographs for every one of the wide-eyed youngsters, and then climbs into his cab. As the taxi speeds off into the darkness the Little Leaguers chatter happily among themselves and carefully place their autographed George Brett cards back into their boxes.

That gesture is as an important a contribution to the All-Star Game and big league baseball as Brett's two hits against National League pitching.

Dave Winfield's Party

It's difficult to refuse someone who stands 6'6" and weighs 225 pounds. It's equally difficult to refuse someone who stands 3'6" and tugs at your sleeve.

Which explains why Jim Sundberg of the Texas Rangers and a half-dozen other participants in the 1978 All-Star Game happened to find themselves signing autographs and chatting with what appeared to be half the youngsters in San Diego the day before the big game.

Dave Winfield asked them to, that's why. For kids.

The occasion was Winfield's "All-Star Open House" staged at the sprawling Master Hosts Inn, an event which attracted no more attention than, say, your average visit by the Pied Piper. In all shapes, sizes, colors, and condition of dress, nearly 15,000 boys and girls assembled in hopes of seeing a major leaguer up close. Also to consume cookies, doughnuts, fruit punch, and ice cream.

Long before the appointed hour of 10 A.M., a line of excited youngsters four or five abreast snaked its way along the parking lot. By 10, it stretched around the hotel to the golf pro shop in the rear and doubled back out into the parking lot again.

When Dave Winfield throws a party, everyone comes.

"I was very gratified by the response," Winfield said later. "It was something I wanted to do. It was the perfect opportunity to do something for a lot of people who wouldn't have been able to have anything to do with the game otherwise."

Winfield was unable to fix the exact size of the crowd. "But," he noted,

"I had 10,000 pictures to give away, and I ran out early on." His agent, Al Frohman, estimated that the turnout easily approached 15,000. The line still stretched the length of the parking lot at 11:15, when Frohman asked that no more be permitted to join the festivities.

By this time, those athletes inside had contracted almost terminal writer's cramp after inscribing a wide array of articles including baseball gloves, jackets, balls, bubble gum cards, photos, posters, programs, and, of course, autograph books.

But none complained. "When Dave Winfield asks you to do something, it's almost impossible to say no," said Sundberg.

Also sharing their time with the throng of youngsters were Ross Grimsley and Steve Rogers, Montreal Expos; Pat Zachry, New York Mets; Jack Clark, San Francisco Giants; and Rollie Fingers, Ozzie Smith, and Bill Almon, all of the San Diego Padres.

"I keep thinking how I would have felt if I had an opportunity to come to something like this when I was a kid," said Winfield. "I couldn't even get into a ballgame. I wanted these kids to have a chance to be a part of this event."

If Winfield had any regrets, it was only that he didn't think of the idea sooner. The event was conceived and staged in less than two weeks.

"We were having dinner one night and Dave said, 'I want to have an All-Star party for the kids. Make me a party,' " recalled Frohman.

"You can quote me on this. I think Dave Winfield is crazy." But Frohman's complaint was obviously born of affection.

In the short time available to him, he rented the Master Hosts Inn's Stardust Room, rounded up hundreds of volunteers to police the traffic (largely American Legion members and local sandlot baseball players), and laid in provisions. These included 1,000 dozen doughnuts, 36,000 ice cream bars, 50,000 cookies, and hundreds of gallons of punch.

"Twenty-five thousand of the cookies were donated, but we paid for all the rest of it," said Frohman, who estimated the expense at "between $5,000 and $10,000." He added, "That's the way Dave wanted it. This was no charity thing. It's something he wanted to do."

Winfield has regularly picked up the tab for similar events—but never on such a grand scale. The San Diego slugger also donates $25,000 for tickets that enable underprivileged children to attend Padre games at "Winfield's Pavilion" at San Diego Stadium.

Pregame Workout Draws Crowd of 30,000-Plus

Dave Winfield's party may have attracted a crowd of 15,000 youngsters, but on that same afternoon the All-Stars' workout at San Diego Stadium drew more than twice as many baseball fans. When the turnstile count reached 30,008, Padres officials stopped tabulating as the fans kept pouring into the park.

Ray Kroc, Padres' owner, decided to allow the public to attend the workouts without charge because thousands of willing customers had been unable to purchase tickets for the big game itself. "At least we gave a lot of our fans a chance to see the All-Stars in uniform," declared Kroc.

The sight of all those happy people pleased American League president Lee MacPhail.

"It's the first time we've ever opened the workouts to the public, and it's a great idea," said MacPhail. "Why didn't we think of it before?"

When sluggers like George Foster, Greg Luzinski, Jim Rice, Willie Stargell and Richie Zisk kept slamming batting practice baseballs into the bleachers, the fans hooped and hollered as if the game were in progress.

During the course of the afternoon, the All-Stars must have collectively signed several thousand autographs for boys and girls of all ages.

A Ballplayer Makes His Mother Happy

Is the All-Star Game something really special? Dorothy Sorenson of Mount Clemens, Michigan thinks it is. Mrs. Sorenson and her husband Leonard traveled to San Diego all the way from Mount Clemens on the chance that their son Lary, the 22-year-old Milwaukee Brewers' righthander, might get into the game. There was certainly no guarantee that Lary would see any action, since the American League had eight pitchers on its staff, and manager Billy Martin probably couldn't have cared less if the Sorensons had come from Timbuktu to see their boy.

As it turned out, however, Martin called upon the youngster in the fourth inning, and he shut out the National Leaguers for three complete innings while giving up a single hit. Sorenson's solid performance was one of the few bright spots for the A.L. on a basically dismal evening.

Dorothy Sorenson confided shortly after the game: "Baseball came rather easily to Lary because he's a natural athlete, but none of us thought he'd be pitching in a major league All-Star Game so early in his career. Tonight's events were so wonderful that they were almost unreal—and the only thing Lary could do to make me happier would be to find the right girl to settle down with."

Mothers are mothers wherever you find them!

The Japanese Have This Yen for Joe DiMaggio

The two Japanese major leagues put on an annual midseason All-Star series consisting of three games, with squads chosen from the Central and Pacific leagues. The Japanese have also long followed the U.S. All-Star Game with intense interest, and for the 1978 contest at San Diego they sent over a delegation of more than 40 journalists.

A Japanese televison network even beamed the game back home with Joe DiMaggio doing the color commentary. No, Joe doesn't speak Japanese, but an interpreter sat beside the old Yankee Clipper in the press box and translated all of his bits of wisdom right on the spot.

Joe is a baseball star of major magnitude in Japan, having gone there with the Yankees on an exhibition tour in the fall of 1951, and since then he's traveled to Nippon several times on special coaching assignments. When Emperor Hirohito stages his fiftieth wedding anniversary celebration at his Imperial Palace in Tokyo, who do you suppose was invited to attend as an honored guest? Why Joltin' Joe, of course.

Hamburger King Saves Big League Ball in San Diego

Ray Kroc, owner of the San Diego Padres and founder of the McDonald's hamburger empire, threw out the ceremonial first pitch for the 19th All-Star Game. Kroc deserved that honor because he's the man who saved major league baseball for San Diego.

During the first five years of the franchise's existence in the National League (1969–1973), the Padres home attendance averaged an anemic 610,000, and it appeared that the team would be shifted to Washington, D.C. Commissioner Bowie Kuhn, in fact, strongly favored the move to Washington.

Buzzie Bavasi, then president of the Padres and charged with the success of the franchise, decided there was no hope.

"Baseball in San Diego," he ruefully announced, "is the wrong game in the wrong town."

There was Mexico to the south, desert to the east, ocean to the west, and the Dodgers to the north. No way.

C. Arnholt Smith, owner of the club, was beset by overwhelmiing financial and legal problems. He had to sell.

Joseph Danzansky, a Washington, D.C. grocery chain owner, was eager to buy, and he was assisted in his efforts by Commissioner Kuhn.

A last-minute attempt to save the franchise for San Diego failed when California horsewoman Marj Everett was rejected by the National League as a potential owner.

The Danzansky takeover now seemed to be certain—and everything in the club's offices was packed for shipment to Washington.

Spanking new uniforms—white with a red "Washington" across the chest—had been designed and created by a sporting goods manufacturer. Several Padres even were photographed in them for bubble gum cards, which since have become collector's items.

A funny thing happened then. Ray Kroc took an airplane from Chicago to Los Angeles. En route he read in the newspapers that Marj Everett's offer to buy the Padres had been turned down, and he decided to get into the act. A lifetime Cubs' fan, he had attempted several times to purchase that team from the late Phil Wrigley. No sale, but he retained a strong desire to own a major league baseball team one day.

Almost as soon as he got off the plane, he got hold of Arnholt Smith, offered him a reported $12 million in *cash* for the Padres. The offer was quickly accepted, the National League gave the deal a green light, and Ray Kroc was now a big league club owner.

Kroc, incidentally, had no trouble at all finding $12 million lying around loose in his bank vault since his personal fortune is estimated to be well in excess of $500 million. After all, the man has sold billions of hamburgers.

He's also been successful in selling baseball in San Diego. In his first year as owner in 1974, he saw Padres attendance climb to 1,075,000, and since 1975 the number of paid admissions has been averaging well over 1.3 million.

Ray Kroc is a natural born showman . . . he's been known to grab the public address microphone and apologize to the fans for "some of the stupidest baseball playing I've ever seen." Was this any way to sell a game? You bet it was, though league officials told him to cool it a little.

Because Kroc had done such an outstanding job for baseball in San Diego, his Padres were chosen by the major leagues to host the 1978 All-Star Game.

At a banquet sponsored by the commissioner's office at San Diego's Sheraton Harbor Island Hotel, the Padres' owner was duly feted for his efforts with Bowie Kuhn saying, "Major league baseball in San Diego is alive and well today because of Ray Kroc."

20

A Pirate Reigns
in the Kingdome:
1979

A SELLOUT crowd of nearly 59,000 baseball fans jammed their way into Seattle's Kingdome on July 17, 1979, and before everyone had a chance to be seated, the Nationals nicked the Americans for two quick runs in the top of the first inning.

Fireballer Nolan Ryan struck out the first two men to face him, but Steve Garvey didn't flinch and drew a walk on a 3–2 count. Garvey raced home as Mike Schmidt lined a triple off the right-center field wall, and Schmidt trotted across the plate when George Foster sliced a double down the right field line.

The Americans responded in their half of the inning by working Steve Carlton over for three markers. After Roy Smalley popped out, George Brett walked, and Don Baylor, who worked the count to three and two, doubled just inside third base down the left field line to score Brett. Fred Lynn then drove a 2–2 pitch into the right-center field seats for a homer, Baylor scoring ahead of him.

The senior circuit knotted the score at 3–3 in the second when Bob Boone, Lou Brock, and Davey Lopes all singled to fill the bases, with Boone tallying on Dave Parker's sacrifice fly to center. Then in the third the N.L. took the lead when Schmidt doubled to right center and eventually scored on Dave Winfield's groundout.

The Americans came right back in their half of the third to scratch out two runs and regain the lead at 5–4. After Brett grounded out, Baylor singled to left, and took second on Joaquin Andujar's wild pitch. Baylor moved to third as Jim Rice grounded out to short. Chet Lemon was hit by a pitch, and Carl Yastrzemski singled through the middle scoring Baylor, Lemon stopping at second. When Schmidt, after fielding Darrell Porter's grounder, threw wildly to first base, Lemon crossed the plate.

With only three innings completed, the game was already more than one and one-half hours old, and the fans appeared to be ready to settle down for a long evening.

The fourth and fifth innings went scoreless, but in the top of the sixth Winfield doubled to right center and scored on Gary Carter's line single to left. The game was again deadlocked now at 5–5.

The junior circuit came storming back in its half of the stanza to pick up a run against the offerings of the San Diego Padres' 40-year-old Gaylord Perry and take the lead for the third time in this seesaw affair. Yastrzemski led off with a ground single to right, and the Red Sox veteran was given a rousing ovation as he left the field when Rick Burleson came in to run for him. Porter lined a double to right center; Burleson stopped at third.

At this point manager Bob Lemon called on Bruce Bochte, hard-hitting Seattle first baseman, to bat for Frank White. Bochte, the only Mariners' player to be named an All-Star, was cheered wildly by the home crowd as he went to the plate, and he responded by bouncing a single over shortstop Larry Bowa's head to score Burleson.

N.L. manager Tom Lasorda yanked Perry, who had failed to retire anybody, in favor of Joe Sambito. Before the frame ended, Sambito himself needed relief help from Mike LaCoss to get the third out with the bases loaded. The Americans had threatened to make the sixth their big inning, but they had to settle for the single marker.

Jim Kern, the Texas Rangers' relief ace, came out of the bull pen to blank the Nationals in the seventh.

In the A.L. seventh, Jim Rice, 1 for 9 in All-Star play, popped a fly that dropped just inside the right field foul line, but he was thrown out at third on a rifle peg from Dave Parker. Parker, who apparently lost sight of the ball in the lights, lost no time in recovering it and uncorking his Herculean heave. LaCoss retired the next two batters to end the inning.

Left-handed swinger Lee Mazzilli, pinch-hitting for Gary Matthews, led off the N.L. half of the eighth by tagging a Jim Kern fastball for a "wrong field" homer into the left field bleachers to tie the game at 6–6. This was only the second homer of the 1979 season yielded by the Texas fireman in 86 innings of work. Kern proceeded to retire the next three men in order.

Bruce Sutter, the Chicago Cubs' star reliever and master of the deceptive "split-finger" fastball, took the mound against the A.L. in the eighth. Brian Downing greeted Sutter with a sharp ground single to center. Bochte sacrificed Downing to second, and Reggie Jackson was intentionally passed. Bobby Grich struck out swinging.

Graig Nettles lined a smoking single to right field. As Downing was making the mad dash to score, Dave Parker scooped up the ball, and the 6′ 5″ 230-pound outfielder unleashed a cannonlike throw of some 300-odd feet that carried all the way to home plate on the line. Catcher Gary

Carter caught the ball in plenty of time to put the tag on the sliding Downing to retire the side.

Pete Rose led off the top of the ninth by lining out to Rice in left. Joe Morgan walked and was awarded second on Kern's balk. Parker was intentionally passed, Craig Reynolds fouled out to Nettles, and when Ron Cey walked to fill the bases Manager Lemon pulled Kern in favor of Ron Guidry.

The Yankees brilliant left-hander, who had compiled an amazing 25-3 record in 1978, walked Mazzilli, forcing in Morgan to give the Nationals a 7-6 margin. Winfield forced Mazzilli, Burleson to Grich, to end the inning in which the Nationals had picked up their run on no hits and four walks.

Bruce Sutter disposed of the Americans in the bottom of the ninth with little difficulty. Ken Singleton, batting for Guidry, grounded out to Morgan. Rice struck out swinging, and after Lemon walked, Burleson also went down swinging to end the game on the usual tragic note for the American League.

Dave Parker was awarded Most Valuable Player honors primarily for his defensive work. His two assists from the outfield, both game-saving throws, marked the first such performance by an All-Star outer-gardener. Parker also collected a single, drove in a run with a sacrifice fly, and drew an intentional walk.

Asked why he had not substituted for Parker, Manager Tom Lasorda said emphatically: "We'd have kept him in if the game had gone 20 innings. He's just one of the best defensive players in the business."

The All-Star victory was the second for Bruce Sutter in as many years, matching the achievement of Don Drysdale of the Los Angeles Dodgers in 1967 at Anaheim and 1968 at Houston.

The 3 hour and 11 minute contest was one minute longer than the previous record for a nine-inning game, which had been set at Cleveland in 1954. The seven pitchers used by the National League tied an All-Star record.

Baseball experts pondered this latest defeat for the Americans—their eighth loss in a row and 16 out of the last 17 games. The junior circuit, which one held a commanding 12-4 lead over the N.L., had managed over the years to slip to a 18-31-1 disadvantage.

"Sure, the American League lost another tough one, but the 1979 game was one of the most exciting and best-played affairs in All-Star history," said Ron Bergman, veteran baseball writer for *The Oakland Tribune.* "The fans enjoyed every minute of it, and that's what baseball is all about."

Nevertheless, American League relief pitching failed at a critical point in the game. Loser Jim Kern, noted for his excellent control and overpowering strikeout pitch, gave up three walks in the fateful ninth, and Ron Guidry walked the winning run across the plate.

Guidry, who had been warming up in the bull pen intermittently since the second inning, admitted he was tired since he had thrown 130 pitches in a losing effort against the California Angels at Anaheim only two days before. "I didn't have anything when I came in and said so to Graig Nettles when I walked by him going to the mound," Guidry told reporters after the game.

When Bob Lemon was asked why he didn't call upon Tommy John to pitch in the ninth, he answered: "I was saving him because I thought we were going into extra innings."

Winning the game on four walks was entirely acceptable to Tommy Lasorda. "That's great," beamed the Dodger manager. "I'll take them any way I can get 'em."

When Pete Rose was inserted at first base in the sixth inning, he became the first All-Star player to see action at five different positions. He had previously played at second, third, left field, and right field. Stan Musial (1b, lf, cf, rf) and Hank Aaron (also 1b, lf, cf, rf) had shared the four-position mark with Rose.

For the first time in All-Star history three players from the same team were elected to outfield starting positions: the Boston Red Sox trio of Jim Rice, Fred Lynn, and Carl Yastrzemski.

California Angels' first baseman Rod Carew led all players from both leagues in the fan balloting with nearly four million votes, but the perennial A.L. batting champion didn't see action at the Kingdome because of a severe thumb injury.

The 1980 game has been scheduled for Los Angeles' Dodger Stadium, the 1981 contest will be played at Cleveland's Municipal Stadium.

21

National League
Supremacy:
What Does It Mean?

"DOES the dominance of the National League in the All-Star Game over the past couple of decades mean anything? I'll say it does—it means that the National League has had the superior pool of top caliber players," crows Sparky Anderson, former Cincinnati Reds' manager, who piloted the N.L. All-Stars four times between 1971 and 1977.

"Take a look at the 1973 game we played in Kansas City as one example," continued Anderson. "Even our 7–1 victory margin doesn't begin to tell the whole story of how decisively we outclassed the American League. On our roster, we had players like Pete Rose, Joe Morgan, Cesar Cedeno, Hank Aaron, Joe Torre, Billy Williams, Bobby Bonds, Johnny Bench, Ted Simmons, Ron Santo, Willie Stargell, Bob Watson, Willie Davis, Tom Seaver, and Don Sutton. The American League just didn't have that many first-class stars. In our league we've had a helluva lot more depth."

During a period of more than a year I interviewed over 150 big league players, managers, coaches, and team executives. Each interview included the same question: "Has the National League proven it is superior because of all those All-Star victories?"

Some agreed with Anderson; others took vigorous exception, Baltimore Orioles' manager, Earl Weaver, snapped: "I don't see how you can prove that one league might have a clear edge over the other on the basis of a single annual game—and an exhibition game at that."

Weaver went on to say:

"In this kind of exhibition, you try to use as many of your players as you can, and there's a lot of shifting going on all the time. You're still trying to win, of course, but in the All-Star Game managers are faced with a unique set of circumstances that aren't present in regular season or World Series games. And don't forget that the American League has been losing a lot of very close games lately," he concluded.

Weaver has the distinction of having managed the American League to its last All-Star victory, a 6–4 decision at Detroit in 1971.

While the A.L. has been compiling an embarrassingly poor All-Star record (16 losses out of the last 17 games), it has nevertheless held its own in World Series play. For the last 16 years the Series is even at 8–8, while since 1947 the A.L. is ahead by a comfortable 19–13 margin. How do you explain this phenomenon in the light of the All-Star results? The question was tossed to Bill Virdon, the thoughtful manager of the Houston Astros.

"The World Series and the All-Star Game are entirely different situations," explained Virdon. "In the World Series you merely have the top *single teams* from each league squaring off against each other, but in the All-Star Game your rosters are made up of *the best players from all teams.* Consequently, the National League's superiority really shows up in All-Star competition. And the record indicates that for the past two decades or so the American League has been clearly overmatched in All-Star play."

Frank Robinson, who's appeared for both leagues in All-Star play, doesn't agree with Virdon's line of thinking. "I've always thought the All-Star Game has been a great showcase for talent, and it's really an important part of baseball as a whole . . . but no one can convince me that one league can prove its superiority through a single game which is basically an exhibition," he emphasized.

"If you're hell bent on determining the relative strengths of the two leagues, then put on a round robin series at the end of the season in which the best three or four teams from each league take part. At the conclusion of the round robin, you might be able to make a judgment."

Robinson, now a Baltimore Orioles' coach, savored the memories of the many All-Star games in which he participated, especially the 1971 contest at Detroit where his two-run homer was a key factor in the A.L. victory.

Richie Zisk, Texas Rangers' outfielder, and another veteran who's played in both circuits: "I honestly can't see any real difference in the caliber of the two leagues. Maybe beginning in 1977, though, the American League's talent was stretched a little thin because those two expansion teams were added in Seattle and Toronto.

"Again, as far as differences between the two leagues are concerned, you really don't have that many . . . you just see the same jackasses wearing different uniforms."

When asked if the string of National League victories in the All-Star Game meant anything, Johnny Bench, Cincinnati Reds' catcher, squared his big shoulders and blurted, almost as a reflex: "It means we're better'n they are!" Bench then caught himself and went on to say:

"Don't misunderstand me . . . the American League has some real great talent, but we've been so successful because we've had the depth. Just look at third base—at that position during the past several years we've had guys like Pete Rose, Mike Schmidt, Ron Cey, and Bill Madlock to choose from.

"For a long stretch we had so many repeat players on the N.L. squad that we had almost a set lineup for the All-Star Game from one year to another. With all those veterans on our side we were damned tough to beat.

"Still, we could never afford to get cocky and overconfident because we always knew we had to face tough opposition. And none of us want to make fools of ourselves before 50 to 75 million people watching us on national television."

Freddie Patek, Kansas City Royals' shortstop, didn't seem to be happy with a number of aspects of the All-Star Game: "I think the American League fans have been making a lot of mistakes in voting for players, and I can cite plenty of cases where they've shown poor judgment," he declared.

"For example, Bobby Bonds, one of the best players you'll ever see wasn't given a place on the 1976 team when he was with California and having a great year until he got injured in August. Then Robin Yount, a super shortstop, hasn't made the team yet because he plays for Milwaukee, one of the league's small towns. He just doesn't get enough votes in Milwaukee.

"The fans kept voting for Brooks Robinson as starting third baseman late in his career when he was definitely past his peak. Don't misunderstand me. I'm not rapping Brooksie at all, because in his prime he was probably the best third baseman ever—but things like that wouldn't happen if the players themselves, or the managers, chose the teams.

Then the managers don't always make the wisest pitching selections. In 1977, for example, Kansas City had two of the most effective pitchers in the league, Dennis Leonard and Paul Splittorf. They both had great records, but they were not chosen as All-Stars. If the American League fielded its best possible teams, then maybe we wouldn't be losing all those games year after year."

Patek went on to emphasize: "The All-Star voting is really a gigantic popularity contest. Players who get the big press coverage are the ones who get voted in . . . and those with the most ability and top performance records are left out in the cold all too often. There's a lot of politics involved in the whole All-Star Game business."

Joe Morgan, Cincinnati Reds' second baseman and veteran All-Star performer: "Fans don't always pick the best players from either league for the All-Star Game. The fans may not scrutinize player performance as closely as they should, and they wind up voting for second liners, or for veterans late in their careers getting by on reputation. Who knows if the American League could have done better if the fans had chosen more wisely."

We've already heard from Pete Rose, but the longtime Cincinnati Reds' star, now with the Philadelphia Phillies has more to say: "I think the National League always gets better psyched up for these games. The league president usually makes it a point to visit our clubhouse and give us a pep talk before the game. When Warren Giles was president, he used to come in and make like Knute Rockne—and that helped us. A little screaming from Giles and the adrenalin really flowed."

Stan Musial, too, testifies, ". . . even the most grizzled veterans responded to [Giles'] exhortations." During a pre-All-Star Game party held at the Sheraton Harbor Island Hotel at San Diego in July 1978, Warren Giles talked about those pep talks. Giles had served as National League president for a record 18 years from 1951 to 1969 and maintained his keen interest in baseball until his death in February 1979. He confided: "Sure, I went into the clubhouse before the All-Star Games to talk to the boys a little. Don't forget that we once had a tough time trying to beat the American League, and we had to make up for that. I told my boys to play tough aggressive baseball and not to let up for a minute. I told them to slide hard into second base and, if necessary, to knock American League asses out into left field while doing so. We've been going along pretty well lately."
Immediately after the 1978 Game at San Diego, Warren Giles and Chub Feeney were walking down the runway from the dugout to the clubhouse. The 81-year-old Giles was in fine form as he chuckled, "Goddam it . . . we beat 'em again!"

On the subject of fans not always choosing players wisely for the midsummer classic, Warren Giles claimed emphatically, "The All-Star Game really belongs to the fans. This is the one time the fans can exercise a direct influence on the game because they choose the starting lineups. Sure, they make mistakes, because sometimes they don't always pick the best player for each position. But let them continue to vote, let them participate, and allow them their mistakes because that's a part of baseball, too, If we took away the fan All-Star vote now, we would do baseball as a whole a lot damage."

Brooks Robinson, former Baltimore Orioles' third baseman, surefire future Hall of Famer, and performer in 18 All-Star games: "I think we have to admit that the National League was just a little tougher for about a 15-year period in the 1960s and 1970s, just as the American League was a little tougher in an earlier period, especially in the 1930s and 1940s. The National League kept coming up with so many big stars, men like Aaron, Mays, Clemente, Brock, Rose, Bench, Morgan, Garvey, Koufax, Drysdale, and Seaver . . . they've been very hard to beat."

Connie Ryan, Texas Rangers' coach: "At one time a lot of people in baseball said that the American League did poorly in the All-Star Games because the Nationals got the jump in signing the best black players. But that's all ancient history now . . . there must be other reasons why the American Leaguers are still doing poorly."

Don Zimmer, Boston Red Sox manager: "The American League wants to win that All-Star Game badly, and the players have been pressing since they got into that losing streak. A victory or two would be a real tonic for them."

George Brett, Kansas City Royals' third baseman: "When the National Leaguers take the field, they're all gung ho and seem eager to draw a little blood. We go out there a little more relaxed, treat the game as an exhibition, and get beat."

Joe Torre, New York Mets' manager and a National League veteran with 16 years' playing experience: "American Leaguers have never been pushovers, but I think the National League has held the edge in the power department, and that's been the difference. During the past 20 years or so, our league had more of the really consistent long ball hitters, and we capitalized on that plus factor in the All-Star Games."

Ted Kluszewski, Cincinnati Reds' batting coach with 14 years' playing experience in both major leagues: "We have things known as 'cycles' in professional baseball, and the American League seems to be in a long losing cycle as far as the All-Star Game is concerned. The A.L. is certainly not nearly as bad as its record for the past 20 years indicates."

Yogi Berra, New York Yankees' coach, Hall of Famer, and a veteran of 15 All-Star Games: "I still don't see how you can judge one league against the other on the basis of one game. A lot of the games I've played in and seen were close and were decided by a single key play. If the Nationals start whipping the Americans in the World Series regularly, then I'll start to worry."

Reggie Jackson, New York Yankees' outfielder and a veteran of All-Star Games against the National League which the Americans lost: "The National League must be better, because we keep getting the shit kicked out of us all the time."

Jackson made this frank statement at spring training in 1978 when his five home runs against the Los Angeles Dodgers in the 1977 World Series were still the talk of the baseball world. Jackson's three homers and five RBIs in the sixth and deciding game wrecked the Dodgers.

Steve Garvey, Los Angeles Dodgers: "The National League seems to go into the All-Star Game with a great deal of confidence since we've been on a long winning streak. We're not under any real pressure, and because we're loose we play better ball.

"I don't want to criticize the American League, but I think we go into these games with more real spirit and enthusiasm . . . maybe the A.L. has become disheartened at losing so often.

"The All-Star Game is special to all of us since this is the only time when the fans have a voice in directing the play by choosing the starting lineups . . . no ballplayer ever forgets how important the fans are."

Johnny Pesky, Boston Red Sox coach and former outstanding player: "The American League has too much talent, especially great young talent, to keep losing these All-Star Games indefinitely. Things are bound to start evening out. Consider that during the past years the Americans have been coming up with a lot of first-class ballplayers like Jim Rice, Fred Lynn, Carlton Fisk, Jason Thompson, Ron LeFlore, Ron Guidry, George Brett, and others.

"The Nationals may well have had the edge during the 1960s and 1970s . . . they've been amazingly deep in player talent. Of all their pitchers, I've especially liked this kid Tom Seaver . . . he not only has that overpowering fastball but throws a variety of pitches and throws them *all* well. He's an artist on the mound with lots of moxie. Seaver always looked damned good in All-Star competition, and he's just one of the reasons the Americans have had trouble winning those games.

"Remember, though, that the American League dominated the All-Star series in the 1930s and 1940s. . . . Maybe these things run in cycles, and maybe we'll have a different kind of cycle in the 1980s.

"Keep in mind also that the American League was top dog when the New York Yankees were a powerhouse and winning all those pennants.

When the Yankees began declining in the early-to-mid-1960s, the whole league seemed to decline right with them. The Yankees are strong once again right now, and that means the A.L. as a whole is a lot tougher as well."

Al Hrabosky, veteran relief pitcher with extensive experience in both major leagues: "I don't think anyone can really argue the fact that the National League has been quite a bit deeper in talent. Despite all that, however, the Americans should have done better in the more recent All-Star Games, but I think they've been pressing too much. They feel like they've gotten themselves into a corner and want to fight their way out.

"The National League has been more progressive in a variety of ways . . . for example, it has more first-class and modern stadiums, while the American League has too many rundown parks in the poorer ghetto sections of its towns. The Americans would like interleague play to help spur attendance, but the Nationals don't need gimmicks of that sort to drum up more business."

Eddie Yost, Boston Red Sox coach and a veteran of 35 years in big league baseball: "I don't feel it's just a coincidence that the National League has been winning all those All-Star Games for so many years. This may be a clear indication that the Nationals are indeed superior—at least for the moment—because they have more all-'round talent."

Billy Gardner, Montreal Expos' coach and a veteran of both major leagues as a player: "During the past 20-odd years the National League has obviously succeeded in getting a big edge in player talent. Their long string of successes in the All-Star Game simply reflects their ability in rounding up so many exceptional players."

Pete Runnels, 14-year big league veteran and two-time American League batting champion: "The All-Star Game should not be considered as a test of league superiority. I make that statement for lots of reasons: players from both leagues often treat the game as an exhibition, there are lineup changes galore, fans choose the starting teams—and they frequently do that in a haphazard way—and top players on many occasions decline to come after they've been chosen."

Lou Brock, St. Louis Cardinals: "How many times do we have to beat the American Leaguers in the All-Star Game to prove that we're the superior league? The record speaks for itself.

"Players on the N.L. All-Star teams seem to have developed a genuine sense of camaraderie. I played in so many games with boys like Pete Rose, Joe Morgan, Johnny Bench, Tom Seaver, Steve Carlton, and others that All-Star time seemed like old home week."

Walter Alston, Los Angeles Dodgers manager for 23 years: "The National League has been dominant because overall it's had superior power, speed, pitching, and defense. To state it quite frankly, we've just had the better players."

Mickey Vernon, New York Yankees' minor league batting coach and a veteran of 43 years in professional baseball: "No doubt about it . . . the National League has had the outstanding talent. Still, the American League always tries damned hard to win the All-Star Game because almost everyone takes these match-ups seriously."

George Scott, former Boston Red Sox first baseman and now with the New York Yankees, was defiant: "You can't judge the relative merits of either league on the basis of the All-Star Game because it's an exhibition and there's no money involved. Players don't get all that excited playing for the pension fund—as important as our pensions are. The World Series—that's the ultimate test of baseball superiority because that's where they load the money on the table."

Without mentioning the Billy Martin-Nolan Ryan feud,* stemming from Martin's statement that he wouldn't pick Ryan for the 1978 All-Star squad even if the California fireballer had 20 victories by midseason, I asked Tommy Lasorda, the National League's All-Star manager, if he would ever allow himself to get into a position of not selecting a particular player because of a personality clash.

"Absolutely not!" boomed the Los Angeles skipper. "The fans vote for the eight starting players, and then it's my job to choose the pitchers and the reserve squad. I want the National League's top talent on the All-Star roster, and I'm not going to pass over any player because of personal reasons. In fact, in no way would I want to jeopardize our league's chances for a victory."

Bill Veeck, Chicago White Sox president: "As far as the All-Star Game is concerned, I really can't place any significance in the fact that the National League has been victorious most of the time in recent years. Rather, I would place much more importance in the World Series results, and everyone is well aware of what the American League has done

---

* When Frank Tanana, California Angels' right-hander, an original Billy Martin choice for the A.L.'s 1977 All-Star pitching staff, was forced to cancel out because of an injury, the Yankee manager picked Nolan Ryan in his place. Ryan, piqued at not being a first choice, refused to accept the designation as a substitute, did not report, and went off to sulk. Martin's pique was aroused in kind.

in the fall classic. For example, note two recent World Series, 1977–1978, won by the New York Yankees from the best the National League has had to offer."

Lee MacPhail, American League president: "Of course, it's been an embarrassment to the American League that we've done so poorly in the All-Star Game for so many years now. The A.L. has an excellent World Series record, and we've got more of our players from the modern era in the Hall of Fame . . . in fact, for a long time we were considered as the superior league . . . but we keep losing the All-Star Game. This is really a mystery, but how can you explain a lot of things about baseball?

"It seems as if the National League has been trying to make up for lost time, and yet I think we're now in a position to turn things around very quickly and start evening up our All-Star record."

Charles S. "Chub" Feeney, National League president: "For a long time it was customary for the National League president to visit the clubhouse before the All-Star Game and give his players an inspired pep talk to spur them on. For the last couple of years, however, I haven't felt that a pregame pep talk is necessary. Just look at our record."

Jack Buck, St. Louis Cardinals' play-by-play announcer, KMOX radio: "The National League's long succession of victories in the All-Star Game is just one very obvious indication that this league is superior to the American in many respects. The Nationals have been deeper in player talent for a long time now, and perhaps this phenomenon has occurred because the club owners and executives seem to have been a bit more aggressive and imaginative. But in order to be entirely fair we ought to emphasize that the American League seems to be gaining a little ground now that a man with extraordinary drive like George Steinbrenner has taken charge of the New York Yankees. Gene Autry of the California Angels is also willing to spend big money and take risks in order to build a winning team.

"Nonetheless, I think that the American League has a long way to go before it will catch up. I've always liked the spirit the National Leaguers show on the playing field, and that quality also becomes evident at All-Star time. I even think that the National League has a clear edge in regard to the caliber of its umpires."

Hank Peters, Baltimore Orioles' general manager: "The Nationals have been winning a lot of All-Star games in recent years, but at the same time the Americans have been more than holding their own in the World Series—so how can you say one league is superior to the other?

"A great deal has been said about the American League's decision to institute the designated hitter rule in 1973, a move that some people say was made primarily to help boost attendance. The National League has been adamant, of course, in not adopting the DH. . . . Actually, the National League tends to cling to its traditional ways more. However, the DH rule hasn't made all that much difference in the game insofar as the American League is concerned. The introduction of artificial playing surfaces within the past decade or so has for all intents and purposes made a much greater impact on the way major league baseball is played."

Sparky Anderson names Branch Rickey as the one man most responsible for the National League's great success of the past two generations. Rickey originated the "farm system" as a source of major league talent while manager and then general manager of the St. Louis Cardinals in the 1920s, and he later served as general manager for the Brooklyn Dodgers and Pittsburgh Pirates. It was Rickey who broke baseball's color line when he signed infielder Jackie Robinson to a contract with the Brooklyn Dodgers' organization in 1946.

Sparky says of the N.L.'s superiority: "The only solid reason I can point to is that one man ran through this league and never touched the other league: Branch Rickey. He built the Cardinals, the Dodgers, and the Pirates, and his influence is still around. There are still a lot of people here who are Rickey's disciples who are still doing things his way.

"Doing things Rickey's way means well-organized scouting and a good system of farm clubs. Mr. Rickey always put the highest priority on speed. He always wanted players who could throw hard, run fast, and play defense. That's the kind of players we have in our league."

22

"I Remember the Glory"

A NUMBER of big leaguers, past and present, have shared their memories of games on All-Star-studded diamonds. Here is a small treasure chest full.

Brooks Robinson explained why he always did particularly well in the World Series and in eighteen All-Star contests: "Both the World Series and All-Star match-ups are very special situations. Don't misunderstand me—any true major leaguer bears down as hard as he can every time he takes the field. But when I played in that long series of All-Star Games over the years—knowing that I was representing my league before packed houses, and with additional tens of millions of fans watching on television—something inside me just kept clicking, and maybe that gave me a little extra push."

Despite Brooks Robinson's outstanding efforts in behalf of the American League at All-Star time, he still holds the dubious distinction of having played for the most losing teams in the history of the interleague rivalry, 15.

Rod Carew established himself as the major league's premier hitter during the 1970s, and at the end of the 1978 season his lifetime batting average was .335, highest by far of any active player. Over the years 1969 to '78, Carew had captured no less than seven league batting titles. Strangely, however, he could manage only 3 for 27 (all singles) in his first ten All-Star Games. The day before the 1978 game at San Diego he was asked, "How come?"

"I just can't understand it. . . I've always taken my usual swings, but

126

the balls haven't been dropping in," answered the Panamanian-born Carew, certainly one of the finest left-handed line drive hitters in baseball history. "I really can't figure why I haven't done better against National League pitching," he mused.

At San Diego, however, Carew lashed line drive triples to left-center field in his first two trips to the plate. This was the first game he got more than one hit in any All-Star encounter and raised his eleven-game average to the .151 level.

When Minnesota Twins' owner Calvin Griffith was in the process of unloading Rod Carew at the end of the 1978 campaign, the offers came in thick and fast from teams in both leagues. Bob Lurie, owner of the San Francisco Giants, for example, waved a multiyear contract worth several millions in front of Carew, but it was respectfully declined. Later the A.L.'s perennial batting champion admitted, "I'd rather not change leagues because I don't want to face National League pitching every day." There's a confession that speaks volumes.

Do any of Willie Mays's All-Star Games stand out in his memory? After all, with 24 appearances he holds the record for having played in the most midsummer games. Actually, he's tied with Stan Musial and Hank Aaron in this category.

(Mays does, however, own a batch of All-Star offensive records all by himself. Among these are: most hits, 23; most runs scored, 20; most triples, 6; and most stolen bases, 6. He is also tied with Hank Aaron for most times playing on a winning team, 17.)

"I played in so many All-Star Games that it's hard to remember them all now," Mays admitted, but after a little reflection he said, "Of course, I can't forget 1960 because in the two games that year I got six hits."

In the first game at Kansas City on July 11, he went 3 for 4, and in the second game two days later at Yankee Stadium, he again went 3 for 4. In both contests it was Mays's hitting that drove the National League to victory. No other player has ever collected six All-Star hits in one year.

Mays, in fact, enjoyed his greatest stretch as an All-Star performer from 1959 to '62, when two games were played each year. He was the starting center fielder in all eight of the contests, played five complete games, and went 12 for 29, good for a .414 average. He handled 55 chances in the outfield without an error, too. In that era he was clearly *the* dominant All-Star.

Hall of Famer Mickey Mantle, the New York Yankees' great slugger from 1951 to '68 now says, "I wish I had gotten into more All-Star Games when I had the chance and had done better in those I did play in."

Mantle really shouldn't feel all that bad about his record in the midsummer classic. From 1953 through 1968 he played in 16 games and managed to rap 10 hits, including a brace of homers, in 43 at bats for a .233 average. Not outstanding by any means, but nothing to sulk about either. About those games missed: he was picked for the 1952 squad, but didn't hear the call for action; sat out the second game in the 1962 set of two; missed the 1963 game because of a fractured left foot; and sat on the bench for the 1965 clash. Still, few players got into more All-Star classics than Mickey Mantle did.

Mantle was particularly unhappy about his performance in the 1967 game at Anaheim where the N.L. won 2-1 in 15 innings. As a pinch hitter in the fifth inning, with two out and a runner in scoring position, he ignominiously took a called third strike. "I flew from coast to coast just to strike out . . . 3,000 miles, and then I get caught looking," Mantle grumbled.

Mighty Mickey also struck out as a pinch hitter in his final All-Star appearance in 1968. This time, however, he only had to travel half a continent; the game was played at Houston. He does, incidentally, hold the All-Star strikeout record, 17.

It should be said for Mantle that he was definitely past his peak in 1967-68, and was chosen for those two squads largely on the basis of his brilliant overall record in the majors.

While Mantle may have been a bit subpar in All-Star competition, he shone like a meteor in a dozen World Series against the best the National League could offer. He established a hatful of Series offensive records, including: most home runs, 18; most total bases, 123; most runs scored, 42; and most runs batted in, 40.

Ed "Whitey" Ford, Yankee left-hander, who won a record ten World Series games, did much worse in All-Star competition. In six games he was 0–2, pitched 12 innings, gave up 19 hits, and wound up with a bloated ERA of 8.25.

(left) Mickey Mantle holds the strikeout records for both the World Series (54) and All-Star Games (17). Mickey's strikeout total is especially high for interleague competition because he made an extra effort to hit home runs in those really big games.

Maury Wills batted .357 in six All-Star Games. His baserunning was decisive in the N.L.'s 1962 victory.

(above right) Jim Bouton may be best remembered for his controversial book about baseball, *Ball Four,* but he did pitch in an All-Star Game. He hurled a scoreless inning for the American League in the 1963 contest. That's the year Bouton was 21–7 with the Yankees, his best year in the majors.

(right) Orioles' third baseman Brooks Robinson took part in 18 All-Star Games from 1960 through 1974. *(Baltimore Orioles)*

Jim "Catfish" Hunter, representing the Oakland A's, was the losing pitcher in the 1967 game at Anaheim that went a record 15 innings. Catfish pitched four scoreless innings in relief and then gave up a homer to Tony Perez in the 15th as the Nationals won 2–1. Hunter eventually went to the Yankees via the free agent route. *(Topps Chewing Gum Co.)*

(right) The San Francisco Giant's big first baseman Willie McCovey blasted two home runs to lead the National League to its 9–3 victory in the 1969 game at Washington. *(Topps Chewing Gum Co.)*

(below) Pete Rose has played in the midseason classic 12 times from 1965 through 1979. His aggressive baserunning in the 1970 game was decisive in the N.L.'s 5–4 victory in 12 innings. After 16 years with the Cincinnati Reds, Rose went to the Philadelphia Phillies in 1979.

Willie Mays holds many All-Star lifetime records, including: most hits, 23; most runs scored, 20; most triples, 6; and most stolen bases, 6.

(below) From 1963 through 1979 the National League whipped the Americans in 16 of 17 All-Star Games. During that stretch Baltimore Orioles' manager Earl Weaver piloted the junior circuit to their lone victory, the 1971 contest at Detroit. *(Baltimore Orioles)*

(lower right) Frank Robinson slammed a decisive two-run homer in the 1971 game at Tiger Stadium and paced the American League to a 6–4 victory. Robinson won the Arch Ward Trophy as the game's Most Valuable Player. *(Baltimore Orioles)*

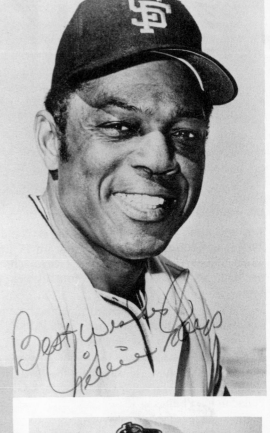

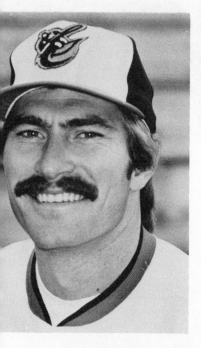
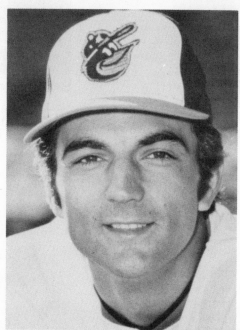

(top) The American League featured such outstanding infielders as Bobby Grich *(left)* and Mark Belanger on its All-Star squads of the 1970s, but it still kept losing. *(Baltimore Orioles)*

(above) Joe Morgan took MVP honors in the 1972 game won by the Nationals 4–3. *(Topps Chewing Gum Co.)*

(left) Longtime Pittsburgh Pirates' star outfielder Roberto Clemente batted .324 in 14 All-Star Games. He was elected to the Hall of Fame in 1973 after his tragic death in an airplane crash.

In seven All-Star Games between 1967 and 1977 Tom Seaver wasn't given a decision, but he succeeded for the most part in keeping A.L. bats in check, striking out 15 in 12 innings of work. After more than a decade with the New York Mets, Seaver went to Cincinnati in a June 1977 trade.

(above right) Rich Gossage, the super relief pitcher, keeps jumping from one league to another in the All-Star Game. As a member of the Chicago White Sox he hurled for the A.L. in 1975; as a Pittsburgh Pirate, he threw for the N.L. in 1977; and as a New York Yankee, for the A.L. again in 1978.

(right) Steve Garvey receives the 1974 All-Star Game Most Valuable Player trophy from Commissioner Bowie Kuhn at Pittsburgh's Three Rivers Stadium. Garvey paced his squad to a 7–2 win with two key hits and several sparkling fielding plays. *(Baseball Commissioner's Office, New York City)*

Secretary of State Henry Kissinger seems to be enjoying himself thoroughly as he throws out the first ball for the 1975 game in Milwaukee. After the game Kissinger confessed that he was a lifelong Yankees fan. *(Baseball Commissioner's Office, New York City)*

(left) Hank Aaron shares the record with Willie Mays for having played on the greatest number of winning All-Star teams, 17. When Aaron played for the American League as a member of the Milwaukee Brewers in 1975, he was on the losing team, naturally.

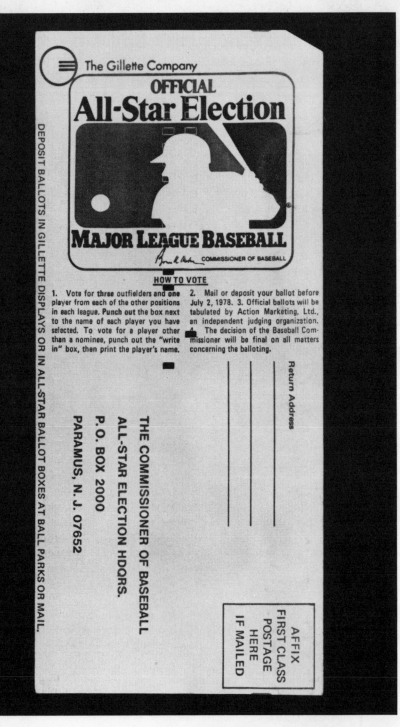

The official ballot for the 1978 game at San Diego. The Gillette Company underwrites the cost of printing—a major undertaking because of the huge numbers involved.

Gillette
1978 All-Star Game Official Ballot

NATIONAL LEAGUE   AMERICAN LEAGUE

1st Base

National League		American League	
Burroughs	Montanez	Carew	L. May
Driessen	T. Perez	Chambliss	Mayberry
Garvey	Stargell	Cooper	G. Scott
K. Hernandez	Watson	Hargrove	J. Thompson

2nd Base

Cash	Sizemore	Grich	Randolph
Lopes	Stennett	Kuiper	Remy
Madlock	Trillo	Money	F. White
Morgan	Tyson	Orta	Wills

Shortstop

Bowa	Russell	Belanger	Mulliniks
Concepcion	Speier	Burleson	Patek
DeJesus	Taveras	Campaneris	Smalley
Foli	Templeton	Dent	Yount

3rd Base

Cabell	Randle	B. Bell	Howell
Cey	Reitz	G. Brett	Murray
Garner	Rose	Harrah	Nettles
Ontiveros	Schmidt	Hobson	Soderholm

Catcher

Bench	Pocoroba	Fisk	Porter
Boone	Simmons	Fosse	Downing
Carter	Stearns	M. May	Sundberg
Ferguson	Yeager	Munson	Wynegar

Outfield

D. Baker	Luzinski	Bailor	Manning
Brock	G. Maddox	Bonds	A. Oliver
Cedeno	Matthews	Bostock	Otis
Jose Cruz	McBride	Cowens	Page
Dawson	Monday	Hisle	Rice
Foster	Jerry Morales	Reg. Jackson	Rivers
Gamble	Murcer	Rup. Jones	Rudi
Geronimo	Parker	Kemp	Singleton
Griffey	Wm. Robinson	LeFlore	Staub
S. Henderson	R. Smith	Lemon	C. Washington
Hendrick	Winfield	Lezcano	Yastrzemski
Kingman	E. Valentine	Lynn	Zisk

PUNCH OUT ONLY IF YOU WRITE IN VOTE BELOW

Pos.	Player	Pos.	Player
Andre Norton			

PRINTED IN U.S.A.

Billy Martin was on the winning side in the World Series five times out of six in his playing days with the New York Yankees, but lost to the Nationals two years in a row when he managed the Americans in the 1977 and 1978 All-Star Games. He's shown here as manager of the 1971 Detroit Tigers when he served as a coach of the American All-Star squad that won its only victory within a span of nearly two decades.

(below) Reggie Jackson, then of the Oakland A's, clubbed a two-run 520-foot homer in the 1971 game— one of the longest smashes in All-Star history. Reggie now plays for the New York Yankees. *(Topps Chewing Gum Co.)*

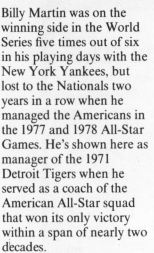

(top left) Carlton Fisk was one of the most prominent catchers in the All-Star Games of the 1970s. *(Topps Chewing Gum Co.)*

(top right) In ten All-Star Games Johnny Bench has hit three homers and averaged .385.

(left) When California Angels' fireballer Nolan Ryan refused to be named to the 1977 All-Star squad as a "second choice," he aroused A.L. manager Billy Martin's ire. *(Topps Chewing Gum Co.)*

(right) Shortstop Larry Bowa of the Phillies played a major role in the N.L.'s 7–3 victory in the 1978 game. *(Topps Chewing Gum Co.)*

Outfielder Chet Lemon of the Chicago White Sox was first named to the All-Stars in 1978. He is one of the few big leaguers around whose hobby is Greek mythology. *(Chicago White Sox)*

(below) St. Louis Cardinals' general manager Branch Rickey (center) inspecting his top farm team at Rochester in 1940. With Rickey are Red Wings' manager Billy Southworth (left) and club president Oliver French (right). Many baseball experts believe that Rickey's long tenure as an executive of National League clubs enabled the senior circuit to catch and then pass the American League as the dominant force in major league ball. Southworth, one of Rickey's many protégés, managed the N.L. All-Stars in 1943, 1944, and 1949. *(The National Baseball Hall of Fame and Museum, Cooperstown, N.Y.)*

Box Scores

July 6, 1933   At Comiskey Park, Chicago

Nationals	AB	R	H	PO	A	E	Americans	AB	R	H	PO	A	E
Martin (Cardinals), 3b ..	4	0	0	0	0	0	Chapman (Yankees), lf-						
Frisch (Cardinals), 2b ..	4	1	2	5	3	0	rf	5	0	1	1	0	0
Klein (Phillies), rf	4	0	1	3	0	0	Gehringer (Tigers), 2b .	3	1	0	1	3	0
P. Waner (Pirates), rf ..	0	0	0	0	0	0	Ruth (Yankees), rf	4	1	2	1	0	0
Hafey (Reds), lf	4	0	1	0	0	0	West (Browns), cf	0	0	0	0	0	0
Terry (Giants), 1b	4	0	2	7	0	0	Gehrig (Yankees), 1b ..	2	0	0	12	0	1
Berger (Braves), cf	4	0	0	4	0	0	Simmons (White Sox),						
Bartell (Phillies), ss	2	0	0	0	3	0	cf-lf	4	0	1	4	0	0
(c)Traynor (Pirates)	1	0	1	0	0	0	Dykes (White Sox), 3b .	3	1	2	2	4	0
Hubbell (Giants), p	0	0	0	0	0	0	Cronin (Senators), ss ..	3	1	1	2	4	0
(e)Cuccinello (Dodgers)	1	0	0	0	0	0	R. Ferrell (Red Sox), c .	3	0	0	4	0	0
Wilson (Cardinals), c ...	1	0	0	2	0	0	Gomez (Yankees), p ...	1	0	1	0	0	0
(a)O'Doul (Giants)	1	0	0	0	0	0	Crowder (Senators), p .	1	0	0	0	0	0
Hartnett (Cubs), c	1	0	0	2	0	0	(b)Averill (Indians)	1	0	1	0	0	0
Hallahan (Cardinals), p .	1	0	0	1	0	0	Grove (Athletics) p	1	0	0	0	0	0
Warneke (Cubs), p	1	1	1	0	0	0							
(d)English (Cubs), ss ..	1	0	0	0	0	0							
Totals	34	2	8	24	11	0	Totals	31	4	9	27	11	1

National League	0	0	0		0	0	2		0	0	0—2
American League	0	1	2		0	0	1		0	0	x—4

Pitching Summary

National League	IP	H	R	ER	BB	SO	American League	IP	H	R	ER	BB	SO
Hallahan (L)	2*	2	3	3	5	1	Gomez (W)	3	2	0	0	0	1
Warneke	4	6	1	1	0	2	Crowder	3	3	2	2	0	0
Hubbell	2	1	0	0	1	1	Grove	3	3	0	0	0	3

* Pitched to three batters in third.

(a) Grounded out for Wilson in sixth. (b) Singled for Crowder in sixth. (c) Doubled for Bartell in seventh. (d) Flied out for Warneke in seventh. (e) Fanned for Hubbell in ninth. Runs batted in—Martin, Frisch, Ruth 2, Gomez, Averill. Two-base hit—Traynor. Three-base hit—Warneke. Home runs—Ruth, Frisch. Sacrifice hit—Ferrell. Stolen base—Gehringer. Double plays—Bartell, Frisch, and Terry; Dykes and Gehrig. Left on bases—Americans 10, Nationals 5.

Managers—Connie Mack, Philadelphia (A.L.); John McGraw, New York (N.L.).

Umpires—Dinneen and McGowan (A.L.), Klem and Rigler (N.L.) Time—2:05. Attendance—47,595.

July 10, 1934   At Polo Grounds, New York

Americans	AB	R	H	PO	A	E	Nationals	AB	R	H	PO	A	E
Gehringer (Tigers), 2b .	3	0	2	2	1	0	Frisch (Cardinals), 2b ..	3	3	2	0	1	0
Manush (Senators), lf ..	2	0	0	0	0	0	(a)Herman (Cubs), 2b ..	2	0	1	0	1	0
Ruffing (Yankees), p ...	1	0	1	0	0	0	Traynor (Pirates), 3b ...	5	2	2	1	0	0
Harder (Indians), p	2	0	0	1	0	0	Medwick (Cardinals), lf .	2	1	1	0	0	0
Ruth (Yankees), lf	2	1	0	0	0	0	(d)Klein (Cubs), lf	3	0	1	1	0	0
Chapman (Yankees), rf	2	0	1	0	1	0	Cuyler (Cubs), rf	2	0	0	2	0	0
Gehrig (Yankees), 1b ..	4	1	0	11	1	1	(e)Ott (Giants), rf	2	0	0	0	1	0
Foxx (Athletics), 3b	5	1	2	1	2	0	Berger (Braves), cf	2	0	0	0	0	1
Simmons (White Sox),							(f)P. Waner (Pirates), cf	2	0	0	1	0	0
cf-lf	5	3	3	3	0	0	Terry (Giants), 1b	3	0	1	4	0	0
Cronin (Senators), ss .	5	1	2	2	8	0	Jackson (Giants), ss ...	2	0	0	0	1	0
Dickey (Yankees), c ...	2	1	1	4	0	0	(g)Vaughan (Pirates),						
(h)Cochrane (Tigers), c	1	0	0	1	1	0	ss	2	0	0	4	0	0
Gomez (Yankees), p ...	1	0	0	0	0	0	Hartnett (Cubs), c	2	0	0	9	0	0
(b)Averill (Indians), cf ..	4	1	2	1	0	0	Lopez (Dodgers), c	2	0	0	5	1	0
West (Browns), cf	0	0	0	1	0	0	Hubbell (Giants), p	0	0	0	0	0	0
							Warneke (Cubs), p	0	0	0	0	0	0
							Mungo (Dodgers), p ...	0	0	0	0	0	0
							(c)Martin (Cardinals) ...	0	1	0	0	0	0
							Dean (Cardinals), p	1	0	0	0	0	0
							Frankhouse (Braves), p	1	0	0	0	0	0
Totals	39	9	14	27	14	1	Totals	36	7	8	27	5	1

```
American League ....................  0  0  0     2  6  1     0  0  0—9
National League ....................  1  0  3     0  3  0     0  0  0—7
```

Pitching Summary

American League	IP	H	R	ER	BB	SO	National League	IP	H	R	ER	BB	SO
Gomez	3	3	4	4	1	3	Hubbell	3	2	0	0	2	6
Ruffing	1†	4	3	3	1	0	Warneke	1*	3	4	4	3	1
Harder (W)	5	1	0	0	0	0	Mungo (L)	1	4	4	4	2	1
							Dean	3	5	1	1	1	4
							Frankhouse	1	0	0	0	1	0

* Pitched to two batters in fifth.
† Pitched to four batters in fifth.

(a) Popped out for Hubbell in third but was allowed to replace Frisch in seventh.
(b) Tripled for Gomez in fourth. (c) Walked for Mungo in fifth. (d) Singled for Medwick
in fifth. (e) Flied out for Cuyler in fifth. (f) Fanned for Berger in fifth. (g) Forced runner
for Jackson in fifth. (h) Ran for Dickey in sixth. Runs batted in—Frisch, Medwick 3,
Cronin 2, Averill 3, Foxx, Simmons, Ruffing 2, Traynor, Klein. Two-base hits—Foxx,
Simmons 2, Cronin, Averill, Herman. Three-base hits—Chapman, Averill. Home
runs—Frisch, Medwick. Stolen bases—Gehringer, Manush, Traynor, Ott. Double
play—Lopez and Vaughan. Left on bases—Americans 12, Nationals 5.

Managers—Joe Cronin, Washington (A.L.); Bill Terry, New York (N.L.)
Umpires—Pfirman and Stark (N.L.), Owens and Moriarty (A.L.) Time—2:44. Attendance—48,363.

July 8, 1935   At Municipal Stadium, Cleveland

Nationals	AB	R	H	PO	A	E	Americans	AB	R	H	PO	A	E
Martin (Cardinals), 3b ..	4	0	1	0	0	1	Vosmik (Indians), rf	4	1	1	1	0	0
Vaughan (Pirates), ss ..	3	1	1	2	2	0	Gehringer (Tigers), 2b .	3	0	2	1	3	0
Ott (Giants), rf	4	0	0	1	0	0	Gehrig (Yankees), 1b ..	3	1	0	12	0	0
Medwick (Cardinals), lf .	3	0	0	0	0	0	Foxx (Athletics), 3b	3	1	2	0	0	0
Terry (Giants), 1b	3	0	1	5	1	0	Bluege (Senators), 3b ..	0	0	0	0	0	0
Collins (Cardinals), 1b .	1	0	0	2	0	0	Johnson (Athletics), lf ..	4	0	0	4	0	0
Berger (Braves), cf	2	0	0	1	0	0	Chapman (Yankees), lf .	0	0	0	0	0	0
(b)Moore (Giants), cf ..	2	0	0	1	0	0	Simmons (White Sox),						
Herman (Cubs), 2b	3	0	0	1	4	0	cf	4	0	2	2	0	0
Wilson (Phillies), c	3	0	1	8	0	0	Cramer (Athletics), cf ..	0	0	0	0	0	0
(c)Whitehead							Hemsley (Browns), c ...	4	1	1	6	0	0
(Cardinals)	0	0	0	0	0	0	Cronin (Red Sox), ss ...	4	0	0	1	4	0
Hartnett (Cubs), c	0	0	0	3	0	0	Gomez (Yankees), p ...	2	0	0	0	2	0
Walker (Cardinals), p ..	0	0	0	0	0	0	Harder (Indians), p	1	0	0	0	1	0
(a)Mancuso (Giants) ...	1	0	0	0	0	0							
Schumacher (Giants), p	1	0	0	0	1	0							
(d)P. Waner (Pirates) ..	1	0	0	0	0	0							
Derringer (Reds), p	0	0	0	0	0	0							
Dean (Cardinals), p	0	0	0	0	0	0							
Totals	31	1	4	24	8	1	Totals	32	4	8	27	10	0

National League .... 0 0 0   1 0 0   0 0 0—1
American League .... 2 1 0   0 1 0   0 0 x—4

Pitching Summary

National League	IP	H	R	ER	BB	SO	American League	IP	H	R	ER	BB	SO
Walker (L)	2	3	3	3	1	2	Gomez (W)	6	3	1	1	2	4
Schumacher	4	4	1	1	1	5	Harder	3	1	0	0	0	1
Derringer	1	1	0	0	0	1							
Dean	1	1	0	0	1	1							

(a) Flied out for Walker in third. (b) Flied out for Berger in seventh. (c) Ran for Wilson in seventh. (d) Grounded out for Schumacher in seventh. Runs batted in—Foxx 3, Cronin, Terry. Two-base hits—Vaughan, Wilson, Gehringer, Simmons. Three-base hit—Hemsley. Home run—Foxx. Left on bases—Americans 7, Nationals 5.

Managers—Mickey Cochrane, Detroit (A.L.); Frank Frisch, St. Louis (N.L.).

Umpires—Ormsby and Geisel (A.L.), Magerkurth and Sears (N.L.) Time—2:06. Attendance—69,831.

July 7, 1936   At Braves Field, Boston

Americans	AB	R	H	PO	A	E	Nationals	AB	R	H	PO	A	E
Appling (White Sox), ss	4	0	1	2	2	0	Galan (Cubs), cf	4	1	1	1	0	0
Gehringer (Tigers), 2b .	3	0	2	2	1	0	Herman (Cubs), 2b	3	1	2	3	4	0
DiMaggio (Yankees), rf .	5	0	0	1	0	1	Collins (Cardinals), 1b .	2	0	0	9	1	0
Gehrig (Yankees), 1b ..	2	1	1	7	0	0	Medwick (Cardinals), lf .	4	0	1	0	0	0
Averill (Indians), cf	3	0	0	3	1	0	Demaree (Cubs), rf	3	1	1	1	0	0
Chapman (Senators), cf	1	0	0	0	0	0	(d)Ott (Giants), rf	1	0	1	0	0	0
Ferrell (Red Sox), c	2	0	0	4	0	0	Hartnett (Cubs), c	4	1	1	7	0	0
(a)Dickey (Yankees), c .	2	0	0	2	0	0	Whitney (Phillies), 3b ..	3	0	1	0	2	0
Radcliff (White Sox), lf .	2	0	1	2	0	0	(e)Riggs (Reds), 3b	1	0	0	0	0	0
Goslin (Tigers), lf	1	1	1	1	0	0	Durocher (Cardinals),						
Higgins (Athletics), 3b .	2	0	0	0	1	0	ss	3	0	1	4	0	0
(b)Foxx (Red Sox), 3b .	2	1	1	0	1	0	J. Dean (Cardinals), p ..	1	0	0	0	2	0
Grove (Red Sox), p	1	0	0	0	0	0	Hubbell (Giants), p	1	0	0	2	1	0
Rowe (Tigers), p	1	0	0	0	0	0	Davis (Cubs), p	0	0	0	0	1	0
(c)Selkirk (Yankees) ...	0	0	0	0	0	0	Warneke (Cubs), p	1	0	0	0	0	0
Harder (Indians), p	0	0	0	0	1	0							
(f)Crosetti (Yankees) ...	1	0	0	0	0	0							
Totals	32	3	7	24	7	1	Totals	31	4	9	27	11	0

American League .... 0 0 0   0 0 0   3 0 0—3
National League .... 0 2 0   0 2 0   0 0 x—4

Pitching Summary

American League	IP	H	R	ER	BB	SO	National League	IP	H	R	ER	BB	SO
Grove (L)	3	3	2	2	2	2	J. Dean (W)	3	0	0	0	2	3
Rowe	3	4	2	1	1	2	Hubbell	3	2	0	0	1	2
Harder	2	2	2	0	0	2	Davis	⅔	4	3	3	1	0
							Warneke	2⅓	1	0	0	3	2

(a) Grounded out for Ferrell in seventh. (b) Singled for Higgins in seventh. (c) Walked for Rowe in seventh. (d) Singled for Demaree in eighth. (e) Fanned for Whitney in eighth. (f) Fanned for Harder in ninth. Runs batted in—Hartnett, Whitney, Medwick, Galan, Appling 2, Gehrig. Two-base hit—Gehringer. Three-base hit—Hartnett. Home runs—Galan, Gehrig. Double plays—Whitney, Herman, and Collins; Appling, Gehringer, and Gehrig. Wild pitch—Hubbell. Left on bases—Americans 9, Nationals 7.

Managers—Joe McCarthy, New York (A.L.); Charles Grimm, Chicago (N.L.)

Umpires—Reardon and Stewart (N.L.), Summers and Kolls (A.L.) Time—2:00. Attendance—25,556.

July 7, 1937   At Griffith Stadium, Washington

Nationals	AB	R	H	PO	A	E	Americans	AB	R	H	PO	A	E
P. Waner (Pirates), rf ..	5	0	0	0	0	0	Rolfe (Yankees), 3b	4	2	2	0	1	2
Herman (Cubs), 2b	5	1	2	1	4	0	Gehringer (Tigers), 2b .	5	1	3	2	5	0
Medwick (Cardinals), lf .	5	1	4	1	0	0	DiMaggio (Yankees), rf .	4	1	1	1	1	0
Demaree (Cubs), cf	5	0	1	3	1	0	Gehrig (Yankees), 1b ..	4	1	2	10	1	0
Mize (Cardinals), 1b ...	4	0	0	7	0	0	Averill (Indians), cf	3	0	1	2	0	0
Hartnett (Cubs), c	3	1	1	6	0	0	Cronin (Red Sox), ss ...	4	1	1	4	3	0
(b)Whitehead (Giants) .	0	0	0	0	0	0	Dickey (Yankees), c ...	3	1	2	2	0	0
Mancuso (Giants), c ...	1	0	0	1	0	0	West (Browns), lf	4	1	1	5	0	0
Bartell (Giants), ss	4	0	1	2	3	0	Gomez (Yankees), p ...	1	0	0	0	0	0
J. Dean (Cardinals), p ..	1	0	0	0	1	0	Bridges (Tigers), p	1	0	0	0	1	0
Hubbell (Giants), p	0	0	0	0	0	0	(d)Foxx (Red Sox)	1	0	0	0	0	0
Blanton (Pirates), p	0	0	0	0	0	0	Harder (Indians), p	1	0	0	1	1	0
(a)Ott (Giants)	1	0	1	0	0	0							
Grissom (Reds), p	0	0	0	0	0	0							
(c)Collins (Cubs)	1	0	1	0	0	0							
Mungo (Dodgers), p ...	0	0	0	0	1	0							
(e)Moore (Giants)	1	0	0	0	0	0							
Walters (Phillies), p	0	0	0	0	1	0							
Totals	41	3	13	24	11	0	Totals	35	8	13	27	13	2

National League	0	0	0	1	1	1	0	0	0—3
American League	0	0	2	3	1	2	0	0	x—8

Pitching Summary

National League	IP	H	R	ER	BB	SO	American League	IP	H	R	ER	BB	SO
J. Dean (L)	3	4	2	2	1	2	Gomez (W)	3	1	0	0	0	0
Hubbell	⅔	3	3	3	1	1	Bridges	3	7	3	3	0	0
Blanton	⅓	0	0	0	0	1	Harder	3	5	0	0	0	0
Grissom	1	2	1	1	0	2							
Mungo	2	2	2	2	2	1							
Walters	1	2	0	0	0	0							

(a) Doubled for Blanton in fifth. (b) Ran for Hartnett in sixth. (c) Singled for Grissom in sixth. (d) Grounded out for Bridges in sixth. (e) Forced runner for Mungo in eighth. Runs batted in—Gehrig 4, Rolfe 2, Gehringer, Dickey, P. Waner, Medwick, Mize. Two-base hits—Gehrig, Dickey, Cronin, Ott, Medwick 2. Three-base hit—Rolfe. Home run—Gehrig. Double play—Bartell and Mize. Left on bases—Nationals 11, Americans 7.

Managers—Joe McCarthy, New York (A.L.); Bill Terry, New York (N.L.)

Umpires—McGowan and Quinn (A.L.), Barr and Pinelli (N.L.) Time—2:30. Attendance—31,391.

July 6, 1938   At Crosley Field, Cincinnati

Americans	AB	R	H	PO	A	E	Nationals	AB	R	H	PO	A	E
Kreevich (White Sox), lf	2	0	0	1	0	0	Hack (Cubs), 3b	4	1	1	1	2	0
(c)Cramer (Red Sox), lf	2	0	0	0	0	0	Herman (Cubs), 2b	4	0	1	3	4	0
Gehringer (Tigers), 2b .	3	0	1	2	2	0	Goodman (Reds), rf ...	3	0	0	2	0	0
Averill (Indians), cf	4	0	0	5	0	0	Medwick (Cardinals), lf .	4	0	1	2	0	0
Foxx (Red Sox), 1b-3b .	4	0	1	5	1	1	Ott (Giants), cf	4	1	1	3	0	0
DiMaggio (Yankees), rf .	4	1	1	2	0	1	Lombardi (Reds), c	4	0	2	5	0	0
Dickey (Yankees), c ...	4	0	1	8	0	1	McCormick (Reds), 1b .	4	1	1	11	0	0
Cronin (Red Sox), ss ...	3	0	2	0	2	1	Durocher (Dodgers), ss	3	1	1	0	3	0
Lewis (Senators), 3b ...	1	0	0	0	1	0	Vander Meer (Reds), p .	0	0	0	0	3	0
(b)Gehrig (Yankees), 1b	3	0	1	1	0	0	(a)Leiber (Giants)	1	0	0	0	0	0
Gomez (Yankees), p ...	1	0	0	0	0	0	Lee (Cubs), p	1	0	0	0	0	0
Allen (Indians), p	1	0	0	0	0	0	Brown (Pirates), p	1	0	0	0	1	0
(d)York (Tigers)	1	0	0	0	0	0							
Grove (Red Sox), p	0	0	0	0	0	0							
(e)Johnson (Athletics) .	1	0	0	0	0	0							
Totals	34	1	7	24	6	4	Totals	33	4	8	27	13	0

American League ....   0 0 0   0 0 0   0 0 1—1
National League ....   1 0 0   1 0 0   2 0 x—4

Pitching Summary

American League	IP	H	R	ER	BB	SO	National League	IP	H	R	ER	BB	SO
Gomez (L)	3	2	1	0	0	1	Vander Meer (W)	3	1	0	0	0	1
Allen	3	2	1	1	0	3	Lee	3	1	0	0	1	2
Grove	2	4	2	0	0	3	Brown	3	5	1	1	1	2

(a) Lined out for Vander Meer in third. (b) Grounded out for Lewis in fifth. (c) Grounded out for Kreevich in sixth. (d) Fanned for Allen in seventh. (e) Struck out for Grove in ninth. Runs batted in—Medwick, Lombardi, Cronin. Two-base hits—Dickey, Cronin. Three-base hit—Ott. Stolen bases—Goodman, DiMaggio. Hit by pitcher—By Allen (Goodman). Left on bases—Americans 8, Nationals 6.

Managers: Joe McCarthy, New York (A.L.); Bill Terry, New York (N.L.).

Umpires—Ballanfant and Klem (N.L.), Basil and Geisel (A.L.) Time—1:58. Attendance—27,067.

July 11, 1939   At Yankee Stadium, New York

Nationals	AB	R	H	PO	A	E	Americans	AB	R	H	PO	A	E
Hack (Cubs), 3b	4	0	1	1	1	0	Cramer (Red Sox), rf ...	4	0	1	3	0	0
Frey (Reds), 2b	4	0	1	0	4	0	Rolfe (Yankees), 3b	4	0	1	1	0	0
Goodman (Reds), rf ...	1	0	0	0	0	0	DiMaggio (Yankees), cf	4	1	1	1	0	0
(c)Herman (Cubs)	1	0	0	0	0	0	Dickey (Yankees), c ...	3	1	0	10	0	0
Moore (Cardinals), cf ..	1	0	0	0	0	0	Greenberg (Tigers), 1b .	3	1	1	7	1	0
McCormick (Reds), 1b .	4	0	0	7	1	0	Cronin (Red Sox), ss ...	4	0	1	2	3	1
Lombardi (Reds), c	4	0	2	6	0	0	Selkirk (Yankees), lf ...	2	0	1	0	0	0
Medwick (Cardinals), lf .	4	0	0	1	0	0	Gordon (Yankees), 2b ..	4	0	0	2	5	0
Ott (Giants), cf-rf	4	0	2	4	0	0	Ruffing (Yankees), p ...	0	0	0	0	0	0
Vaughan (Pirates), ss ..	3	1	1	4	1	1	(a)Hoag (Browns)	1	0	0	0	0	0
Derringer (Reds), p	1	0	0	0	0	0	Bridges (Tigers), p	1	0	0	0	1	0
(b)Camilli (Dodgers) ...	1	0	0	0	0	0	Feller (Indians), p	1	0	0	0	0	0
Lee (Cubs), p	0	0	0	0	0	0							
(d)Phelps (Dodgers) ...	1	0	0	0	0	0							
Fette (Braves), p	0	0	0	1	0	0							
(e)Mize (Cardinals)	1	0	0	0	0	0							
Totals	34	1	7	24	7	1	Totals	31	3	6	27	9	1

National League .... 0 0 1   0 0 0   0 0 0—1
American League .... 0 0 0   2 1 0   0 0 x—3

Pitching Summary

National League	IP	H	R	ER	BB	SO	American League	IP	H	R	ER	BB	SO
Derringer	3	2	0	0	0	1	Ruffing	3	4	1	1	1	4
Lee (L)	3	3	3	2	3	4	Bridges (W)	2⅓	2	0	0	1	3
Fette	2	1	0	0	1	1	Feller	3⅔	1	0	0	1	2

(a) Fanned for Ruffing in third. (b) Struck out for Derringer in fourth. (c) Struck out for Goodman in fifth. (d) Grounded out for Lee in seventh. (e) Struck out for Fette in ninth. Runs batted in—DiMaggio, Selkirk, Frey. Two-base hit—Frey. Home run—DiMaggio. Double play—Gordon, Cronin, and Greenberg. Left on bases—Nationals 9, Americans 8.

Managers: Joe McCarthy, New York (A.L.); Charles "Gabby" Hartnett, Chicago (N.L.)

Umpires—Hubbard and Rommel (A.L.), Goetz and Magerkurth (N.L.) Time—1:55. Attendance—62,892.

July 9, 1940   At Sportsman's Park, St. Louis

Americans	AB	R	H	PO	A	E	Nationals	AB	R	H	PO	A	E
Travis (Senators), 3b ..	3	0	0	0	0	0	Vaughan (Pirates), ss ..	3	1	1	0	1	0
Keltner (Indians), 3b ...	1	0	0	2	1	0	Miller (Braves), ss	1	0	0	2	1	0
Williams (Red Sox), lf ..	2	0	0	3	0	0	Herman (Cubs), 2b	3	1	3	0	3	0
Finney (Red Sox), rf ...	0	0	0	0	0	0	Coscarart (Dodgers),						
Keller (Yankees), rf	2	0	0	4	0	0	2b	1	0	0	0	2	0
Greenberg (Tigers), lf ..	2	0	0	0	0	0	West (Braves), rf	1	1	1	0	0	0
DiMaggio (Yankees), cf	4	0	0	1	0	0	Nicholson (Cubs), rf ...	2	0	0	1	0	0
Foxx (Red Sox), 1b	3	0	0	4	2	0	Ott (Giants), rf	0	1	0	0	0	0
Appling (White Sox), ss	3	0	2	0	0	0	Mize (Cardinals), 1b ...	2	0	0	8	0	0
Boudreau (Indians), ss .	0	0	0	0	0	0	F. McCormick (Reds),						
Dickey (Yankees), c ...	1	0	0	2	0	0	1b	1	0	0	2	0	0
Hayes (Athletics), c	1	0	0	1	0	0	Lombardi (Reds), c	2	0	1	3	0	0
Hemsley (Indians), c ...	1	0	0	3	0	1	Phelps (Dodgers), c ...	0	0	0	1	0	0
Gordon (Yankees), 2b .	2	0	0	3	1	0	Danning (Giants), c	1	0	1	6	0	0
(a)Mack (Dodgers), 2b ..	1	0	0	0	0	0	Medwick (Dodgers), lf ..	2	0	0	1	0	0
Ruffing (Yankees), p ...	1	0	0	0	0	0	J. Moore (Giants), lf ...	2	0	0	1	0	0
Newsom (Tigers), p	1	0	1	0	0	0	Lavagetto (Dodgers),						
Feller (Indians), p	1	0	0	1	0	0	3b	2	0	0	0	1	0
							May (Phillies), 3b	1	0	0	0	0	0
							T. Moore (Cardinals), cf	3	0	0	2	0	0
							Derringer (Reds), p	1	0	0	0	1	0
							Walters (Reds), p	0	0	0	0	1	0
							Wyatt (Dodgers), p	1	0	0	0	0	0
							French (Cubs), p	0	0	0	0	0	0
							Hubbell (Giants), p	0	0	0	0	0	0
Totals	29	0	3	24	4	1	Totals	29	4	7	27	10	0

American League .... 0 0 0   0 0 0   0 0 0—0
National League .... 3 0 0   0 0 0   0 1 x—4

Pitching Summary

American League	IP	H	R	ER	BB	SO	National League	IP	H	R	ER	BB	SO
Ruffing (L)	3	5	3	3	0	2	Derringer (W)	2	1	0	0	1	3
Newsom	3	1	0	0	1	1	Walters	2	0	0	0	0	0
Feller	2	1	1	1	2	3	Wyatt	2	1	0	0	0	1
							French	2	1	0	0	0	2
							Hubbell	1	0	0	0	1	1

(a) Struck out for Gordon in eighth. Runs batted in—West, 3, Danning. Two-base hit—Appling. Home run—West. Sacrifice hits—F. McCormick, French. Double play—Coscarart, Miller, and F. McCormick. Hit by pitcher—By Feller (May). Left on bases—Nationals 7, Americans 4.

Managers: Joe Cronin, Boston (A.L.); Bill McKechnie, Cincinnati (N.L.).

Umpires—Reardon and Stewart (N.L.), Pipgras and Basil (A.L.) Time—1:53. Attendance—32,373.

July 8, 1941   At Briggs Stadium, Detroit

Nationals	AB	R	H	PO	A	E	Americans	AB	R	H	PO	A	E
Hack (Cubs), 3b	2	0	1	3	0	0	Doerr (Red Sox), 2b ...	3	0	0	0	0	0
(f)Lavagetto (Dodgers),							Gordon (Yankees), 2b .	2	1	1	2	0	0
3b	1	0	0	0	0	0	Travis (Senators), 3b ..	4	1	1	1	2	0
T. Moore (Cardinals), lf	5	0	0	0	0	0	J. DiMaggio (Yanks), cf	4	3	1	1	0	0
Reiser (Dodgers), cf ...	4	0	0	6	0	2	Williams (Red Sox), lf ..	4	1	2	3	0	1
Mize (Cardinals), 1b ...	4	1	1	5	0	0	Heath (Indians), rf	2	0	0	1	0	1
F. McCormick (Reds),							D. DiMaggio (R. Sox), rf	1	0	1	1	0	0
1b	0	0	0	0	0	0	Cronin (Red Sox), ss ...	2	0	0	3	0	0
Nicholson (Cubs), rf ...	1	0	0	1	0	0	Boudreau (Indians), ss .	2	0	2	0	1	0
Elliot (Pirates), rf	1	0	0	0	0	0	York (Tigers), 1b	3	0	1	6	2	0
Slaughter (Cardinals), rf	2	1	1	0	0	0	Foxx (Red Sox), 1b	1	0	0	2	2	0
Vaughan (Pirates), ss ..	4	2	3	1	2	0	Dickey (Yankees), c ...	3	0	1	4	2	0
Miller (Braves), ss	0	0	0	0	1	0	Hayes (Athletics), c	1	0	0	2	0	0
Frey (Reds), 2b	1	0	1	1	3	0	Feller (Indians), p	0	0	0	0	1	0
(c)Herman (Dodgers),							(b)Cullenbine (Browns)	1	0	0	0	0	0
2b	3	0	2	3	0	0	Lee (White Sox), p	1	0	0	0	1	0
Owen (Dodgers), c	1	0	0	0	0	0	Hudson (Senators), p ..	0	0	0	0	0	0
Lopez (Pirates), c	1	0	0	3	0	0	(e)Keller (Yankees)	1	0	0	0	0	0
Danning (Giants), c	1	0	0	3	0	0	Smith (White Sox), p ...	0	0	0	1	0	1
Wyatt (Dodgers), p	0	0	0	0	0	0	(g)Keltner (Indians)	1	1	1	0	0	0
(a)Ott (Giants)	1	0	0	0	0	0							
Derringer (Reds), p	0	0	0	0	1	0							
Walters (Reds), p	1	1	1	0	0	0							
(d)Medwick (Dodgers) .	1	0	0	0	0	0							
Passeau (Cubs), p	1	0	0	0	0	0							
Totals	35	5	10	26	7	2	Totals	36	7	11	27	11	3

National League	0	0	0	0	0	1	2	2	0—5
American League	0	0	0	1	0	1	0	1	4—7

Two out when winning run scored.

Pitching Summary

National League	IP	H	R	ER	BB	SO	American League	IP	H	R	ER	BB	SO
Wyatt	2	0	0	0	1	0	Feller	3	1	0	0	0	4
Derringer	2	2	1	0	0	1	Lee	3	4	1	1	0	0
Walters	2	3	1	1	2	2	Hudson	1	3	2	2	1	1
Passeau (L)	2⅔	6	5	4	1	3	Smith (W)	2	2	2	2	0	2

(a) Struck out for Wyatt in third. (b) Grounded out for Feller in third. (c) Singled for Frey in fifth. (d) Grounded out for Walters in seventh. (e) Struck out for Hudson in seventh. (f) Grounded out for Hack in ninth. (g) Singled for Smith in ninth. Runs batted in—Williams 4, Moore, Boudreau, Vaughan 4, D. DiMaggio, J. DiMaggio. Two-base hits—Travis, Williams, Walters, Herman, Mize, J. DiMaggio. Home runs—Vaughan 2, Williams. Sacrifice hits—Hack, Lopez. Double plays—Frey, Vaughan, and Mize; York and Cronin. Left on bases—Americans 7, Nationals 6.

Managers: Del Baker, Detroit (A.L.); Bill McKechnie, Cincinnati (N.L.).

Umpires—Summers and Grieve (A.L.), Jorda and Pinelli (N.L.) Time—2:23. Attendance—54,674.

July 6, 1942   At Polo Grounds, New York

Americans	AB	R	H	PO	A	E	Nationals	AB	R	H	PO	A	E
Boudreau (Indians), ss .	4	1	1	4	5	0	Brown (Cardinals), 2b ..	2	0	0	1	0	1
Henrich (Yankees), rf ..	4	1	1	2	0	0	Herman (Dodgers), 2b .	1	0	0	0	0	0
Williams (Red Sox), lf ..	4	0	1	0	0	0	Vaughan (Dodgers), 3b	2	0	0	1	2	0
J. DiMaggio (Yanks), cf	4	0	2	2	0	0	Elliot (Pirates), 3b	1	0	1	1	2	0
York (Tigers), 1b	4	1	1	11	3	0	Reiser (Dodgers), cf ...	3	0	1	3	0	0
Gordon (Yankees), 2b .	4	0	0	1	4	0	Moore (Cardinals), cf ..	1	0	0	1	0	0
Keltner (Indians), 3b ...	4	0	0	0	1	0	Mize (Giants), 1b	2	0	0	3	0	0
Tebbetts (Tigers), c	4	0	0	4	1	0	F. McCormick (Reds),						
Chandler (Yankees), p .	1	0	0	3	1	0	1b	2	0	0	3	0	0
(b)Johnson (Athletics) .	1	0	1	0	0	0	Ott (Giants), rf	4	0	0	1	0	0
Benton (Tigers), p	1	0	0	0	1	0	Medwick (Dodgers), lf ..	2	0	0	1	0	0
							Slaughter (Cardinals), lf	2	0	1	1	0	0
							W. Cooper (Cardinals),						
							c	2	0	1	7	0	0
							Lombardi (Braves), c ..	1	0	0	2	0	0
							Miller (Braves), ss	2	0	0	2	1	0
							Reese (Dodgers), ss ...	1	0	0	0	1	0
							M. Cooper (Cardinals),						
							p	0	0	0	0	0	0
							(a)Marshall (Giants)	1	0	0	0	0	0
							Vander Meer (Reds), p .	0	0	0	0	1	0
							(c)Litwhiler (Phillies) ...	1	0	1	0	0	0
							Passeau (Cubs), p	0	0	0	0	0	0
							(d)Owen (Dodgers)	1	1	1	0	0	0
							Walters (Reds), p	0	0	0	0	0	0
Totals	35	3	7	27	16	0	Totals	31	1	6	27	7	1

American League .... 3 0 0   0 0 0   0 0 0—3
National League .... 0 0 0   0 0 0   0 1 0—1

Pitching Summary

American League	IP	H	R	ER	BB	SO	National League	IP	H	R	ER	BB	SO
Chandler (W)	4	2	0	0	0	2	M. Cooper (L)	3	4	3	3	0	2
Benton	5	4	1	1	2	1	Vander Meer	3	2	0	0	0	4
							Passeau	2	1	0	0	0	1
							Walters	1	0	0	0	0	1

(a) Forced runner for M. Cooper in third. (b) Singled for Chandler in fifth. (c) Singled for Vander Meer in sixth. (d) Homered for Passeau in eighth. Runs batted in—Boudreau, York 2, Owen. Two-base hit—Henrich. Home runs—Boudreau, York, Owen. Double plays—Gordon, Boudreau, and York; Boudreau and York. Hit by pitcher—By Chandler (Brown). Passed ball—Tebbetts. Left on bases—Nationals 6, Americans 5.

Managers: Joe McCarthy, New York (A.L.); Leo Durocher, Brooklyn (N.L.)

Umpires—Ballanfant and Barlick (N.L.), Stewart and McGowan (A.L.) Time—2:07. Attendance—34,178.

July 13, 1943   At Shibe Park, Philadelphia (Night)

Nationals	AB	R	H	PO	A	E	Americans	AB	R	H	PO	A	E
Hack (Cubs), 3b	5	1	3	0	2	1	Case (Senators), rf	2	1	0	0	0	0
Herman (Dodgers), 2b .	5	0	2	3	3	2	Keltner (Indians), 3b ...	4	1	1	2	2	0
Musial (Cardinals), lf-rf .	4	0	1	0	0	0	Wakefield (Tigers), lf ...	4	0	2	3	0	0
Nicholson (Cubs), rf ...	2	0	0	0	0	0	R.Johnson (Senators),						
(a)Galan (Dodgers), lf ..	1	0	0	1	0	0	lf	0	0	0	1	0	0
Fletcher (Pirates), 1b ..	2	0	0	3	0	0	Stephens (Browns), ss .	3	0	1	1	3	1
(d)Dahlgren (Phillies),							Siebert (Athletics), 1b ..	1	0	0	3	1	0
1b	2	0	0	3	0	0	(a)York (Tigers), 1b	3	0	1	4	0	0
W. Cooper (Cardinals),							Laabs (Browns), cf	3	1	0	7	0	0
c	2	0	1	7	1	0	Early (Senators), c	2	1	0	3	0	0
(e)Lombardi (Giants), c	2	0	0	3	0	0	Doerr (Red Sox), 2b ...	4	1	2	3	3	0
H. Walker (Cards), cf ..	1	0	0	1	0	0	Leonard (Senators), p ..	1	0	1	0	1	0
(b)DiMaggio (Pirates),							Newhouser (Tigers), p ..	1	0	0	0	0	0
cf	3	2	3	1	0	0	(f)Heath (Indians)	1	0	0	0	0	0
Marion (Cardinals), ss .	2	0	0	2	2	0	Hughson (Red Sox), p .	0	0	0	0	0	0
(g)Ott (Giants)	1	0	0	0	0	0							
Miller (Reds), ss	1	0	0	0	1	0							
M. Cooper (Cardinals),													
p	1	0	0	0	1	0							
Vander Meer (Reds), p .	1	0	0	0	1	0							
Sewell (Pirates), p	0	0	0	0	1	0							
(h)F.Walker (Dodgers) .	1	0	0	0	0	0							
Javery (Braves), p	0	0	0	0	0	0							
(i)Frey (Reds)	1	0	0	0	0	0							
Totals	37	3	10	24	12	3	Totals	29	5	8	27	10	1

National League	1	0	0		0	0	0		1	0	1—3
American League	0	3	1		0	1	0		0	0	x—5

Pitching Summary

National League	IP	H	R	ER	BB	SO	American League	IP	H	R	ER	BB	SO
M. Cooper (L)	2⅓	4	4	4	2	1	Leonard (W)	3	2	1	1	0	0
Vander Meer	2⅔	2	1	0	1	6	Newhouser	3	3	0	0	1	1
Sewell	1	0	0	0	0	0	Hughson	3	5	2	2	0	2
Javery	2	2	0	0	0	3							

(a) Struck out for Siebert in third. (b) Singled for H. Walker in fourth. (c) Walked for Nicholson in sixth. (d) Grounded into double play for Fletcher in sixth. (e) Flied out for W. Cooper in sixth. (f) Flied out for Newhouser in sixth. (g) Struck out for Marion in seventh. (h) Flied out for Sewell in seventh. (i) Flied out for Javery in ninth. Runs batted in—Musial, F. Walker, DiMaggio, Doerr 3, Wakefield. Two-base hits—Musial, Keltner, Wakefield. Three-base hit—DiMaggio. Home runs—Doerr, DiMaggio. Sacrifice hits—Stephens, Early. Double plays—Hack, Herman, and Fletcher; Vander Meer, Marion, and Herman; Miller, Herman, and Dahlgren; Stephens, Doerr, and York. Hit by pitcher—By M. Cooper (Case). Left on bases—Nationals 8, Americans 6.

Managers: Joe McCarthy, New York (A.L.); Billy Southworth, St. Louis (N.L.)

Umpires—Rommel and Rue (A.L.), Conlan and Dunn (N.L.) Time—2:07. Attendance—31,938.

July 11, 1944   At Forbes Field, Pittsburgh (Night)

Americans	AB	R	H	PO	A	E	Nationals	AB	R	H	PO	A	E
Tucker (White Sox), cf .	4	0	0	4	0	0	Galan (Dodgers), lf	4	1	1	2	0	0
Spence (Senators), rf ..	4	0	2	2	1	0	Cavarretta (Cubs), 1b ..	2	1	2	12	0	0
McQuinn (Browns), 1b .	4	0	1	5	1	1	Musial (Cardinals), cf-rf	4	1	1	2	1	0
Stephens (Browns), ss .	4	0	1	1	0	0	W.Cooper (Cardinals),						
Johnson (Red Sox), lf ..	3	0	0	2	1	0	c	5	1	2	5	2	0
Keltner (Indians), 3b ...	4	1	1	0	4	0	Mueller (Reds), c	0	0	0	0	0	0
Doerr (Red Sox), 2b ...	3	0	0	4	1	1	Walker (Dodgers), cf ...	4	0	2	0	0	0
Hemsley (Yankees), c ..	2	0	0	2	0	0	DiMaggio (Pirates), cf ..	0	0	0	0	0	0
Hayes (Athletics), c	1	0	0	3	0	1	Elliot (Pirates), 3b	3	0	0	0	3	0
Borowy (Yankees), p ...	1	0	1	0	0	0	Kurowski (Cards), 3b ..	1	0	1	0	1	0
Hughson (Red Sox), p .	1	0	0	0	0	0	Ryan (Braves), 2b	4	1	2	4	4	1
Muncrief (Browns), p ..	0	0	0	1	0	0	Marion (Cardinals), ss .	3	1	0	2	3	0
(c)Higgins (Tigers)	1	0	0	0	0	0	Walters (Reds), p	0	0	0	0	1	0
Newhouser (Tigers), p .	0	0	0	0	1	0	(a)Ott (Giants)	1	0	0	0	0	0
Newsom (Athletics), p ..	0	0	0	0	0	0	Raffensberger (Phils), p	0	0	0	0	0	0
							(b)Nicholson (Cubs) ...	1	1	1	0	0	0
							Sewell (Pirates), p	1	0	0	0	0	0
							(d)Medwick (Giants) ...	0	0	0	0	0	0
							Tobin (Braves), p	0	0	0	0	0	0
Totals	32	1	6	24	9	3	Totals	33	7	12	27	15	1

American League .... 0 1 0   0 0 0   0 0 0—1
National League .... 0 0 0   0 4 0   2 1 x—7

Pitching Summary

American League	IP	H	R	ER	BB	SO	National League	IP	H	R	ER	BB	SO
Borowy	3	3	0	0	1	0	Walters	3	5	1	1	0	1
Hughson (L)	1⅔	5	4	3	1	2	Raffensberger (W)	2	1	0	0	0	2
Muncrief	1⅓	1	0	0	0	1	Sewell	3	0	0	0	1	2
Newhouser	1⅔	3	3	2	2	1	Tobin	1	0	0	0	0	0
Newsom	⅓	0	0	0	0	0							

(a) Flied out for Walters in third. (b) Doubled for Raffensberger in fifth. (c) Grounded out for Muncrief in seventh. (d) Sacrificed for Sewell in eighth. Runs batted in—Kurowski 2, Nicholson, Galan, W. Cooper, Walker, Musial, Borowy. Two-base hits—Nicholson, Kurowski. Three-base hit—Cavarretta. Sacrifice hits—Marion, Musial, Medwick. Stolen base—Ryan. Double plays—Spence and Hemsley; Marion, Ryan, and Cavarretta. Wild pitch—Muncrief. Left on bases—Nationals 9, Americans 5.

Managers: Joe McCarthy, New York (A.L.); Billy Southworth, St. Louis (N.L.)

Umpires—Barr and Sears (N.L.), Berry and Hubbard (A.L.) Time—2:11. Attendance—29,589.

July 9, 1946   At Fenway Park, Boston

Nationals	AB	R	H	PO	A	E	Americans	AB	R	H	PO	A	E
Schoendienst (Cards),							D.DiMaggio (Red Sox),						
2b	2	0	0	0	2	0	cf	2	0	1	1	0	0
(c)Gustine (Pirates), 2b	1	0	0	1	1	0	Spence (Senators), cf ..	0	1	0	1	0	0
Musial (Cardinals), lf ...	2	0	0	0	0	0	Chapman (Athletics), cf	2	0	0	1	0	0
(d)Ennis (Phillies), lf ...	2	0	0	0	0	0	Pesky (Red Sox), ss ...	2	0	0	1	0	1
Hopp (Braves), cf	2	0	1	0	0	0	Stephens (Browns), ss .	3	1	2	0	4	0
(e)Lowrey (Cubs), cf ...	2	0	1	3	0	0	Williams (Red Sox), lf ..	4	4	4	1	0	0
Walker (Dodgers), rf ...	3	0	0	1	0	0	Keller (Yankees), rf	4	2	1	1	0	0
Slaughter (Cards), rf ...	1	0	0	0	0	0	Doerr (Red Sox), 2b ...	2	0	0	1	1	0
Kurowski (Cards), 3b ..	3	0	0	2	1	0	Gordon (Yankees), 2b .	2	0	1	0	1	0
(i)Verban (Phillies)	1	0	0	0	0	0	Vernon (Senators), 1b .	2	0	0	2	1	0
Mize (Giants), 1b	1	0	0	7	0	0	York (Red Sox), 1b	2	0	1	5	0	0
(b)McCormick (Phillies),							Keltner (Indians), 3b ...	0	0	0	0	0	0
1b	1	0	0	1	1	0	Stirnweiss (Yankees),						
(g)Cavarretta (Cubs),							3b	3	1	1	0	0	0
1b	1	0	0	1	0	0	Hayes (Indians), c	1	0	0	3	0	0
Cooper (Giants), c	1	0	1	0	0	0	Rosar (Athletics), c	2	1	1	5	0	0
Masi (Braves), c	2	0	0	4	1	0	Wagner (Red Sox), c ..	1	0	0	4	0	0
Marion (Cardinals), ss .	3	0	0	4	6	0	Feller (Indians), p	0	0	0	0	0	0
Passeau (Cubs), p	1	0	0	0	1	0	(a)Appling (White Sox) .	1	0	0	0	0	0
Higbe (Dodgers), p	1	0	0	0	0	0	Newhouser (Tigers), p .	1	1	1	1	0	0
Blackwell (Reds), p	0	0	0	0	0	0	(f)Dickey (Yankees)	1	0	0	0	0	0
(h)Lamanno (Reds)	1	0	0	0	0	0	Kramer (Browns) p	1	1	1	0	0	0
Sewell (Pirates), p	0	0	0	0	0	0							
Totals	31	0	3	24	13	0	Totals	36	12	14	27	7	1

```
National League .....................   0  0  0     0  0  0     0  0 0—0
American League ....................   2  0  0     1  3  0     2  4 x—12
```

Pitching Summary

National League	IP	H	R	ER	BB	SO	American League	IP	H	R	ER	BB	SO
Passeau (L)	3	2	2	2	2	0	Feller (W)	3	2	0	0	0	3
Higbe	1⅓	5	4	4	1	2	Newhouser	3	1	0	0	0	4
Blackwell	2⅔	3	2	2	1	1	Kramer	3	0	0	0	1	3
Sewell	1	4	4	4	0	0							

(a) Grounded out for Feller in third. (b) Flied out for Mize in fourth. (c) Struck out for Schoendienst in sixth. (d) Struck out for Musial in sixth. (e) Singled for Hopp in sixth. (f) Struck out for Newhouser in sixth. (g) Struck out for McCormick in seventh. (h) Grounded out for Blackwell in eighth. (i) Fouled out for Kurowski in ninth. Runs batted in—Keller 2, Williams 5, Stephens 2, Gordon 2, Chapman. Two-base hits—Stephens, Gordon. Home runs—Williams 2, Keller. Double plays—Marion and Mize; Schoendienst, Marion, and Mize. Wild pitch—Blackwell. Left on bases—Nationals 5, Americans 4.

Managers: Steve O'Neill, Detroit (A.L.); Charles Grimm, Chicago (N.L.).

Umpires—Summers and Rommel (A.L.), Boggess and Goetz (N.L.) Time—2:19. Attendance—34,906.

July 8, 1947   At Wrigley Field, Chicago

Americans	AB	R	H	PO	A	E	Nationals	AB	R	H	PO	A	E
Kell (Tigers), 3b	4	0	0	0	0	0	H.Walker (Phillies), cf ..	2	0	0	1	0	0
Johnson (Yankees), 3b	0	0	0	0	0	0	Pafko (Cubs), cf	2	0	1	2	0	0
Lewis (Senators), rf	2	0	0	1	0	0	F.Walker (Dodgers), rf .	2	0	0	1	0	0
(b)Appling (White Sox) .	1	1	1	0	0	0	Marshall (Giants), rf ...	1	0	0	3	0	0
Henrich (Yankees), rf ..	1	0	0	3	0	0	W.Cooper (Giants), c ..	3	0	0	6	0	0
Williams (Red Sox), lf ..	4	0	2	3	0	0	Edwards (Dodgers), c ..	0	0	0	2	0	0
DiMaggio (Yankees), cf	3	0	1	1	0	0	Cavarretta (Cubs), 1b ..	1	0	0	1	0	0
Boudreau (Indians), ss .	4	0	1	4	4	0	Mize (Giants), 1b	3	1	2	8	0	0
McQuinn (Yankees), 1b	4	0	0	9	1	0	Masi (Braves), c	0	0	0	0	0	0
Gordon (Yankees), 2b .	2	0	1	0	4	0	Slaughter (Cards), lf ...	3	0	0	1	0	0
Doerr (Red Sox), 2b ...	2	1	1	0	2	0	Gustine (Pirates), 3b ...	2	0	0	0	2	0
Rosar (Athletics), c	4	0	0	6	0	0	Kurowski (Cards), 3b ..	2	0	0	0	1	0
Newhouser (Tigers), p ..	1	0	0	0	0	0	Marion (Cardinals), ss .	2	0	1	0	1	0
Shea (Yankees), p	1	0	0	0	0	0	Reese (Dodgers), ss ...	1	0	0	0	2	0
(c)Spence (Senators) ..	1	0	1	0	0	0	Verban (Phillies), 2b ...	2	0	0	0	0	0
Masterson (Senators), p	0	0	0	0	0	0	Stanky (Dodgers), 2b ..	2	0	0	2	2	0
Page (Yankees), p	0	0	0	0	0	0	Blackwell (Reds), p	0	0	0	0	0	0
							(a)Haas (Reds)	1	0	1	0	0	0
							Brecheen (Cards), p ...	1	0	0	0	1	0
							Sain (Braves), p	0	0	0	0	0	1
							(d)Musial (Cardinals) ...	1	0	0	0	0	0
							Spahn (Braves), p	0	0	0	0	0	0
							(g)Rowe (Phillies)	1	0	0	0	0	0
Totals	34	2	8	27	11	0	Totals	32	1	5	27	9	1

American League .... 0 0 0   0 0 1   1 0 0—2
National League .... 0 0 0   1 0 0   0 0 0—1

Pitching Summary

American League	IP	H	R	ER	BB	SO	National League	IP	H	R	ER	BB	SO
Newhouser	3	1	0	0	0	0	Blackwell	3	1	0	0	0	4
Shea (W)	3	3	1	1	2	2	Brecheen	3	5	1	1	0	2
Masterson	1⅔	0	0	0	1	2	Sain (L)	1	2	1	1	0	1
Page	1⅓	1	0	0	1	0	Spahn	2	0	0	0	1	1

(a) Singled for Blackwell in third. (b) Singled for Lewis in sixth. (c) Singled for Shea in seventh. (d) Grounded out for Sain in seventh. (e) Struck out for Edwards in eighth. (f) Ran for Mize in eighth. (g) Flied out for Spahn in ninth. Runs batted in—Mize, Spence. Two-base hits—Williams, Gordon. Home run—Mize. Stolen base—Doerr. Double play—Reese, Stanky, and Mize. Wild pitch—Blackwell. Passed ball—W. Cooper. Left on bases—Nationals 8, Americans 6.

Managers: Joe Cronin, Boston (A.L.); Eddie Dyer, St. Louis (N.L.)

Umpires—Boyer and Passarella (A.L.), Conlan and Henline (N.L.) Time—2:19. Attendance—41,123.

July 13, 1948   At Sportsman's Park, St. Louis

Nationals	AB	R	H	PO	A	E	Americans	AB	R	H	PO	A	E
Ashburn (Phillies), cf ..	4	1	2	1	0	0	Mullin (Tigers), rf	1	0	0	0	0	0
Kiner (Pirates), lf	1	0	0	1	0	0	(c)DiMaggio (Yankees) .	1	0	0	0	0	0
Schoendienst (Cards),							Zarilla (Browns), rf	2	0	0	2	0	0
2b	4	0	0	0	1	0	Henrich (Yankees), lf ..	3	0	0	1	0	0
Rigney (Giants), 2b	0	0	0	2	0	0	Boudreau (Indians), ss .	2	0	0	2	0	0
Musial (Cardinals), lf-cf .	4	1	2	3	0	0	Stephens (Red Sox), ss	2	0	1	0	0	0
Mize (Giants), lb	4	0	1	4	1	0	Gordon (Indians), 2b ...	2	0	0	1	2	0
Slaughter (Cards), rf ...	2	0	1	2	0	0	Doerr (Red Sox), 2b ...	2	0	0	0	3	0
Holmes (Braves), rf	1	0	0	1	0	0	Evers (Tigers), cf	4	1	1	0	0	0
Pafko (Cubs), 3b	2	0	0	0	0	0	Keltner (Indians), 3b ...	3	1	1	1	6	0
Elliot (Braves), 3b	2	0	1	0	0	0	McQuinn (Yankees), 1b	4	1	2	14	0	0
Cooper (Braves), c	2	0	0	3	0	0	Rosar (Athletics), c	1	0	0	1	0	0
Masi (Braves), c	2	0	1	4	0	0	Tebbetts (Red Sox), c ..	1	1	0	5	1	0
Reese (Dodgers), ss ...	2	0	0	2	2	0	Masterson (Senators), p	0	0	0	0	0	0
Kerr (Giants), ss	2	0	0	1	0	0	(a)Vernon (Senators) ..	0	1	0	0	0	0
Branca (Dodgers), p ...	1	0	0	0	0	0	Raschi (Yankees), p ...	1	0	1	0	0	0
(b)Gustine (Pirates)	1	0	0	0	0	0	(e)Williams (Red Sox) ..	0	0	0	0	0	0
Schmitz (Cubs), p	0	0	0	0	0	0	(f)Newhouser (Tigers) ..	0	0	0	0	0	0
Sain (Braves), p	0	0	0	0	0	0	Coleman (Athletics), p .	0	0	0	0	1	0
(d)Waitkus (Cubs)	0	0	0	0	0	0							
Blackwell (Reds), p	0	0	0	0	0	0							
(g)Thomson (Giants) ...	1	0	0	0	0	0							
Totals	35	2	8	24	4	0	Totals	29	5	6	27	14	0

```
National League .....................   2  0  0     0  0  0     0  0 0—2
American League ....................   0  1  1     3  0  0     0  0 x—5
```

Pitching Summary

National League	IP	H	R	ER	BB	SO	American League	IP	H	R	ER	BB	SO
Branca	3	1	2	2	3	3	Masterson	3	5	2	2	1	1
Schmitz (L)	⅓	3	3	3	1	0	Raschi (W)	3	3	0	0	1	3
Sain	1⅔	0	0	0	0	3	Coleman	3	0	0	0	2	3
Blackwell	3	2	0	0	3	1							

(a) Walked for Masterson in third. (b) Struck out for Branca in fourth. (c) Flied out for Mullin in fourth, scoring Tebbetts from third. (d) Walked for Sain in sixth. (e) Walked for Raschi in sixth. (f) Ran for Williams in sixth. (g) Struck out for Blackwell in ninth. Runs batted in—Musial 2, Evers, Boudreau, Raschi 2, DiMaggio. Home runs—Musial, Evers. Sacrifice hit—Coleman. Stolen bases—Ashburn, Vernon, Mullin, McQuinn. Wild pitch—Masterson. Left on bases—Nationals 10, Americans 8.

Managers: Stanley "Bucky" Harris, New York (A.L.); Leo Durocher, Brooklyn (N.L.) Umpires—Berry and Paparella (A.L.), Reardon and Stewart (N.L.) Time—2:27. Attendance—34,009.

July 12, 1949   At Ebbets Field, Brooklyn

Americans	AB	R	H	PO	A	E	Nationals	AB	R	H	PO	A	E
D.DiMaggio (Red Sox),							Reese (Dodgers), ss ...	5	0	0	3	3	1
rf-cf	5	2	2	2	0	0	J.Robinson (Dodgers),						
Raschi (Yankees), p ...	1	0	0	0	1	0	2b	4	3	1	1	1	0
Kell (Tigers), 3b	3	2	2	0	1	0	Musial (Cardinals), cf-rf	4	1	3	2	0	0
(d)Dillinger (Browns),							Kiner (Pirates), lf	5	1	1	3	0	0
3b	1	2	1	0	2	0	Mize (Giants), 1b	2	0	1	1	0	1
Williams (Red Sox), lf ..	2	1	0	1	0	0	(a)Hodges (Dodgers),						
Mitchell (Indians), lf	1	0	1	1	0	1	1b	3	1	1	8	2	0
J.DiMaggio (Yanks), cf .	4	1	2	0	0	0	Marshall (Giants), rf ...	1	1	0	1	0	1
(e)Doby (Indians), rf-cf .	1	0	0	2	0	0	Bickford (Braves), p ...	0	0	0	0	0	0
Joost (Athletics), ss	2	1	1	2	2	0	(f)Thomson (Giants) ...	1	0	0	0	0	0
Stephens (Red Sox), ss	2	0	0	2	0	0	Pollet (Cardinals), p ...	0	0	0	1	0	0
E.Robinson (Senators),							Blackwell (Reds), p	0	0	0	0	0	0
1b	5	1	1	8	0	0	(h)Slaughter (Cardinals),						
Goodman (Red Sox),							....	1	0	0	0	0	0
1b	0	0	0	1	1	0	Roe (Dodgers), p	0	0	0	0	0	0
Michaels (White Sox),							Kazak (Cardinals), 3b ..	2	0	2	0	1	0
2b	2	0	0	1	3	0	S.Gordon (Giants), 3b .	2	0	1	0	4	0
J.Gordon (Indians), 2b .	2	1	1	3	3	0	Seminick (Phillies), c ..	1	0	0	3	0	1
Tebbetts (Red Sox), c ..	2	0	2	2	0	0	Campanella (Dodgers),						
Berra (Yankees), c	3	0	0	2	1	0	c	2	0	0	2	0	1
Parnell (Red Sox), p ...	1	0	0	0	1	0	Spahn (Braves), p	0	0	0	0	0	0
Trucks (Tigers), p	1	0	0	0	0	0	Newcombe (Dodgers),						
Brissie (Athletics), p ...	1	0	0	0	0	0	p	1	0	0	0	0	0
(g)Wertz (Tigers), rf	2	0	0	0	0	0	(b)Schoendienst (Cards)						
							....	1	0	1	0	0	0
							Munger (Cardinals), p ..	0	0	0	0	0	0
							(c)Pafko (Cubs), cf	2	0	1	2	0	0
Totals	41	11	13	27	15	1	Totals	37	7	12	27	11	5

American League .... 4 0 0   2 0 2   3 0 0—11
National League .... 2 1 2   0 0 2   0 0 0—7

Pitching Summary

American League	IP	H	R	ER	BB	SO	National League	IP	H	R	ER	BB	SO
Parnell	1*	3	3	3	1	1	Spahn	1⅓	4	4	0	2	3
Trucks (W)	2	3	2	2	2	0	Newcombe (L)	2⅔	3	2	2	1	0
Brissie	3	5	2	2	2	1	Munger	1	0	0	0	1	0
Raschi	3	1	0	0	3	1	Bickford	1	2	2	2	1	0
							Pollet	1	4	3	3	0	0
							Blackwell	1	0	0	0	0	2
							Roe	1	0	0	0	0	0

* Pitched to three batters in second inning.

(a) Ran for Mize in third. (b) Singled for Newcombe in fourth. (c) Struck out for Munger in fifth. (d) Ran for Kell in sixth. (e) Ran for J. DiMaggio in sixth. (f) Flied out for Bickford in sixth. (g) Flied out for Brissie in seventh. (h) Flied out for Blackwell in eighth. Runs batted in—J. DiMaggio 3, E. Robinson, Tebbetts, Musial 2, Newcombe, Kazak, Joost 2, Kiner 2, D. DiMaggio, Dillinger, Mitchell. (Joost scored on Reese's error in first; J. Robinson scored when Kiner grounded into a double play in third.) Two-base hits—J. Robinson, Tebbetts, S. Gordon, D. DiMaggio, J. DiMaggio, J. Gordon, Mitchell. Home runs—Musial, Kiner. Stolen base—Kell. Double plays—Michaels, Joost, and E. Robinson; Joost, Michaels, and E. Robinson; J. Robinson, Reese, and Hodges. Hit by pitcher—By Parnell (Seminick). Left on bases—Nationals 12, Americans 8.

Managers: Lou Boudreau, Cleveland (A.L.); Billy Southworth, Boston (N.L.)

Umpires—Barlick, Gore, and Ballanfant (N.L.), Hubbard, Summers, and Grieve (A.L.) Time—3:04. Attendance—32,577.

July 11, 1950   At Comiskey Park, Chicago

Nationals	AB	R	H	PO	A	E	Americans	AB	R	H	PO	A	E
Jones (Phillies), 3b	7	0	1	2	3	0	Rizzuto (Yankees), ss ..	6	0	2	2	2	0
Kiner (Pirates), lf	6	1	2	1	0	0	Doby (Indians), cf	6	1	2	9	0	0
Musial (Cardinals), 1b ..	5	0	0	11	1	0	Kell (Tigers), 3b	6	0	0	2	4	0
Robinson (Dodgers), 2b	4	1	1	3	2	0	Williams (Red Sox), lf ..	4	0	1	2	0	0
(f)Wyrostek (Reds), rf ..	2	0	0	0	0	0	D.DiMaggio (R. Sox), lf .	2	0	0	1	0	0
Slaughter (Cards), cf-rf	4	1	2	3	0	0	Dropo (Red Sox), 1b ...	3	0	1	8	1	0
Schoendienst (Cards),							(e)Fain (Athletics), 1b ..	3	0	1	2	1	0
2b	1	1	1	1	1	0	Evers (Tigers), rf	2	0	0	1	0	0
Sauer (Cubs), rf	2	0	0	1	0	0	J.DiMaggio (Yanks), rf .	3	0	0	3	0	0
Pafko (Cubs), cf	4	0	2	4	0	0	Berra (Yankees), c	2	0	0	2	0	0
Campanella (Dodgers),							(b)Hegan (Indians), c ..	3	0	0	7	1	0
c	6	0	0	13	2	0	Doerr (Red Sox), 2b ...	3	0	0	1	4	0
Marion (Cardinals), ss .	2	0	0	0	2	0	Coleman (Yankees), 2b	2	0	0	0	0	1
Konstanty (Phillies), p ..	0	0	0	0	0	0	Raschi (Yankees), p ...	0	0	0	0	0	0
Jansen (Giants), p	2	0	0	1	0	0	(a)Michaels (Senators) .	1	1	1	0	0	0
(g)Snider (Dodgers) ...	1	0	0	0	0	0	Lemon (Indians), p	0	1	0	1	0	0
Blackwell (Reds), p	1	0	0	0	1	0	Houtteman (Tigers), p ..	1	0	0	1	0	0
Roberts (Phillies), p	1	0	0	0	0	0	Reynolds (Yankees), p .	1	0	0	0	0	0
Newcombe (Dodgers),							Henrich (Yankees)	1	0	0	0	0	0
p	0	0	0	0	1	0	Gray (Tigers), p	0	0	0	0	0	0
(c)Sisler (Phillies)	1	0	1	0	0	0	Feller (Indians), p	0	0	0	0	0	0
(d)Reese (Dodgers), ss	3	0	0	2	4	0							
Totals	52	4	10	42	17	0	Totals	49	3	8	42	13	1

National League .... 0 2 0   0 0 0   0 0 1   0 0 0   0 1—4
American League ...... 0 0 1   0 2 0   0 0 0   0 0 0   0 0—3

Pitching Summary

National League	IP	H	R	ER	BB	SO	American League	IP	H	R	ER	BB	SO
Roberts	3	3	1	1	1	1	Raschi	3	2	2	2	0	1
Newcombe	2	3	2	2	1	1	Lemon	3	1	0	0	0	2
Konstanty	1	0	0	0	0	2	Houtteman	3	3	1	1	1	0
Jansen	5	1	0	0	0	6	Reynolds	3	1	0	0	1	2
Blackwell (W)	3	1	0	0	0	2	Gray (L)	1⅓	3	1	1	0	1
							Feller	⅔	0	0	0	1	1

(a) Doubled for Raschi in third. (b) Ran for Berra in fourth. (c) Singled for New-combe in sixth. (d) Ran for Sisler in sixth. (e) Popped out for Dropo in eighth. (f) Flied out for Robinson in eleventh. (g) Flied out for Jansen in twelfth. (h) Flied out for Reynolds in twelfth. Runs batted in—Slaughter, Sauer, Kell 2, Williams, Kiner, Schoendienst. Two-base hits—Michaels, Doby, Kiner. Three-base hits—Slaughter, Dropo. Home runs—Kiner, Schoendienst. Double plays—Rizzuto, Doerr, and Dropo; Jones, Schoendienst, and Musial. Wild pitch—Roberts. Passed ball—Hegan. Left on bases—Nationals 9, Americans 6.

Managers: Casey Stengel, New York (A.L.); Burt Shotton, Brooklyn (N.L.)

Umpires—McGowan, Rommel, and Stevens (A.L.), Pinelli, Conlan, and Robb (N.L.) Time—3:19. Attendance—46,127.

July 10, 1951   At Briggs Stadium, Detroit

Nationals	AB	R	H	PO	A	E	Americans	AB	R	H	PO	A	E
Ashburn (Phillies), cf ..	4	2	2	4	1	0	D.DiMaggio (Red Sox),						
Snider (Dodgers), cf ...	0	0	0	0	0	0	cf	5	0	1	1	0	0
Dark (Giants), ss	5	0	1	0	3	0	Fox (White Sox), 2b ...	3	0	1	3	1	1
Reese (Dodgers), ss ...	0	0	0	0	1	0	(e)Doerr (Red Sox), 2b .	1	0	1	1	0	0
Musial (Cards), lf-rf-lf ..	4	1	2	0	0	0	Kell (Tigers), 3b	3	1	1	4	2	0
Westlake (Cardinals), lf .	0	0	0	0	0	0	Williams (Red Sox), lf ..	3	0	1	3	0	0
J.Robinson (Dodgers),							Busby (White Sox), lf ..	0	0	0	0	0	0
2b	4	1	2	3	1	1	Berra (Yankees), c	4	1	1	4	2	1
Schoendienst (Cards),							Wertz (Tigers), rf	3	1	1	2	0	0
2b	0	0	0	0	0	0	Rizzuto (Yankees), ss ..	1	0	0	1	2	0
Hodges (Dodgers), 1b .	5	2	2	6	0	0	Fain (Athletics), 1b	3	0	1	5	0	0
Elliot (Braves), 3b	2	1	1	1	1	0	(f)E.Robinson (White						
Jones (Phillies), 3b	2	0	0	3	0	0	Sox), 1b	1	0	0	0	1	0
Ennis (Phillies), rf	2	0	0	0	0	0	Carrasquel (White Sox),						
Kiner (Pirates), lf	2	1	1	1	0	0	ss	2	0	1	0	3	0
Wyrostek (Reds), lf	1	0	0	0	0	0	(c)Minoso (White Sox),						
Campanella (Dodgers),							rf	2	0	0	2	0	0
c	4	0	0	9	1	0	Garver (Browns), p	1	0	0	0	0	0
Roberts (Phillies), p	0	0	0	0	0	0	Lopat (Yankees), p	0	0	0	0	0	0
(a)Slaughter (Cardinals)	1	0	0	0	0	0	(b)Doby (Indians)	1	0	0	0	0	0
Maglie (Giants), p	1	0	0	0	0	0	Hutchinson (Tigers), p .	0	0	0	0	0	0
Newcombe (Dodgers),							(d)Stephens (Red Sox) .	1	0	0	0	0	0
p	2	0	1	0	1	0	Parnell (Red Sox), p ...	0	0	0	0	0	0
Blackwell (Reds), p	0	0	0	0	0	0	Lemon (Indians), p	0	0	0	1	0	0
							(g)Hegan (Indians)	1	0	1	0	0	0
Totals	39	8	12	27	9	1	Totals	35	3	10	27	11	2

```
National League ....................   1  0  0    3  0  2    1  1  0—8
American League ....................   0  1  0    1  1  0    0  0  0—3
```

Pitching Summary

National League	IP	H	R	ER	BB	SO	American League	IP	H	R	ER	BB	SO
Roberts	2	4	1	1	1	1	Garver	3	1	1	0	1	1
Maglie (W)	3	3	2	2	1	1	Lopat (L)	1	3	3	3	0	0
Newcombe	3	2	0	0	0	3	Hutchinson	3	3	3	2	0	
Blackwell	1	1	0	0	1	2	Parnell	1	3	1	1	1	1
							Lemon	1	2	0	0	1	1

(a) Lined out for Roberts in third. (b) Popped out for Lopat in fourth. (c) Grounded out for Carrasquel in sixth. (d) Struck out for Hutchinson in seventh. (e) Singled for Fox in seventh. (f) Grounded out for Fain in eighth. (g) Doubled for Lemon in ninth. Runs batted in—Fain, Musial, Elliot 2, Wertz, Kell, Hodges 2, J. Robinson, Kiner. Two-base hits—Ashburn, Hegan. Three-base hits—Fain, Williams. Home runs—Musial, Elliot, Wertz, Kell, Hodges, Kiner. Sacrifice hit—Kell. Double play—Berra and Kell. Passed ball—Campanella. Left on bases—Nationals 8, Americans 9.

Managers: Casey Stengel, New York (A.L.); Edwin Sawyer, Philadelphia (N.L.).

Umpires—Passarella, Hurley, and Honochick (A.L.), Robb, Jorda, and Dascoli (N.L.) Time—2:41. Attendance—52,075.

July 8, 1952   At Shibe Park, Philadelphia

Americans	AB	R	H	PO	A	E	Nationals	AB	R	H	PO	A	E
D.DiMaggio (Red Sox),							Lockman (Giants), 1b ..	3	0	0	5	0	0
cf	2	0	1	1	0	0	J.Robinson (Dodgers),						
Doby (Indians), cf	0	0	0	0	0	0	2b	3	1	1	2	2	0
Bauer (Yankees), rf	3	0	1	2	0	0	Musial (Cardinals), cf ..	2	1	0	1	0	0
Jensen (Senators), rf ..	0	0	0	0	0	0	Sauer (Cubs), lf	2	1	1	0	0	0
Mitchell (Indians), lf	1	0	0	1	0	0	Campanella (Dodgers),						
(c)Minoso (White Sox),							c	1	0	0	5	1	0
lf	1	1	1	0	0	0	Slaughter (Cardinals), rf	2	0	1	0	0	0
Rosen (Indians), 3b	1	1	0	3	1	0	Thomson (Giants), 3b ..	2	0	0	1	1	0
Berra (Yankees), c	2	0	0	6	0	0	Hamner (Phillies), ss ...	1	0	0	1	3	0
E.Robinson (White Sox)							Simmons (Phillies), p ..	0	0	0	0	0	0
1b	2	0	1	1	0	0	(b)Reese (Dodgers)	1	0	0	0	0	0
Avila (Indians), 2b	2	0	1	0	0	0	Rush (Cubs), p	1	0	0	0	0	0
Rizzuto (Yankees), ss ..	2	0	0	1	0	0							
Raschi (Yankees), p ...	0	0	0	0	0	0							
(a)McDougald													
(Yankees)	1	0	0	0	0	0							
Lemon (Indians), p	1	0	0	0	0	0							
Shantz (Athletics), p ...	0	0	0	0	0	0							
Totals	18	2	5	15	1	0	Totals	18	3	3	15	7	0

American League .... 0 0 0   2 0—2

National League .... 1 0 0   2 0—3

Game shortened by rain.

Pitching Summary

American League	IP	H	R	ER	BB	SO	National League	IP	H	R	ER	BB	SO
Raschi	2	1	1	1	0	3	Simmons	3	1	0	0	1	3
Lemon (L)	2	2	2	2	2	0	Rush (W)	2	4	2	2	1	1
Shantz	1	0	0	0	0	3							

(a) Grounded out for Raschi in third. (b) Flied out for Simmons in third. (c) Doubled for Mitchell in fourth. Runs batted in—J. Robinson, E. Robinson, Avila, Sauer 2. Two-base hits—DiMaggio, Minoso, Slaughter. Home runs—J. Robinson, Sauer. Double play—Hamner, J. Robinson, and Sauer. Hit by pitcher—By Lemon (Musial). Left on bases—Americans 3, Nationals 3.

Managers: Casey Stengel, New York (A.L.); Leo Durocher, New York (N.L.)

Umpires—Barlick, Boggess, and Warneke (N.L.), Berry, Summers, and Soar (A.L.) Time—1:29. Attendance—32,785.

July 14, 1953   At Crosley Field, Cincinnati

Americans	AB	R	H	PO	A	E
Goodman (Red Sox), 2b	2	0	0	1	1	0
Fox (White Sox), 2b ...	1	0	0	1	0	0
Vernon (Senators), 1b .	3	0	0	6	0	0
Fain (White Sox), 1b ...	1	1	1	1	1	0
Bauer (Yankees), rf	2	0	0	3	0	0
(j)Mize (Yankees)	1	0	1	0	0	0
Mantle (Yankees), cf ...	2	0	0	0	0	0
(e)Hunter (Browns)	0	0	0	0	0	0
Doby (Indians), cf	1	0	0	1	1	0
Rosen (Indians), 3b	4	0	0	2	4	0
Zernial (Athletics), lf ...	2	0	1	1	0	0
Minoso (White Sox), lf .	2	0	2	0	0	0
Berra (Yankees), c	4	0	0	4	0	0
Carrasquel (White Sox), ss	2	0	0	2	1	0
(g)Kell (Red Sox)	1	0	0	0	0	0
Rizzuto (Yankees), ss ..	0	0	0	0	1	0
Pierce (White Sox), p ..	1	0	0	0	0	0
Reynolds (Yankees), p .	0	0	0	0	0	0
(c)Kuenn (Tigers)	1	0	0	0	0	0
Garcia (Indians), p	0	0	0	1	0	0
(h)E. Robinson (Athletics)	1	0	0	0	0	0
Paige (Browns), p	0	0	0	0	0	0
Totals	31	1	5	24	8	0

Nationals	AB	R	H	PO	A	E
Reese (Dodgers), ss ...	4	0	2	1	1	0
Hamner (Phillies), ss ...	0	0	0	0	0	0
Schoendienst (Cards), 2b	3	0	0	0	3	0
Williams (Giants), 2b ...	0	0	0	2	0	0
Musial (Cardinals), lf ...	4	0	2	3	0	0
Kluszewski (Reds), 1b .	3	0	1	5	0	0
(d)Hodges (Dodgers), 1b	1	0	0	1	0	0
Campanella (Dodgers), c	4	1	1	6	2	0
Mathews (Braves), 3b ..	3	1	0	0	0	0
Bell (Reds), cf	3	0	0	4	0	0
(i)Snider (Dodgers), cf .	0	1	0	1	0	0
Slaughter (Cards), rf ...	3	2	2	4	0	0
Roberts (Phillies), p	0	0	0	0	1	0
(a)Kiner (Cubs)	1	0	0	0	0	0
Spahn (Braves), p	0	0	0	0	0	0
(b)Ashburn (Phillies) ...	1	0	1	0	0	0
Simmons (Phillies), p ..	0	0	0	0	0	0
(f)J. Robinson (Dodgers)	1	0	0	0	0	0
Dickson (Pirates), p	1	0	1	0	0	0
Totals	32	5	10	27	7	0

American League .... 0 0 0   0 0 0   0 0 1—1
National League .... 0 0 0   0 2 0   1 2 x—5

Pitching Summary

American League	IP	H	R	ER	BB	SO
Pierce	3	1	0	0	0	1
Reynolds (L)	2	2	2	2	1	0
Garcia	2	4	1	1	1	2
Paige	1	3	2	2	1	0

National League	IP	H	R	ER	BB	SO
Roberts	3	1	0	0	1	2
Spahn (W)	2	0	0	0	1	2
Simmons	2	1	0	0	1	1
Dickson	2	3	1	1	0	0

(a) Struck out for Roberts in third. (b) Singled for Spahn in fifth. (c) Lined out for Reynolds in sixth. (d) Ran for Kluszewski in sixth. (e) Ran for Mantle in seventh. (f) Popped out for Simmons in seventh. (g) Flied out for Carrasquel in eighth. (h) Lined out for Garcia in eighth. (i) Walked for Bell in eighth. (j) Singled for Bauer in ninth. Runs batted in—Ashburn, Reese 2, Slaughter, Dickson, Minoso. Two-base hit—Reese. Stolen base—Slaughter. Double play—Carrasquel and Vernon. Hit by pitcher—By Reynolds (Mathews). Left on bases—Nationals 7, Americans 6.

Managers: Casey Stengel, New York (A.L.); Chuck Dressen, Brooklyn (N.L.).

Umpires—Conlan, Donatelli, and Engeln (N.L.), Stevens, McKinley, and Napp (A.L.). Time—2:19. Attendance—30,846.

July 13, 1954   At Municipal Stadium, Cleveland

Nationals	AB	R	H	PO	A	E
Hamner (Phillies), 2b ..	3	0	0	0	0	0
Schoendienst						
(Cardinals), 2b	2	0	0	1	0	0
Dark (Giants), ss	5	0	1	1	2	0
Snider (Dodgers), cf-rf .	4	2	3	2	0	0
Musial (Cardinals), rf-lf .	5	1	2	2	1	0
Kluszewski (Reds), 1b .	4	2	2	5	0	0
Hodges (Dodgers), 1b .	1	0	0	1	0	0
Jablonski (Cards), 3b ..	3	1	1	0	1	0
Jackson (Cubs), 3b	2	0	0	1	1	0
Robinson (Dodgers), lf ..	2	1	1	0	0	0
Mays (Giants), cf	2	1	1	1	0	0
Campanella (Dodgers),						
c	3	0	1	9	0	0
Burgess (Phillies), c ...	0	0	0	1	0	0
Roberts (Phillies), p	1	0	0	0	0	0
(a)Mueller (Giants)	1	0	1	0	0	0
Antonelli (Giants), p ...	0	0	0	0	0	0
(c)Thomas (Pirates)	1	0	0	0	0	0
Spahn (Braves), p	0	0	0	0	0	0
Grissom (Giants), p	0	0	0	0	0	0
(e)Bell (Reds)	1	1	1	0	0	0
Conley (Braves), p	0	0	0	0	0	0
Erskine (Dodgers), p ...	0	0	0	0	0	0
Totals	40	9	14	24	5	0

Americans	AB	R	H	PO	A	E
Minoso (White Sox),						
lf-rf	4	1	2	1	0	1
Piersall (Red Sox), rf ...	0	0	0	0	0	0
Avila (Indians), 2b	3	1	3	1	1	0
Keegan (White Sox), p .	0	0	0	0	0	0
Stone (Senators), p	0	0	0	0	0	0
(f)Doby (Indians), cf ...	1	1	1	0	0	0
Mantle (Yankees), cf ...	5	1	2	2	0	0
Trucks (White Sox), p ..	0	0	0	0	0	0
Berra (Yankees), c	4	2	2	5	0	0
Rosen (Indians), 1b-3b .	4	2	3	7	0	0
Boone (Tigers), 3b	4	1	1	1	3	0
(g)Vernon (Senators),						
1b	1	0	0	1	0	0
Bauer (Yankees), rf	2	0	1	1	0	0
Porterfield (Senators), p	1	0	0	0	0	0
(d)Fox (White Sox), 2b .	2	0	1	1	0	0
Carrasquel (White Sox),						
ss	5	1	1	5	4	0
Ford (Yankees), p	1	0	0	0	0	0
Consuegra (White Sox),						
p	0	0	0	0	0	0
Lemon (Indians), p	0	0	0	0	0	0
(b)Williams (Red Sox),						
lf	2	1	0	0	0	0
Noren (Yankees), lf	0	0	0	0	0	0
Totals	39	11	17	27	8	1

National League .... 0 0 0 5 2 0 0 0 2—9
American League .... 0 0 4 1 2 1 0 3 x—11

Pitching Summary

National League	IP	H	R	ER	BB	SO
Roberts	3	5	4	4	2	5
Antonelli	2	4	3	3	0	2
Spahn	⅔	4	1	1	1	0
Grissom	1⅓	0	0	0	2	0
Conley (L)	⅓	3	3	3	1	0
Erskine	⅔	1	0	0	0	1

American League	IP	H	R	ER	BB	SO
Ford	3	1	0	0	1	0
Consuegra	⅓	5	5	5	0	0
Lemon	⅔	1	0	0	0	0
Porterfield	3	4	2	2	0	1
Keegan	⅔	3	2	2	0	1
Stone (W)	⅓	0	0	0	0	0

(a) Doubled for Roberts in fourth. (b) Struck out for Lemon in fourth. (c) Struck out for Antonelli in sixth. (d) Struck out for Porterfield in seventh. (e) Homered for Grissom in eighth. (f) Homered for Stone in eighth. (g) Struck out for Boone in eighth. Runs batted in—Rosen 5, Boone, Kluszewski 3, Jablonski, Robinson 2, Mueller, Avila 2, Bell 2, Doby, Fox 2. Two-base hits—Robinson, Mueller, Snider. Home runs—Rosen 2, Boone, Kluszewski, Bell, Doby. Sacrifice fly—Avila. Double play—Avila, Carrasquel, and Rosen. Left on bases—Nationals 6, Americans 9.

Managers: Casey Stengel, New York (A.L.); Walter Alston, Brooklyn (N.L.).

Umpires—Rommel (A.L.), plate; Ballanfant (N.L.), first base; Honochick (A.L.), second base; Stewart (N.L.), third base; Gorman (N.L.), left field; Paparella (A.L.), right field (first 4½ innings). Stewart (N.L.), plate; Honochick (A.L.), first base; Ballanfant (N.L.), second base; Rommel (A.L.), third base; Gorman (N.L.), left field; Paparella (A.L.), right field (last four innings). Time—3:10. Attendance—68,751.

July 12, 1955   At Milwaukee County Stadium, Milwaukee

Americans	AB	R	H	PO	A	E	Nationals	AB	R	H	PO	A	E
Kuenn (Tigers), ss	3	1	1	1	0	0	Schoendienst						
Carrasquel (White Sox),							(Cardinals), 2b	6	0	2	3	2	0
ss	3	0	2	1	3	1	Ennis (Phillies), lf	1	0	0	1	0	0
Fox (White Sox), 2b ...	3	1	1	2	0	0	(c)Musial (Cardinals), lf	4	1	1	0	0	0
Avila (Indians), 2b	1	0	0	1	2	0	Snider (Dodgers), cf ...	2	0	0	3	0	0
Williams (Red Sox), lf ..	3	1	1	1	0	0	Mays (Giants), cf	3	2	2	3	0	0
Smith (Indians), lf	1	0	0	0	0	0	Kluszewski (Reds), 1b .	5	1	2	9	1	0
Mantle (Yankees), cf ...	6	1	2	3	0	0	Mathews (Braves), 3b ..	2	0	0	0	3	1
Berra (Yankees), c	6	1	1	8	2	0	Jackson (Cubs), 3b	3	1	1	0	0	0
Kaline (Tigers), rf	4	0	1	6	0	0	Mueller (Giants), rf	2	0	1	0	0	0
Vernon (Senators), 1b .	5	0	1	8	0	0	(d)Aaron (Braves), rf ...	2	1	2	0	0	0
Finigan (Athletics), 3b .	3	0	0	2	0	0	Banks (Cubs), ss	2	0	0	2	1	0
Rosen (Indians), 3b	2	0	0	0	0	1	Logan (Braves), ss	3	0	1	1	1	0
Pierce (White Sox), p ..	0	0	0	0	0	0	Crandall (Braves), c ...	1	0	0	1	0	0
(b)Jensen (Red Sox) ...	1	0	0	0	0	0	(e)Burgess (Phillies), c .	1	0	0	2	0	0
Wynn (Indians), p	0	0	0	0	1	0	(h)Lopata (Phillies), c ..	3	0	0	10	0	0
(g)Power (Athletics) ...	1	0	0	0	0	0	Roberts (Phillies), p	0	0	0	1	1	0
Ford (Yankees), p	1	0	0	0	1	0	(a)Thomas (Pirates)	1	0	0	0	0	0
Sullivan (Red Sox), p ..	1	0	0	0	0	0	Haddix (Cardinals), p ..	0	0	0	0	2	0
							(f)Hodges (Dodgers) ...	1	0	1	0	0	0
							Newcombe (Dodgers),						
							p	0	0	0	0	0	0
							(i)Baker (Cubs)	1	0	0	0	0	0
							Jones (Cubs), p	0	0	0	0	0	0
							Nuxhall (Reds), p	2	0	0	0	1	0
							Conley (Braves), p	0	0	0	0	0	0
Totals	44	5	10	33	9	2	Totals	45	6	13	36	12	1

American League ....   4 0 0   0 0 1   0 0 0   0 0 0—5
National League ....   0 0 0   0 0 0   2 3 0   0 0 1—6

Pitching Summary

American League	IP	H	R	ER	BB	SO	National League	IP	H	R	ER	BB	SO
Pierce	3	1	0	0	0	3	Roberts	3	4	4	4	1	0
Wynn	3	3	0	0	0	1	Haddix	3	3	1	1	0	2
Ford	1⅔	5	5	3	1	0	Newcombe	1	1	0	0	0	1
Sullivan (L)	3⅓*	4	1	1	1	4	Jones	⅔	0	0	0	2	1
							Nuxhall	3⅓	2	0	0	3	5
							Conley (W)	1	0	0	0	0	3

* Pitched to one batter in twelfth.

(a) Popped out for Roberts in third. (b) Popped out for Pierce in fourth. (c) Struck out for Ennis in fourth. (d) Ran for Mueller in fifth. (e) Hit into force play for Crandall in fifth. (f) Singled for Haddix in sixth. (g) Popped out for Wynn in seventh. (h) Safe on error for Burgess in seventh. (i) Flied out for Newcombe in seventh. Runs batted in—Mantle 3, Vernon, Logan, Jackson, Aaron, Musial. Two-base hits—Kluszewski, Kaline. Home runs—Mantle, Musial. Sacrifice hits—Pierce, Avila. Double plays—Kluszewski, Banks, and Robert; Wynn, Carrasquel, and Vernon. Hit by pitcher—By Jones (Kaline). Wild pitch—Roberts. Passed ball—Crandall. Left on bases—Americans 12, Nationals 8.

Managers: Al Lopez, Cleveland (A.L.); Leo Durocher, New York (N.L.).

Umpires—Barlick, Boggess, and Secory (N.L.), Soar, Summers, and Runge (A.L.). Time—3:17. Attendance—45,643.

July 10, 1956   At Griffith Stadium, Washington

Nationals	AB	R	H	PO	A	E
Temple (Reds), 2b	4	1	2	2	3	0
Robinson (Reds), lf	2	0	0	1	0	0
(d)Snider (Dodgers), cf	3	0	0	1	0	0
Musial (Cards), rf-lf	4	1	1	2	0	0
Aaron (Braves), lf	1	0	0	0	0	0
Boyer (Cardinals), 3b ..	5	1	3	3	1	0
Bell (Reds), cf	1	0	0	2	0	0
(b)Mays (Giants), cf-rf ..	3	2	1	2	0	0
Long (Pirates), 1b	2	0	0	6	0	0
(f)Kluszewski (Reds),						
1b	2	1	2	2	0	0
Bailey (Reds), c	3	0	0	3	1	0
Campanella (Dodgers),						
c	0	0	0	1	0	0
McMillan (Reds), ss	3	1	2	1	5	0
Friend (Pirates), p	0	0	0	0	0	0
(c)Repulski						
(Cardinals), ...	1	0	0	0	0	0
Spahn (Braves), p	1	0	0	0	0	0
Antonelli (Giants), p ...	1	0	0	1	0	0
Totals	36	7	11	27	10	0

Americans	AB	R	H	PO	A	E
Kuenn (Tigers), ss	5	0	1	2	3	0
Fox (White Sox), 2b ...	4	1	2	1	0	0
Williams (Red Sox), lf ..	4	1	1	2	0	0
Mantle (Yankees), cf ...	4	1	1	0	0	0
Berra (Yankees), c	2	0	2	10	1	0
(g)Lollar (White Sox), c	2	0	1	4	0	0
Kaline (Tigers), rf	3	0	1	0	0	0
Piersall (Red Sox), rf ...	1	0	0	1	0	0
Vernon (Red Sox), 1b ..	2	0	0	4	0	0
(h)Power (Athletics), 1b	2	0	1	3	0	0
Kell (Orioles), 3b	4	0	1	0	1	0
Pierce (White Sox), p ..	0	0	0	0	1	0
(a)Simpson (Athletics) .	1	0	0	0	0	0
Ford (Yankees), p	0	0	0	0	0	0
Wilson (White Sox), p ..	0	0	0	0	1	0
(e)Martin (Yankees)....	1	0	0	0	0	0
Brewer (Red Sox), p ...	0	0	0	0	0	0
(i)Boone (Tigers)	1	0	0	0	0	0
Score (Indians), p	0	0	0	0	0	0
Wynn (Indians), p	0	0	0	0	0	0
(j)Sievers (Senators) ...	1	0	0	0	0	0
Totals	37	3	11	27	11	0

National League .... 0 0 1 2 1 1 2 0 0—7
American League .... 0 0 0 0 0 3 0 0 0—3

Pitching Summary

National League	IP	H	R	ER	BB	SO
Friend (W)	3	3	0	0	0	3
Spahn	2*	4	3	3	0	1
Antonelli	4	4	0	0	0	1

American League	IP	H	R	ER	BB	SO
Pierce (L)	3	2	1	1	1	5
Ford	1	3	2	2	1	2
Wilson	1	2	1	1	0	1
Brewer	2	4	3	3	1	2
Score	1	0	0	0	1	1
Wynn	1	0	0	0	0	0

* Pitched to three batters in sixth.

(a) Struck out for Pierce in third. (b) Homered for Bell in fourth. (c) Fouled out for Friend in fourth. (d) Flied out for Robinson in fifth. (e) Grounded out for Wilson in fifth. (f) Doubled for Long in sixth. (g) Singled for Berra in sixth. (h) Flied out for Vernon in sixth. (i) Lined out for Brewer in seventh. (j) Popped out for Wynn in ninth. Runs batted in—Temple, Mays 2, Boyer, Williams 2, Mantle, Musial, Kluszewski. Two-base hits—Kluszewski 2. Home runs—Mays, Williams, Mantle, Musial. Sacrifice hit—Friend. Stolen base—Temple. Double play—McMillan, Temple, and Kluszewski. Wild Pitches—Brewer 2. Left on bases—Nationals 7, Americans 7.

Managers: Casey Stengel, New York (A.L.); Walter Alston, Brooklyn (N.L.).

Umpires—Berry, Hurley, and Flaherty (A.L.), Pinelli, Gore, and Jackowski (N.L.). Time—2:45. Attendance—28,843.

July 9, 1957   At Busch Stadium, St. Louis

Americans	AB	R	H	PO	A	E
Kuenn (Tigers), ss	2	0	0	0	1	0
McDougald (Yankees),						
ss	2	1	0	1	0	0
Fox (White Sox), 2b ...	4	0	0	2	4	0
Kaline (Tigers), rf	5	1	2	1	1	0
Mantle (Yankees), cf ...	4	1	1	4	0	0
Williams (Red Sox), lf ..	3	1	0	2	0	0
Minoso (White Sox), lf .	1	0	1	1	1	0
Wertz (Indians), 1b	2	0	1	3	0	0
Skowron (Yankees), 1b	3	1	2	5	1	0
Berra (Yankees), c	3	0	1	6	0	0
Kell (Orioles), 3b	2	0	0	0	1	0
Malzone (Red Sox), 3b .	2	0	0	1	1	0
Bunning (Tigers), p	1	0	0	0	0	0
(a)Maxwell (Tigers)	1	0	1	0	0	0
Loes (Orioles), p	1	0	0	0	1	0
Wynn (Indians), p	0	0	0	0	0	0
Pierce (White Sox), p ..	1	1	1	1	0	0
Mossi (Indians), p	0	0	0	0	0	0
Grim (Yankees), p	0	0	0	0	0	0
Totals	37	6	10	27	11	0

Nationals	AB	R	H	PO	A	E
Temple (Reds), 2b	2	0	0	3	0	0
(e)Schoendienst						
(Braves), 2b	2	0	0	0	0	1
Aaron (Braves), rf	4	0	1	2	0	0
Musial (Cardinals), 1b ..	3	1	1	9	0	0
Mays (Giants), cf	4	2	2	2	0	0
Bailey (Reds), c	3	1	1	2	0	0
(h)Foiles (Pirates)	1	1	1	0	0	0
Robinson (Reds), lf	2	0	1	5	0	0
(f)Bell (Reds), lf	1	0	1	0	0	0
Hoak (Reds), 3b	1	0	0	1	0	0
(b)Mathews (Braves),						
3b	3	0	0	1	0	0
McMillan (Reds), ss	1	0	0	2	0	0
(c)Banks (Cubs), ss	3	0	1	0	3	0
Simmons (Phillies), p ..	0	0	0	0	0	0
Burdette (Braves), p ...	1	0	0	0	0	0
Sanford (Phillies), p	0	0	0	0	0	0
(d)Moon (Cardinals)	1	0	0	0	0	0
Jackson (Cardinals), p .	0	0	0	0	1	0
(g)Cimoli (Dodgers)	1	0	0	0	0	0
Labine (Dodgers), p ...	0	0	0	0	1	0
(i)Hodges (Dodgers) ...	1	0	0	0	0	0
Totals	34	5	9	27	5	1

American League .... 0 2 0   0 0 1   0 0 3—6
National League .... 0 0 0   0 0 0   2 0 3—5

Pitching Summary

American League	IP	H	R	ER	BB	SO
Bunning (W)	3	0	0	0	0	1
Loes	3	3	0	0	0	1
Wynn	⅓	3	2	2	0	0
Pierce	1⅔†	2	3	3	2	3
Mossi	⅔	1	0	0	0	0
Grim	⅓	0	0	0	0	1

National League	IP	H	R	ER	BB	SO
Simmons (L)	1*	2	2	2	2	0
Burdette	4	2	0	0	1	0
Sanford	1	2	1	1	0	0
Jackson	2	1	0	0	1	0
Labine	1	3	3	1	0	1

* Pitched to four batters in second. † Pitched to four batters in ninth.

(a) Singled for Bunning in fourth. (b) Hit into force play for Hoak in fifth. (c) Grounded into double play for McMillan in fifth. (d) Grounded out for Sanford in sixth. (e) Flied out for Temple in sixth. (f) Doubled for Robinson in seventh. (g) Struck out for Jackson in eighth. (h) Singled for Bailey in ninth. Runs batted in—Wertz, Kuenn, Berra, Bell 2, Kaline 2, Minoso, Mays, Banks. Two-base hits—Musial, Skowron, Bell, Minoso. Three-base hit—Mays. Sacrifice hit—Fox. Double play—Malzone, Fox, and Skowron. Wild pitches—Sanford, Pierce. Left on bases—Americans 9, Nationals 4.

Managers: Casey Stengel, New York (A.L.); Walter Alston, Brooklyn (N.L.)

Umpires—Dascoli, Dixon, and Landes (N.L.), Napp, Stevens, and Chylak (A.L.) Time—2:43. Attendance—30,693.

July 8, 1958   At Memorial Stadium, Baltimore

Nationals	AB	R	H	PO	A	E	Americans	AB	R	H	PO	A	E
Mays (Giants), cf	4	2	1	1	0	0	Fox (White Sox), 2b ...	4	1	2	5	3	1
Skinner (Pirates), lf	3	0	1	2	0	0	Mantle (Yankees), cf ...	2	0	1	3	0	0
(g)Walls (Cubs), lf	1	0	0	0	0	0	Jensen (Red Sox), rf·...	4	0	1	0	0	0
Musial (Cardinals), 1b ..	4	1	1	7	0	0	Cerv (Athletics), lf	2	0	1	4	0	0
Aaron (Braves), rf	2	0	0	2	0	0	O'Dell (Orioles), p	0	0	0	0	0	0
Banks (Cubs), ss	3	0	0	2	3	1	Skowron (Yankees), 1b	4	0	0	8	0	0
Thomas (Pirates), 3b ...	3	0	1	1	3	1	Malzone (Red Sox), 3b .	4	1	1	0	2	0
Mazeroski (Pirates), 2b .	4	0	0	4	5	0	Triandos (Athletics), c .	2	0	1	1	0	1
Crandall (Braves), c ...	4	0	0	5	0	0	(c)Berra (Yankees), c ..	2	0	0	3	0	0
Spahn (Braves), p	0	0	0	0	1	0	Aparicio (White Sox),						
(a)Blasingame (Cards) .	1	0	0	0	0	0	ss	2	1	0	1	1	0
Friend (Pirates), p	0	0	0	0	0	0	(d)Williams (Red Sox),						
Jackson (Cardinals), p .	0	0	0	0	0	0	lf	2	0	0	1	0	0
(f)Logan (Braves)	1	0	0	0	0	0	Kaline (Tigers), lf	0	0	0	0	0	0
Farrell (Phillies), p	0	0	0	0	0	0	Turley (Yankees), p	0	0	0	0	0	0
							Narleski (Indians), p ...	1	0	1	0	0	0
							(b)Vernon (Indians)	1	1	1	0	0	0
							Wynn (White Sox), p ...	0	0	0	0	0	0
							(e)McDougald						
							(Yankees), ss	1	0	1	0	3	0
Totals	30	3	4	24	12	2	Totals	34	4	9	27	9	3

National League	2	1	0		0	0	0		0 0 0—3
American League	1	1	0		0	1	1		0 0 0—4

Pitching Summary

National League	IP	H	R	ER	BB	SO	American League	IP	H	R	ER	BB	SO
Spahn	3	5	2	1	0	0	Turley	1⅓	3	3	3	2	0
Friend (L)	2⅓	4	2	1	2	0	Narleski	3⅓	1	0	0	1	0
Jackson	⅔	0	0	0	0	0	Wynn (W)	1	0	0	0	0	0
Farrell	2	0	0	0	1	4	O'Dell	3	0	0	0	0	2

(a) Flied out for Spahn in fourth. (b) Singled for Narleski in fifth. (c) Popped out for Triandos in sixth. (d) Safe on error for Aparicio in sixth. (e) Singled for Wynn in sixth. (f) Flied out for Jackson in seventh. (g) Grounded out for Skinner in seventh. Runs batted in—Skinner, Aaron, Fox, Jensen, McDougald. Sacrifice hit—O'Dell. Sacrifice fly—Aaron. Stolen base—Mays. Double plays—Thomas, Mazeroski, and Musial; Malzone, Fox, and Skowron; Banks, Mazeroski, and Musial 2. Hit by pitcher—By Turley (Banks). Wild pitch—Turley. Left on bases—Nationals 5, Americans 7.

Managers: Casey Stengel, New York (A.L.); Fred Haney, Milwaukee (N.L.)

Umpires—Rommel, McKinley, and Umont (A.L.), Gorman, Conlan, and Secory (N.L.) Time—2:13. Attendance—48,829.

July 7, 1959   At Forbes Field, Pittsburgh
First Game

Americans	AB	R	H	PO	A	E	Nationals	AB	R	H	PO	A	E
Minoso (Indians), lf	5	0	0	0	1	0	Temple (Reds), 2b	2	0	0	1	3	0
Fox (White Sox), 2b ...	5	1	2	2	0	0	(a)Musial (Cardinals) ...	1	0	0	0	0	0
Kaline (Tigers), cf	1	1	0	1	0	0	Face (Pirates), p	0	0	0	0	0	0
Skowron (Yankees), 1b	3	0	2	3	0	0	Antonelli (Giants), p ...	0	0	0	0	0	0
Power (Indians), 1b	1	1	1	3	0	0	(h)Boyer (Cardinals), 3b	1	1	1	1	0	0
Colavito (Indians), rf ...	3	0	1	1	0	0	Mathews (Braves), 3b ..	3	1	1	2	1	1
(b)Williams (Red Sox) ..	0	0	0	0	0	0	(i)Groat (Pirates)	0	0	0	0	0	0
(c)McDougald							Elston (Cubs), p	0	0	0	0	0	0
(Yankees), ss	0	0	0	0	0	0	Aaron (Braves), rf	4	1	2	2	0	0
Triandos (Orioles), c ...	4	0	1	8	0	0	Mays (Giants), cf	4	0	1	2	0	0
(f)Mantle (Yankees), rf .	0	0	0	0	0	0	Banks (Cubs), ss	3	1	2	1	2	0
Killebrew (Senators), 3b	3	0	0	1	0	0	Cepeda (Giants), 1b ...	4	0	0	6	0	0
Bunning (Tigers), p	0	0	0	0	0	0	Moon (Dodgers), lf	2	0	0	1	0	0
(d)Runnels (Red Sox) ..	0	0	0	0	0	0	Crandall (Braves), c ...	3	1	1	10	0	0
(e)Sievers (Senators) ..	0	0	0	0	0	0	Drysdale (Dodgers), p ..	1	0	0	0	0	0
Ford (Yankees), p	0	0	0	0	1	0	Burdette (Braves), p ...	1	0	0	0	0	0
Daley (Athletics), p	0	0	0	0	0	0	Mazeroski (Pirates), 2b .	1	0	1	1	0	0
Aparicio (White Sox),													
ss	3	0	0	4	2	0							
(g)Lollar (White Sox), c	1	0	0	1	0	0							
Wynn (White Sox), p ...	1	0	0	1	0	0							
Duren (Yankees), p	1	0	0	0	0	0							
Malzone (Red Sox), 3b .	2	0	0	0	0	0							
Totals	36	4	8	24	5	0	Totals	30	5	9	27	6	1

```
American League ....................  0  0  0    1  0  0    0  3 0—4
National League ....................  1  0  0    0  0  0    2  2 x—5
```

Pitching Summary

American League	IP	H	R	ER	BB	SO	National League	IP	H	R	ER	BB	SO
Wynn	3	2	1	1	1	3	Drysdale	3	0	0	0	0	4
Duren	1	1	0	0	1	4	Burdette	3	4	1	1	0	2
Bunning	1	3	2	2	0	1	Face	1⅔	3	3	3	2	2
Ford (L)	⅓	3	2	2	0	0	Antonelli (W)	⅓	0	0	0	1	0
Daley	⅔	0	0	0	0	1	Elston	1	1	0	0	0	1

(a) Popped out for Temple in sixth. (b) Walked for Colavito in eighth. (c) Ran for Williams in eighth. (d) Announced as batter for Bunning in eighth. (e) Walked for Runnels in eighth. (f) Ran for Triandos in eighth. (g) Grounded into force play for Aparicio in eighth. (h) Singled for Antonelli in eighth. (i) Sacrificed for Mathews in eighth. Runs batted in—Kaline, Power, Triandos 2, Mathews, Aaron, Mays, Crandall, Mazeroski. Two-base hits—Banks 2, Triandos. Three-base hit—Mays. Home runs—Mathews, Kaline. Sacrifice hit—Groat. Double play—Aparicio and Skowron. Wild pitch—Elston. Left on bases—Americans 8, Nationals 4.

Managers: Casey Stengel, New York (A.L.); Fred Haney, Milwaukee (N.L.).

Umpires—Barlick, Donatelli, and Crawford (N.L.), Runge, Paparella, and Rice (A.L.) Time—2:33. Attendance—35,277.

August 3, 1959 At Memorial Coliseum, Los Angeles
Second Game

Americans	AB	R	H	PO	A	E	Nationals	AB	R	H	PO	A	E
Runnels (Red Sox), 1b .	3	0	0	9	0	0	Temple (Reds), 2b	2	1	1	1	1	0
Power (Indians), 1b	1	0	0	4	0	0	(d)Gilliam (Dodgers), 3b	2	1	1	0	0	0
Fox (White Sox), 2b ...	4	1	2	3	1	0	Boyer (Cardinals), 3b ..	2	0	0	0	1	0
Williams (Red Sox), lf ..	3	0	0	0	0	0	Neal (Dodgers), 2b	1	0	0	0	2	0
Kaline (Tigers), lf-cf	2	0	0	0	0	0	Aaron (Braves), rf	3	0	0	2	0	0
Berra (Yankees), c	3	1	1	2	0	0	Mays (Giants), cf	4	0	0	3	0	0
Lollar (White Sox), c ...	0	0	0	2	0	0	Banks (Cubs), ss	4	0	0	2	0	1
Mantle (Yankees), cf ...	3	0	1	3	0	0	Musial (Cardinals), 1b ..	0	0	0	3	1	0
O'Dell (Orioles), p	0	0	0	0	0	0	Robinson (Reds), 1b ...	3	1	3	3	0	1
McLish (Indians), p	0	0	0	0	0	0	Moon (Dodgers), lf	2	0	0	1	0	0
Maris (Athletics), rf	2	0	0	1	0	0	Crandall (Braves), c ...	2	0	1	7	1	0
Colavito (Indians), rf ...	2	1	1	0	0	0	Smith (Cardinals), c ...	2	0	0	5	0	0
Malzone (Red Sox), 3b .	4	1	1	1	6	0	Drysdale (Dodgers), p ..	0	0	0	0	0	0
Aparicio (White Sox),							(a)Mathews (Braves) ...	1	0	0	0	0	0
ss	3	0	0	1	2	0	Conley (Phillies), p	0	0	0	0	1	0
Walker (Orioles), p	1	0	0	0	0	0	(c)Cunningham						
(b)Woodling (Orioles) ..	1	0	0	0	0	0	(Cardinals)	1	0	0	0	0	0
Wynn (White Sox), p ...	0	0	0	1	0	0	(e)Pinson (Reds)	0	0	0	0	0	0
Wilhelm (Orioles), p	0	0	0	0	0	0	Jones (Giants), p	0	0	0	0	0	1
(f)Kubek (Yankees), lf ..	1	1	0	0	0	0	(g)Groat (Pirates)	1	0	0	0	0	0
							Face (Pirates), p	0	0	0	0	0	0
							(h)Burgess (Pirates) ...	1	0	0	0	0	0
Totals	33	5	6	27	9	0	Totals	31	3	6	27	7	3

```
American League ....................   0  1  2   0  0  0   1  1 0—5
National League ....................   1  0  0   0  1  0   1  0 0—3
```

Pitching Summary

American League	IP	H	R	ER	BB	SO	National League	IP	H	R	ER	BB	SO
Walker (W)	3	2	1	1	1	1	Drysdale (L)	3	4	3	3	3	5
Wynn	2	1	1	1	3	1	Conley	2	0	0	0	1	2
Wilhelm	1	1	0	0	0	0	Jones	2	1	1	0	2	3
O'Dell	1	1	1	1	0	0	Face	2	1	1	1	0	2
McLish	2	1	0	0	1	2							

(a) Struck out for Drysdale in third. (b) Grounded out for Walker in fourth. (c) Grounded into force play for Conley in fifth. (d) Walked for Temple in fifth. (e) Ran for Cunningham in fifth. (f) Walked for Wilhelm in seventh. (g) Grounded out for Jones in seventh. (h) Grounded out for Face in ninth. Runs batted in—Fox, Berra 2, Colavito, Malzone, Gilliam, Aaron, Robinson. Two-base hit—Temple. Home runs—Malzone, Berra, Robinson, Gilliam, Colavito. Sacrifice fly—Aaron. Stolen base—Aparicio. Double play—Runnels (unassisted). Left on bases—Americans 7, Nationals 7.

Managers: Casey Stengel, New York (A.L.); Fred Haney, Milwaukee (N.L.)

Umpires—Jackowski, Venzon, and Burkhart (N.L.), Berry, Summers, and Soar (A.L.) Time—2:42. Attendance—55,105.

July 11, 1960   At Municipal Stadium, Kansas City
First Game

Nationals	AB	R	H	PO	A	E
Mays (Giants), cf	4	1		4	0	0
Pinson (Reds), cf	1	0	1	1	0	0
Skinner (Pirates), lf	4	1	1	1	0	0
Cepeda (Giants), lf	1	0	0	0	0	0
Mathews (Braves), 3b	4	0	0	1	0	2
Boyer (Cardinals), 3b	0	0	0	0	2	0
Aaron (Braves), rf	4	0	0	0	1	0
Clemente (Pirates), rf	1	0	0	2	0	0
Banks (Cubs), ss	4	2	2	2	2	0
Groat (Pirates), ss	0	0	0	0	1	0
Adcock (Braves), 1b	3	0	2	3	0	0
(b)White (Cardinals), 1b	1	0	0	4	0	0
Mazeroski (Pirates), 2b	2	0	1	2	2	0
(e)Musial (Cardinals)	1	0	1	0	0	0
(f)Taylor (Phillies)	0	0	0	0	0	0
Neal (Dodgers), 2b	0	0	0	0	0	1
Crandall (Braves), c	3	1	2	4	0	0
Burgess (Pirates), c	1	0	0	3	0	1
Friend (Pirates), p	2	0	0	0	0	0
McCormick (Giants), p	1	0	0	0	0	0
Face (Pirates), p	0	0	0	0	0	0
(g)Larker (Dodgers)	1	0	0	0	0	0
Buhl (Braves), p	0	0	0	0	0	0
Law (Pirates)	0	0	0	0	0	0
Totals	38	5	12	27	8	4

Americans	AB	R	H	PO	A	E
Minoso (White Sox), lf	3	0	0	0	0	0
Lemon (Senators), lf	1	0	0	1	0	0
Malzone (Red Sox), 3b	3	0	0	1	1	0
Robinson (Orioles), 3b	2	0	0	0	0	0
Maris (Yankees), rf	2	0	0	1	0	0
Kuenn (Indians), rf	3	1	1	1	0	0
Mantle (Yankees), cf	0	0	0	2	0	0
Kaline (Tigers), cf	2	2	1	1	0	0
Skowron (Yankees), 1b	3	0	1	9	0	0
Lary (Tigers), p	0	0	0	0	0	0
(h)Lollar (White Sox)	1	0	0	0	0	0
B.Daley (Athletics), p	0	0	0	0	0	1
Berra (Yankees), c	2	0	0	5	0	0
Howard (Yankees), c	1	0	0	4	0	0
Runnels (Red Sox), 2b	1	0	0	0	1	0
Fox (White Sox), 2b	2	0	1	1	3	0
Hansen (Orioles), ss	2	0	1	0	0	0
Aparicio (White Sox), ss	2	0	0	1	1	0
Monbouquette (Red Sox), p	0	0	0	0	0	0
(a)Williams (Red Sox)	1	0	0	0	0	0
Estrada (Orioles), p	0	0	0	0	0	0
Coates (Yankees), p	0	0	0	0	1	0
(c)Smith (White Sox)	1	0	0	0	0	0
Bell (Indians), p	0	0	0	0	1	0
(d)Gentile (Orioles), 1b	2	0	1	0	0	0
Totals	34	3	6	27	8	1

National League	3	1	1	0	0	0	0	0	0	—	5
American League	0	0	0	0	0	1	0	2	0	—	3

Pitching Summary

National League	IP	H	R	ER	BB	SO
Friend (W)	3	1	0	0	1	2
McCormick	2⅓	3	1	0	3	2
Face	1⅔	0	0	0	0	2
Buhl	1⅓	2	2	1	1	1
Law	⅔	0	0	0	0	0

American League	IP	H	R	ER	BB	SO
Monbouquette (L)	2	5	4	4	0	2
Estrada	1	4	1	1	0	1
Coates	2	2	0	0	0	0
Bell	2	0	0	0	0	0
Lary	1	1	0	0	0	1
B. Daley	1	0	0	0	1	2

(a) Grounded out for Monbouquette in second. (b) Ran for Adcock in fifth. (c) Flied out for Coates in fifth. (d) Struck out for Bell in seventh. (e) Singled for Mazeroski in eighth. (f) Ran for Musial in eighth. (g) Hit into force play for Face in eighth. (h) Grounded out for Lary in eighth. Runs batted in—Skinner, Banks 2, Mazeroski, Crandall, Kaline 2, Fox. Two-base hits—Banks, Mays, Adcock. Three-base hits—Mays. Home runs—Banks, Crandall, Kaline. Stolen base—Skinner. Double plays—Malzone and Skowron; Banks, Mazeroski, and White. Hit by pitcher—By Coates (Mazeroski). Wild pitch—Friend. Balk—Friend. Left on bases—Nationals 8, Americans 9.

Managers: Al Lopez, Chicago (A.L.); Walter Alston, Los Angeles (N.L.).

Umpires—Honochick, Chylak, and Stevens (A.L.), Gorman, Boggess, and Smith (N.L.) Time—2:30. Attendance—30,619.

July 13, 1960   At Yankee Stadium, New York
Second Game

Nationals	AB	R	H	PO	A	E	Americans	AB	R	H	PO	A	E
Mays (Giants), cf	4	1	3	5	0	0	Minoso (White Sox), lf .	2	0	0	1	0	0
Pinson (Reds), cf	0	0	0	0	0	0	(e)T.Williams (Red Sox)	1	0	1	0	0	0
Skinner (Pirates), lf	3	0	1	2	0	0	(f)Robinson (Orioles),						
Cepeda (Giants), lf	2	0	0	0	0	0	3b..................	1	0	0	0	0	0
Aaron (Braves), rf	3	0	0	1	0	0	Runnels (Red Sox), 2b .	2	0	0	0	1	0
(h)Clemente (Pirates), rf	0	0	0	0	0	0	Staley (White Sox), p ..	0	0	0	1	1	0
Banks (Cubs), ss	3	0	1	2	3	0	(g)Kaline (Tigers), lf ...	1	0	1	3	0	0
(i)Groat (Pirates), ss ...	1	0	0	0	1	0	Maris (Yankees), rf	4	0	0	0	0	0
Adcock (Braves), 1b ...	2	1	1	3	0	0	Mantle (Yankees), cf ...	4	0	1	3	0	0
White (Cardinals), 1b ..	1	0	0	2	0	0	Skowron (Yankees), 1b	1	0	1	6	0	0
(k)Larker (Dodgers), 1b	0	1	0	3	0	0	Power (Indians), 1b	2	0	0	5	1	0
Mathews (Braves), 3b ..	3	1	1	0	1	0	Berra (Yankees), c	2	0	0	4	1	0
Boyer (Cardinals), 3b ..	1	1	1	1	0	0	Lollar (White Sox), c ...	2	0	1	0	0	0
Mazeroski (Pirates), 2b .	2	0	0	0	0	0	Malzone (Red Sox), 3b .	2	0	0	2	2	0
Neal (Dodgers), 2b	1	0	0	1	2	0	Lary (Tigers), p	0	0	0	0	0	0
Taylor (Phillies), 2b	1	0	1	2	1	0	(j)Smith (White Sox) ...	1	0	0	0	0	0
Crandall (Braves), c ...	2	0	0	3	0	0	Bell (Indians), p	0	0	0	0	1	0
S.Williams (Dodgers), p	0	0	0	0	0	0	Hansen (Orioles), ss ...	4	0	2	2	4	0
(d)Musial (Cardinals), ..	1	1	1	0	0	0	Ford (Yankees), p	0	0	0	0	0	0
Jackson (Cardinals), p .	0	0	0	0	0	0	(a)Kuenn (Indians)	1	0	0	0	0	0
Bailey (Reds), c	1	0	0	0	0	0	Wynn (White Sox), p ...	0	0	0	0	0	0
Law (Pirates), p	1	0	0	0	0	0	(c)Fox (White Sox), 2b .	3	0	1	0	1	0
Podres (Dodgers), p ...	0	0	0	0	1	0							
(b)Burgess (Pirates), c .	2	0	0	2	0	0							
Henry (Reds), p	0	0	0	0	0	0							
McDaniel (Cards), p ...	0	0	0	0	0	0							
Totals	34	6	10	27	10	0	Totals	33	0	8	27	12	0

National League	0	2	1	0	0	0	1	0	2–6
American League	0	0	0	0	0	0	0	0	0–0

Pitching Summary

National League	IP	H	R	ER	BB	SO	American League	IP	H	R	ER	BB	SO
Law (W)	2	1	0	0	0	1	Ford (L)	3	5	3	3	0	1
Podres	2	1	0	0	3	1	Wynn	2	0	0	0	0	2
S.Williams	2	2	0	0	1	2	Staley	2	2	1	1	1	0
Jackson	1	1	0	0	2	0	Lary	1	1	0	0	1	0
Henry	1	1	0	0	0	0	Bell	1	2	2	2	2	0
McDaniel	1	1	0	0	0	0							

(a) Flied out for Ford in third. (b) Struck out for Podres in fifth. (c) Singled for Wynn in fifth. (d) Homered for S. Williams in seventh. (e) Singled for Minoso in seventh. (f) Ran for T. Williams in seventh. (g) Walked for Staley in seventh. (h) Walked for Aaron in eighth. (i) Grounded into double play for Banks in eighth. (j) Popped out for Lary in eighth. (k) Walked for White in ninth. Runs batted in—Mays, Mathews 2, Boyer 2, Musial. Two-base hit—Lollar. Home runs—Mathews, Mays, Musial, Boyer. Sacrifice hit—Henry. Stolen base—Mays. Caught stealing—Mays. Double plays—Law, Banks, and Adcock; Banks, Neal, and White; Fox, Hansen, and Power. Left on bases—Nationals 5, Americans 12.

Managers: Al Lopez, Chicago (A.L.); Walter Alston, Los Angeles (N.L.)

Umpires—Chylak, Honochick, and Stevens (A.L.), Boggess, Gorman, and Smith (N.L.) Time—2:42. Attendance—38, 362.

July 11, 1961   At Candlestick Park, San Francisco
First Game

Americans	AB	R	H	PO	A	E	Nationals	AB	R	H	PO	A	E
Temple (Indians), 2b ...	3	0	0	1	2	0	Wills (Dodgers), ss	5	0	1	0	2	0
(f)Gentile (Orioles), 1b .	2	0	0	2	0	1	Mathews (Braves), 3b ..	2	0	0	0	0	0
Cash (Tigers), 1b	4	0	1	6	1	0	Purkey (Reds), p	0	0	0	1	0	0
(g)Fox (White Sox), 2b .	0	2	0	1	0	0	(b)Musial (Cardinals) ...	1	0	0	0	0	0
Mantle (Yankees), cf ...	3	0	0	3	0	0	McCormick (Giants), p .	0	0	0	0	0	0
Kaline (Tigers), cf	2	1	1	1	0	0	(e)Altman (Cubs)	1	1	1	0	0	0
Maris (Yankees), rf	4	0	1	3	0	0	Face (Pirates), p	0	0	0	0	0	0
Colavito (Tigers), lf	4	0	0	1	0	0	Koufax (Dodgers), p ...	0	0	0	0	0	0
Kubek (Yankees), ss ...	4	0	0	1	2	1	Miller (Giants), p	0	0	0	0	0	0
Romano (Indians), c ...	3	0	0	7	0	0	(i)Aaron (Braves)	1	1	1	0	0	0
(h)Berra (Yankees), c ..	1	0	0	0	0	0	Mays (Giants), cf	5	2	2	3	0	0
Howard (Yankees), c ..	0	0	0	0	0	0	Cepeda (Giants), lf	3	0	0	1	0	1
B.Robinson (Orioles),							F. Robinson (Reds), lf ..	1	0	1	2	0	0
3b	2	0	0	0	2	0	Clemente (Pirates), rf ..	4	1	2	2	0	0
Bunning (Tigers), p ...	0	0	0	1	0	0	White (Cardinals), 1b ..	3	0	1	7	1	0
(d)Brandt (Orioles)	1	0	0	0	0	0	Bolling (Braves), 2b	3	0	0	1	3	0
Fornieles (Red Sox), p .	0	0	0	0	0	0	Zimmer (Cubs), 2b	1	0	0	0	0	1
Wilhelm (Orioles), p	1	0	0	0	0	0	Burgess (Pirates), c	4	0	1	13	0	1
Ford (Yankees), p	1	0	0	0	0	0	Spahn (Braves), p	0	0	0	0	1	0
Lary (Tigers), p	0	0	0	0	0	0	(a)Stuart (Pirates)	1	0	1	0	0	0
Donovan (Senators), p .	0	0	0	0	0	0	Boyer (Cardinals), 3b ..	2	0	0	0	1	2
(c)Killebrew (Twins), 3b	2	1	1	0	0	0							
Howser (Athletics), 3b .	1	0	0	0	1	0							
Totals	38	4	4	27	8	2	Totals	37	5	11	30	8	5

American League	0 0 0	0 0 1	0 0 2	1—4
National League	0 1 0	1 0 0	0 1 0	2—5

Pitching Summary

American League	IP	H	R	ER	BB	SO	National League	IP	H	R	ER	BB	SO
Ford	3	2	1	1	0	2	Spahn	3	0	0	0	0	3
Lary	0*	0	1	0	0	0	Purkey	2	0	0	0	0	1
Donovan	2	4	0	0	0	1	McCormick	3	1	1	1	1	3
Bunning	2	0	0	0	0	2	Face	⅓	2	2	2	0	1
Fornieles	⅓	2	1	1	0	0	Koufax	0†	1	0	0	0	0
Wilhelm (L)	1⅔‡	3	2	2	1	1	Miller (W)	1⅔	0	1	0	1	4

* Pitched to one batter in fourth.
† Pitched to one batter in ninth.
‡ Pitched to four batters in tenth.

(a) Doubled for Spahn in third. (b) Flied out for Purkey in fifth. (c) Homered for Donovan in sixth. (d) Struck out for Bunning in eighth. (e) Homered for McCormick in eighth. (f) Struck out for Temple in ninth. (g) Ran for Cash in ninth. (h) Safe on error for Romano in ninth. (i) Singled for Miller in tenth. Runs batted in—Kaline, Colavito, Killebrew, Altman, Mays, Clemente 2, White. Two-base hits—Stuart, Cash, Mays. Three-base hit—Clemente. Home runs—Killebrew, Altman. Sacrifice flies—Clemente, White. Stolen base—F. Robinson. Hit by pitcher—By Wilhelm (F. Robinson). Balk—Miller. Passed ball—Howard. Left on bases—Americans 6, Nationals 9.

Managers: Paul Richards, Baltimore (A.L.); Danny Murtaugh, Pittsburgh (N.L.)

Umpires—Landes, Crawford, and Vargo (N.L.), Umont, Runge, and Drummond (A.L.) Time—2:53. Attendance—44,115.

July 31, 1961   At Fenway Park, Boston
Second Game

Nationals	AB	R	H	PO	A	E	Americans	AB	R	H	PO	A	E
Wills (Dodgers), ss	2	0	1	1	1	0	Cash (Tigers), 1b	4	0	0	11	0	0
Aaron (Braves), rf	2	0	0	1	0	0	Colavito (Tigers), lf	4	1	1	3	0	0
Miller (Giants), p	0	0	0	0	0	0	Kaline (Tigers), rf	4	0	2	1	0	0
Mathews (Braves), 3b ..	3	1	0	0	2	0	Mantle (Yankees), cf ...	3	0	0	2	0	0
Mays (Giants), cf	3	0	1	1	0	0	Romano (Indians), c ...	1	0	0	1	0	0
Cepeda (Giants), lf	3	0	0	0	0	0	(b)Maris (Yankees)	1	0	0	0	0	0
Clemente (Pirates), rf ..	2	0	0	0	0	0	Howard (Yankees), c ...	2	0	0	6	0	0
Kasko (Reds), ss	1	0	1	2	4	0	Aparicio (White Sox),						
(e)Banks (Cubs), ss	1	0	0	0	0	0	ss	2	0	0	1	3	0
White (Cardinals), 1b ..	4	0	2	11	1	0	(f)Sievers (White Sox) ..	1	0	0	0	0	0
Bolling (Braves), 2b	4	0	0	3	2	1	Temple (Indians), 2b ...	2	0	0	2	3	0
Burgess (Pirates), c	1	0	0	2	0	0	B.Robinson (Orioles),						
Roseboro (Dodgers), c .	3	0	0	6	0	0	3b	3	0	1	0	3	0
Purkey (Reds), p	0	0	0	0	1	0	Bunning (Tigers), p	1	0	0	0	0	0
(a)Stuart (Pirates)	1	0	0	0	0	0	Schwall (Red Sox), p ..	1	0	0	0	0	0
Mahaffey (Phillies), p ..	0	0	0	0	0	0	Pascual (Twins), p	1	0	0	0	0	0
(c)Musial (Cardinals) ...	1	0	0	0	0	0							
Koufax (Dodgers), p ...	0	0	0	0	0	0							
(d)Altman (Cubs), rf ...	1	0	0	0	0	0							
Totals	32	1	5	27	11	1	Totals	30	1	4	27	9	0

```
National League .....................   0  0  0    0  0  1    0  0  0—1
American League ....................   1  0  0    0  0  0    0  0  0—1
```

Game called because of rain.

Pitching Summary

National League	IP	H	R	ER	BB	SO	American League	IP	H	R	ER	BB	SO
Purkey	2	1	1	1	2	2	Bunning	3	0	0	0	0	1
Mahaffey	2	0	0	0	1	0	Schwall	3	5	1	1	1	2
Koufax	2	2	0	0	0	1	Pascual	3	0	0	0	1	4
Miller	3	1	0	0	0	5							

(a) Grounded out for Purkey in third. (b) Popped out for Romano in fourth. (c) Struck out for Mahaffey in fifth. (d) Flied out for Koufax in seventh. (e) Struck out for Kasko in eighth. (f) Struck out for Aparicio in ninth. Runs batted in—White, Colavito. Two-base hit—White. Home run—Colavito. Stolen base—Kaline. Double plays—Bolling, Kasko, and White; White, Kasko, and Bolling. Hit by pitcher—By Schwall (Cepeda). Passed ball—Burgess. Left on bases—Nationals 7, Americans 5.

Managers: Paul Richards, Baltimore (A.L.); Danny Murtaugh, Pittsburgh (N.L.)

Umpires—Napp, Flaherty, and Smith (A.L.), Secory, Sudol, and Pelekoudas (N.L.) Time—2:27. Attendance—31,851.

July 10, 1962 At District of Columbia Stadium, Washington
First Game

Nationals	AB	R	H	PO	A	E
Groat (Pirates), ss	3	1	1	3	3	0
Davenport (Giants), 3b .	1	0	1	0	1	0
Clemente (Pirates), rf ..	3	0	3	2	0	0
F. Alou (Giants), rf	0	0	0	0	0	0
Mays (Giants), cf	3	0	0	3	0	0
Cepeda (Giants), 1b ...	3	0	0	2	2	0
Purkey (Reds), p	0	0	0	0	1	0
(e)Callison (Phillies) ...	1	0	1	0	0	0
Shaw (Braves), p	0	0	0	1	0	0
T.Davis (Dodgers), lf ...	4	0	0	2	0	0
Boyer (Cardinals), 3b ..	2	0	0	1	0	0
Banks (Cubs), 1b	2	0	0	4	1	0
Crandall (Braves), c ...	4	0	0	5	0	0
Mazeroski (Pirates), 2b .	2	0	0	1	0	0
Bolling (Braves), 2b ..	2	0	0	1	3	0
Drysdale (Dodgers), p ..	1	0	0	1	0	0
Marichal (Giants), p	0	0	0	0	0	0
(c)Musial (Cardinals) ...	1	0	1	0	0	0
(d)Wills (Dodgers), ss ..	1	2	1	1	1	0
Totals	33	3	8	27	12	0

Americans	AB	R	H	PO	A	E
Rollins (Twins), 2b	2	1	1	1	3	0
Robinson (Orioles), 3b .	0	0	0	1	0	0
Moran (Angels), 2b	3	0	1	0	0	0
Richardson (Yankees), 2b	1	0	0	1	0	0
Maris (Yankees), cf	2	0	0	2	0	0
Landis (White Sox), cf .	1	0	0	2	0	0
Mantle (Yankees), rf ...	1	0	0	0	0	0
(b)Colavito (Tigers), lf ..	1	0	0	1	0	0
Gentile (Orioles), 1b ...	3	0	0	8	0	0
Wagner (Angels), rf-lf ..	4	0	0	4	0	0
Battey (Twins), c	2	0	0	4	1	0
Romano (Indians), c ...	2	0	1	1	0	0
Aparicio (White Sox), ss	4	0	1	3	2	0
Bunning (Tigers), p	0	0	0	0	0	0
(a)L.Thomas (Angels) ..	1	0	0	0	0	0
Pascual (Twins), p	1	0	0	0	1	0
Donovan (Indians), p ..	0	0	0	0	0	0
(f)Siebern (Athletics) ...	1	0	0	0	0	0
Pappas (Orioles), p	0	0	0	0	0	0
Totals	29	1	4	27	7	0

National League	0	0	0		0	0	2		0	1 0—3
American League	0	0	0		0	0	1		0	0 0—1

Pitching Summary

National League	IP	H	R	ER	BB	SO
Drysdale	3	1	0	0	1	3
Marichal (W)	2	0	0	0	1	0
Purkey	2	2	1	1	0	1
Shaw	2	1	0	0	1	1

American League	IP	H	R	ER	BB	SO
Bunning	3	1	0	0	0	2
Pascual (L)	3	4	2	2	1	1
Donovan	2	3	1	1	0	0
Pappas	1	0	0	0	0	0

(a) Popped out for Bunning in third. (b) Ran for Mantle in fourth. (c) Singled for Marichal in sixth. (d) Ran for Musial in sixth. (e) Singled for Purkey in eighth. (f) Grounded out for Donovan in eighth. Runs batted in—Groat, Cepeda, Maris, F. Alou. Two-base hit—Clemente. Three-base hit—Aparicio. Sacrifice flies—Maris, F. Alou. Stolen bases—Mays, Wills. Caught stealing—Clemente. Double plays—Cepeda, Groat, and Drysdale; Battey and Rollins. Hit by pitcher—By Drysdale (Rollins), by Shaw (Robinson). Left on bases—Nationals 5, Americans 7.

Managers: Ralph Houk, New York (A.L.); Fred Hutchinson, Cincinnati (N.L.).

Umpires—Hurley, Stewart, and Schwartz (A.L.), Donatelli, Venzon, and Steiner (N.L.) Time—2:33. Attendance—45,480.

July 30, 1962   At Wrigley Field, Chicago
Second Game

Americans	AB	R	H	PO	A	E		Nationals	AB	R	H	PO	A	E
Rollins (Twins), 3b	3	0	1	0	1	0		Groat (Pirates), ss	3	0	2	3	3	1
B.Robinson (Orioles),								Wills (Dodgers), ss	1	0	0	0	1	0
3b	1	1	0	0	1	0		Clemente (Pirates), rf ..	2	0	0	2	0	0
Moran (Angels), 2b	4	0	1	1	4	0		F.Robinson (Reds), rf ..	3	0	0	1	0	0
(f)Berra (Yankees)	1	0	0	0	0	0		Mays (Giants), cf	2	0	2	2	0	0
(g)Richardson								Aaron (Braves), cf	2	0	0	1	0	0
(Yankees), 2b	0	1	0	2	0	0		Cepeda (Giants), 1b ...	1	0	0	2	0	0
Maris (Yankees), cf ...	4	2	1	4	0	0		Banks (Cubs), 1b	2	1	1	1	1	0
Colavito (Tigers), rf	4	1	1	2	0	0		T.Davis (Dodgers), lf ...	1	0	0	0	1	1
Gentile (Orioles), 1b ...	4	0	1	10	0	0		(b)Musial (Cards), lf	2	0	0	0	1	0
Battey (Twins), c	2	1	0	2	0	0		Williams (Cubs), lf	1	0	0	2	0	0
(d)Kaline (Tigers)	0	1	0	0	0	0		Boyer (Cardinals), 3b ..	3	0	1	1	2	0
Howard (Yankees), c ..	2	0	0	2	0	0		Mathews (Braves), 3b ..	1	0	0	0	0	2
Wagner (Angels), lf	4	1	3	1	0	0		Crandall (Braves), c ...	1	0	0	3	0	0
L.Thomas (Angels), lf ..	0	0	0	1	0	0		Roseboro (Dodgers), c .	3	1	1	6	0	0
Aparicio (White Sox),								Mazeroski (Pirates), 2b .	1	0	0	0	0	0
ss	2	0	0	2	3	0		(c)Altman (Cubs)	1	0	0	0	0	0
Tresh (Yankees), ss ...	2	0	1	0	4	0		Gibson (Cardinals), p ..	0	0	0	0	0	0
Stenhouse (Senators),								Farrell (Colts), p	0	0	0	0	0	0
p	0	0	0	0	0	0		(e)Ashburn (Mets)	1	1	1	0	0	0
(a)Runnels (Red Sox) ..	1	1	1	0	0	0		Marichal (Giants), p	0	0	0	0	0	0
Herbert (White Sox), p .	1	0	0	0	0	0		(h)Callison (Phillies) ...	0	0	0	0	0	0
Aguirre (Tigers), p	2	0	0	0	0	0		Podres (Dodgers), p ...	1	1	1	0	0	0
Pappas (Orioles), p	0	0	0	0	0	0		Mahaffey (Phillies), p ..	0	0	0	0	0	0
								Bolling (Braves), 2b	3	0	1	3	1	0
Totals	37	9	10	27	13	0		Totals	35	4	10	27	10	4

```
American League ....................  0  0  1   2  0  1   3  0  2—9
National League ....................  0  1  0   0  0  0   1  1  1—4
```

Pitching Summary

American League	IP	H	R	ER	BB	SO		National League	IP	H	R	ER	BB	SO
Stenhouse	2	3	1	1	1	1		Podres	2	2	0	0	0	2
Herbert (W)	3	3	0	0	0	0		Mahaffey (L)	2	2	3	3	1	1
Aguirre	3	3	2	2	0	2		Gibson	2	1	1	1	2	1
Pappas	1	1	1	1	1	0		Farrell	1	3	3	3	1	2
								Marichal	2	2	2	1	0	2

(a) Homered for Stenhouse in third. (b) Grounded out for T. Davis in third. (c) Flied out for Mazeroski in fourth. (d) Ran for Battey in sixth. (e) Singled for Farrell in seventh. (f) Safe on error for Moran in ninth. (g) Ran for Berra in ninth. (h) Walked for Marichal in ninth. Runs batted in—Groat 2, Runnels, Wagner 2, Tresh, Colavito 4, Williams, Maris, Roseboro. Two-base hits—Podres, Tresh, Bolling, Maris. Three-base hit—Banks. Home runs—Runnels, Wagner, Colavito, Roseboro. Sacrifice fly—Colavito. Double plays—Aparicio, Moran, and Gentile; Moran, Aparicio, and Gentile. Hit by pitcher—By Stenhouse (Groat). Wild pitches—Marichal 2, Stenhouse. Left on bases—Americans 6, Nationals 7.

Managers: Ralph Houk, New York (A.L.); Fred Hutchinson, Cincinnati (N.L.).

Umpires—Conlan, Burkhart, and Forman (N.L.), McKinley, Rice, and Kinnamon (A.L.) Time—2:28. Attendance—38,359.

July 9, 1963   At Municipal Stadium, Cleveland

Nationals	AB	R	H	PO	A	E	Americans	AB	R	H	PO	A	E
T.Davis (Dodgers), lf ...	3	1	1	2	1	0	Fox (White Sox), 2b ...	3	0	1	3	1	0
(e)Snider (Mets), lf	1	0	0	0	0	0	Richardson (Yankees),						
Aaron (Braves), rf	4	1	0	3	0	0	2b	2	0	0	0	1	0
White (Cardinals), 1b ..	4	1	1	5	3	0	Pearson (Angels), cf ...	4	1	2	4	0	0
Mays (Giants), cf	3	2	1	1	0	0	Tresh (Yankees), cf	0	0	0	0	0	0
Clemente (Pirates), cf ..	0	0	0	0	0	0	Kaline (Tigers), rf	3	0	0	2	0	0
Bailey (Giants), c	1	0	1	4	1	0	Allison (Twins), rf	1	0	0	0	0	0
(a)Musial (Cardinals) ...	1	0	0	0	0	0	Malzone (Red Sox), 3b .	3	1	1	1	3	0
Culp (Phillies), p	0	0	0	0	1	0	Bouton (Yankees), p ...	0	0	0	0	0	0
Santo (Cubs), 3b	1	0	1	0	0	0	Pizarro (White Sox), p .	0	0	0	0	0	0
Boyer (Cardinals), 3b ..	3	0	0	0	0	0	(c)Killebrew (Twins) ...	1	0	0	0	0	0
(d)McCovey (Giants) ...	1	0	0	0	0	0	Radatz (Red Sox), p ...	0	0	0	0	0	0
Drysdale (Dodgers), p ..	0	0	0	0	0	0	Wagner (Athletics), lf ..	3	1	2	1	0	0
Groat (Cardinals), ss ...	4	0	1	2	2	0	Howard (Yankees), c ..	1	0	0	5	0	0
Javier (Cardinals), 2b ..	4	0	0	4	1	0	Battey (Twins), c	2	0	1	1	0	0
O'Toole (Reds), p	1	0	0	0	0	0	(b)Yastrzemski (Red						
Jackson (Cubs), p	1	0	0	1	0	0	Sox), lf	2	0	0	1	0	0
Edwards (Reds), c	2	0	0	5	0	0	Pepitone (Yankees), 1b .	4	0	0	8	0	0
							Versalles (Twins), ss ...	1	0	1	0	2	0
							Aparicio (Orioles), ss ..	1	0	0	0	0	0
							McBride (Angels), p ...	1	0	1	0	0	0
							Bunning (Tigers), p	0	0	0	0	0	0
							Robinson (Orioles), 3b .	2	0	2	1	1	0
Totals	34	5	6	27	10	0	Totals	34	3	11	27	8	1

National League	0	1	2	0	1	0	0	1	0—5
American League	0	1	2	0	0	0	0	0	0—3

Pitching Summary

National League	IP	H	R	ER	BB	SO	American League	IP	H	R	ER	BB	SO
O'Toole	2	4	1	1	0	1	McBride	3	4	3	3	2	1
Jackson (W)	2	4	2	2	0	3	Bunning (L)	2	0	1	0	1	0
Culp	1	1	0	0	0	0	Bouton	1	0	0	0	0	0
Woodeshick	2	1	0	0	1	3	Pizarro	1	0	0	0	0	0
Drysdale	2	1	0	0	0	2	Radatz	2	2	1	1	0	5

(a) Lined out for Bailey in fifth. (b) Fouled out for Battey in fifth. (c) Called out for Pizarro in seventh. (d) Struck out for Woodeshick in eighth. (e) Called out on strikes for T. Davis in ninth. Runs batted in—Mays 2, Bailey, Santo, Groat, Malzone, Battey, McBride. Two-base hit—Pearson. Sacrifice hit—Bunning. Stolen bases—Mays 2, White. Double plays—T. Davis and Bailey; Groat, Javier, and White; White, Groat, and White. Hit by pitcher—By O'Toole (Versalles). Left on bases—Nationals 5, Americans 7.

Managers: Ralph Houk, New York (A.L.); Alvin Dark, San Francisco (N.L.)

Umpires—Soar, Smith, and Haller (A.L.), Jackowski, Pryor, and Harvey (N.L.) Time—2:20. Attendance—44,160.

July 7, 1964   At Shea Stadium, New York

Americans	AB	R	H	PO	A	E	Nationals	AB	R	H	PO	A	E
Fregosi (Angels), ss ...	4	1	1	4	1	0	Clemente (Pirates), rf ..	3	1	1	1	0	0
Oliva (Twins), rf	4	0	0	0	0	0	Short (Phillies), p	0	0	0	0	1	0
Radatz (Red Sox), p ...	1	0	0	0	0	0	Farrell (Colts), p	0	0	0	0	0	0
Mantle (Yankees), cf ...	4	1	1	2	0	0	(g)White (Cardinals) ...	1	0	0	0	0	0
Hall (Twins), cf	0	0	0	0	0	0	Marichal (Giants), p	0	0	0	0	0	0
Killebrew (Twins), lf	4	1	3	0	0	0	Groat (Cardinals), ss ...	3	0	1	0	0	0
Hinton (Senators), lf ...	0	0	0	0	0	0	(d)Cardenas (Reds), ss	1	0	0	1	0	0
Allison (Twins), 1b	3	0	0	9	0	0	Williams (Cubs), lf	4	1	1	1	0	0
(f)Pepitone (Yankees),							Mays (Giants), cf	3	1	0	7	0	0
1b	0	0	0	1	0	1	Cepeda (Giants), 1b ...	4	0	1	6	0	0
Robinson (Orioles), 3b .	4	0	2	1	2	0	(h)Flood (Cardinals) ...	0	1	0	0	0	0
Richardson (Yankees),							Boyer (Cardinals), 3b ..	4	1	2	0	2	0
2b	4	0	1	0	4	0	Torre (Braves), c	2	0	0	5	0	0
Howard (Yankees), c ..	3	1	0	9	0	0	Edwards (Reds), c	1	1	0	5	0	0
Chance (Angels), p	1	0	0	0	1	0	Hunt (Mets), 2b	3	0	1	1	0	0
Wyatt (Athletics), p	0	0	0	0	1	0	(i)Aaron (Braves)	1	0	0	0	0	0
(b)Siebern (Orioles)	1	0	0	0	0	0	Drysdale (Dodgers), p ..	0	0	0	0	3	0
Pascual (Twins), p	0	0	0	0	1	0	(a)Stargell (Pirates)	1	0	0	0	0	0
(e)Colavito (Athletics) ..	2	0	1	0	0	0	Bunning (Phillies), p ...	0	0	0	0	0	0
							(c)Callison (Phillies), rf .	3	1	1	0	0	0
Totals	35	4	9	26	10	1	Totals	34	7	8	27	6	0

American League .... 1 0 0   0 0 2   1 0 0—4
National League .... 0 0 0   2 1 0   0 0 4—7

Two out when winning run scored.

Pitching Summary

American League	IP	H	R	ER	BB	SO	National League	IP	H	R	ER	BB	SO
Chance	3	2	0	0	0	2	Drysdale	3	2	1	0	0	3
Wyatt	1	2	2	2	0	0	Bunning	2	2	0	0	0	4
Pascual	2	2	1	1	0	1	Short	1	3	2	2	0	1
Radatz (L)	2⅔	2	4	4	2	5	Farrell	2	2	1	1	1	1
							Marichal (W)	1	0	0	0	0	1

(a) Grounded out for Drysdale in third. (b) Flied out for Wyatt in fifth. (c) Popped out for Bunning in fifth. (d) Ran for Groat in fifth. (e) Doubled for Pascual in seventh. (f) Ran for Allison in eighth. (g) Struck out for Farrell in eighth. (h) Ran for Cepeda in ninth. (i) Struck out for Hunt in ninth. Runs batted in—Killebrew, Williams, Boyer, Groat, Robinson 2, Fregosi, Callison 3. Two-base hits—Groat, Colavito. Three-base hit—Robinson. Home runs—Williams, Boyer, Callison. Sacrifice fly—Fregosi. Stolen base—Mays. Hit by pitcher—By Farrell (Howard). Wild pitch—Drysdale. Passed ball—Torre. Left on bases—Americans 7, Nationals 3.

Managers: Al Lopez, Chicago (A.L.); Walter Alston, Los Angeles (N.L.)

Umpires—Sudol, Secory, and Harvey (N.L.), Paparella, Chylak, and Salerno (A.L.) Time—2:37. Attendance—50,844.

July 13, 1965   At Metropolitan Stadium, Bloomington

Nationals	AB	R	H	PO	A	E
Mays (Giants), cf	3	2	1	4	0	0
Aaron (Braves), rf	5	0	1	0	0	0
Stargell (Pirates), lf	3	2	2	1	0	0
(f)Clemente (Pirates), lf.	2	0	0	0	0	0
Allen (Phillies), 3b	3	0	1	0	1	0
Santo (Cubs), 3b	2	0	1	2	0	0
Torre (Braves), c	4	1	1	5	1	0
Banks (Cubs), 1b	4	0	2	11	0	0
Rose (Reds), 2b	2	0	0	1	5	0
Wills (Dodgers), ss ...	4	0	1	2	3	0
Cardenas (Reds), ss ...	0	0	0	0	0	0
Marichal (Giants), p	1	1	1	0	0	0
(b)Rojas (Phillies)	1	0	0	0	0	0
Maloney (Reds), p	0	0	0	0	0	0
Drysdale (Dodgers), p ..	0	0	0	0	0	0
(d)F.Robinson (Reds) ..	1	0	0	0	0	0
Koufax (Dodgers), p ...	0	0	0	0	0	0
Farrell (Astros), p	0	0	0	0	0	0
(g)Williams (Cubs)	1	0	0	0	0	0
Gibson (Cardinals), p ..	0	0	0	1	0	0
Totals	36	6	11	27	10	0

Americans	AB	R	H	PO	A	E
McAuliffe (Tigers), ss ..	3	2	2	3	0	0
McDowell (Indians), p ..	0	0	0	0	1	0
(e)Oliva (Twins), rf	2	0	1	0	0	0
B.Robinson (Orioles),						
3b	4	1	1	1	2	0
Alvis (Indians), 3b	1	0	0	0	0	0
Killebrew (Twins), 1b ..	3	1	1	7	1	0
Colavito (Indians), rf ...	4	0	1	1	0	0
Fisher (White Sox), p ..	0	0	0	1	1	0
(h)Pepitone (Yankees) .	1	0	0	0	0	0
Horton (Tigers), lf	3	0	0	2	0	0
Mantilla (Red Sox), 2b .	2	0	0	1	1	0
Richardson (Yanks), 2b	2	0	0	2	1	0
Davalillo (Indians), cf ..	2	0	1	1	0	0
Versalles (Twins), ss ...	1	0	0	0	2	0
Battey (Twins), c	2	0	0	4	1	0
Freehan (Tigers), c	1	0	1	4	0	0
Pappas (Orioles), p	0	0	0	0	1	0
Grant (Twins), p	0	0	0	0	0	0
(a)Kaline (Tigers)	1	0	0	0	0	0
Richert (Senators), p ..	0	0	0	0	0	0
(c)Hall (Twins), cf	2	1	0	0	0	0
Totals	34	5	8	27	11	0

National League .... 3 2 0   0 0 0   1 0 0—6
American League .... 0 0 0   1 4 0   0 0 0—5

Pitching Summary

National League	IP	H	R	ER	BB	SO
Marichal	3	1	0	0	0	0
Maloney	1⅔	5	5	5	2	1
Drysdale	⅓	0	0	0	0	0
Koufax (W)	1	0	0	0	2	1
Farrell	1	0	0	0	1	0
Gibson	2	2	0	0	1	3

American League	IP	H	R	ER	BB	SO
Pappas	1	4	3	3	1	0
Grant	2	2	2	2	1	3
Richert	2	1	0	0	0	2
McDowell (L)	2	3	1	1	1	2
Fisher	2	1	0	0	0	0

(a) Grounded out for Grant in third. (b) Flied out for Marichal in fourth. (c) Walked for Richert in fifth. (d) Struck out for Drysdale in sixth. (e) Grounded out for McDowell in seventh. (f) Grounded into force play for Stargell in seventh. (g) Grounded out for Farrell in eighth. (h) Struck out for Fisher in ninth. Runs batted in—Mays, Stargell 2, Santo, Torre 2, McAuliffe 2, Killebrew 2, Colavito. Two-base hit—Oliva. Home runs—Mays, Torre, Stargell, McAuliffe, Killebrew. Sacrifice hit—Rose. Double plays—B. Robinson, Mantilla, and Killebrew; Wills, Rose, and Banks; McDowell, Richardson, and Killebrew. Wild pitch—Maloney. Left on bases—Nationals 7, Americans 8.

Managers: Al Lopez, Chicago (A.L.); Gene Mauch, Philadelphia (N.L.).

Umpires—Stevens, DiMuro, and Valentine (A.L.), Weyer, Williams, and Kibler (N.L.). Time—2:45. Attendance—46,706.

July 12, 1966   At Busch Memorial Stadium, St. Louis

Americans	AB	R	H	PO	A	E	Nationals	AB	R	H	PO	A	E
McAuliffe (Tigers), ss ..	3	0	0	1	1	0	Mays (Giants), cf	4	1	1	3	0	0
Stottlemyre (Yanks), p .	0	0	0	0	0	0	Clemente (Pirates), rf ..	4	0	2	2	0	0
(h)Colavito (Indians) ...	1	0	0	0	0	0	Aaron (Braves), lf	4	0	0	2	0	0
Siebert (Indians), p	0	0	0	0	0	0	McCovey (Giants), 1b ..	3	0	0	10	1	0
Richert (Senators), p ..	0	0	0	0	1	0	Santo (Cubs), 3b	4	0	1	2	2	0
Kaline (Tigers), cf	4	0	1	3	0	0	McCarver (Cards), c ...	1	1	1	1	0	0
Agee (White Sox), cf ...	0	0	0	1	0	0	Lefebvre (Dodgers), 2b	2	0	0	2	0	0
F.Robinson (Orioles), lf	4	0	2	2	0	0	Hunt (Mets), 2b	1	0	0	0	1	0
Oliva (Twins), rf	4	0	0	0	0	0	Cardenas (Reds), ss ...	2	0	0	2	2	0
B.Robinson (Orioles),							(f)Stargell (Pirates)	1	0	0	0	0	0
3b	4	1	3	4	4	0	Wills (Dodgers), ss	1	0	1	1	1	0
Scott (Red Sox), 1b	2	0	0	4	1	0	Koufax (Dodgers), p ...	0	0	0	0	0	0
(e)Cash (Tigers), 1b ...	2	0	0	4	0	0	(a)Flood (Cardinals) ...	1	0	0	0	0	0
Freehan (Tigers), c	2	0	1	4	0	0	Bunning (Phillies), p ...	0	0	0	0	0	0
Battey (Twins), c	1	0	0	1	0	0	(b)Allen (Phillies)	1	0	0	0	0	0
Knoop (Angels), 2b	2	0	0	3	1	0	Marichal (Giants), p	0	0	0	0	0	0
(g)Richardson							(i)Hart (Giants)	1	0	0	0	0	0
(Yankees), 2b	2	0	0	1	1	0	Perry (Giants), p	0	0	0	0	0	0
McClain (Tigers), p	1	0	0	0	1	0							
Kaat (Twins), p	0	0	0	0	0	0							
(c)Killebrew (Twins) ...	1	0	1	0	0	0							
(d)Fregosi (Angels), ss .	2	0	0	0	1	0							
Totals	35	1	6	28	11	0	Totals	33	2	6	30	7	0

American League .... 0 1 0   0 0 0   0 0 0   0—1

National League .... 0 0 0   1 0 0   0 0 0   1—2

One out when winning run scored.

Pitching Summary

American League	IP	H	R	ER	BB	SO	National League	IP	H	R	ER	BB	SO
McClain	3	0	0	0	0	3	Koufax	3	1	1	1	0	1
Kaat	2	3	1	1	0	1	Bunning	2	1	0	0	0	2
Stottlemyre	2	1	0	0	1	0	Marichal	3	3	0	0	0	2
Siebert	2	0	0	0	0	1	Perry (W)	2	1	0	0	1	1
Richert (L)	⅓	2	1	1	1	0							

(a) Grounded out for Koufax in third. (b) Struck out for Bunning in fifth. (c) Singled for Kaat in sixth. (d) Ran for Killebrew in sixth. (e) Grounded into double play for Scott in seventh. (f) Fouled out for Cardenas in seventh. (g) Grounded out for Knoop in eighth. (h) Flied out for Stottlemyre in eighth. (i) Struck out for Marichal in eighth. Runs batted in—Santo, Wills. Two-base hit—Clemente. Three-base hit—B. Robinson. Sacrifice hit—Hunt. Double play—McCovey, Cardenas, and McCovey. Wild pitch—Koufax. Left on bases—Americans 5, Nationals 5.

Managers: Sam Mele, Minnesota (A.L.); Walter Alston, Los Angeles (N.L.).

Umpires—Barlick, Vargo, and Engel (N.L.), Umont, Honochick, and Neudecker (A.L.) Time—2:19. Attendance—49,936.

July 11, 1967　At Anaheim, California

Nationals	AB	R	H	PO	A	E	Americans	AB	R	H	PO	A	E
Brock (Cardinals), lf ...	2	0	0	1	0	0	B.Robinson (Orioles),						
(c)Mays (Giants), cf	4	0	0	3	0	0	3b	6	1	1	0	6	0
Clemente (Pirates), rf ..	6	0	1	6	0	0	Carew (Twins), 2b	3	0	0	2	3	0
Aaron (Braves), cf-lf ...	6	0	1	2	0	0	McAuliffe (Tigers), 2b ..	3	0	0	3	2	0
Cepeda (Cardinals), 1b	6	0	0	6	0	0	Oliva (Twins), cf	6	0	2	4	0	0
Allen (Phillies), 3b	4	1	1	0	2	0	Killebrew (Twins), 1b ..	6	0	0	15	1	0
Perez (Reds), 3b	2	1	1	0	3	0	Conigliaro (Red Sox), rf	6	0	0	4	0	0
Torre (Braves), c	2	0	0	4	1	0	Yastrzemski (Red Sox),						
Haller (Giants), c	1	0	0	7	0	0	lf	4	0	3	2	0	0
(g)Banks (Cubs)	1	0	1	0	0	0	Freehan (Tigers), c	5	0	0	13	0	0
McCarver (Cardinals), c	2	0	2	7	1	0	Petrocelli (Red Sox), ss	1	0	0	0	1	0
Mazeroski (Pirates), 2b .	4	0	0	7	1	0	McGlothlin (Angels), p .	0	0	0	0	0	0
Drysdale (Dodgers), p ..	0	0	0	0	0	0	(b)Mantle (Yankees) ...	1	0	0	0	0	0
(k)Helms (Reds)	1	0	0	0	0	0	Peters (White Sox), p ..	0	0	0	0	1	0
Seaver (Mets), p	0	0	0	0	0	0	(d)Mincher (Angels) ...	1	0	1	0	0	0
Alley (Pirates), ss	5	0	0	1	3	0	(e)Agee (White Sox) ...	0	0	0	0	0	0
Marichal (Giants), p	1	0	0	0	0	0	Downing (Yankees), p .	0	0	0	0	0	0
Jenkins (Cubs), p	1	0	0	0	0	0	(h)Alvis (Indians)	1	0	0	0	0	0
Gibson (Cardinals), p ..	0	0	0	0	1	0	Hunter (Athletics), p ...	1	0	0	0	0	0
(f)Wynn (Astros)	1	0	1	0	0	0	(l)Berry (White Sox)	1	0	0	0	0	0
Short (Phillies), p	0	0	0	0	1	0	Chance (Twins), p	0	0	0	0	0	0
(i)Staub (Astros)	1	0	1	0	0	0	(a)Fregosi (Angels), ss .	4	0	1	2	3	0
Cuellar (Astros), p	0	0	0	0	0	0							
(j)Rose (Reds), 2b	1	0	0	1	0	0							
Totals	51	2	9	45	13	0	Totals	49	1	8	45	17	0

```
National League ....   0 1 0   0 0 0   0 0 0   0 0 0   0 0 1—2
American League ...   0 0 0   0 0 1   0 0 0   0 0 0   0 0 0—1
```

Pitching Summary

National League	IP	H	R	ER	BB	SO	American League	IP	H	R	ER	BB	SO
Marichal	3	1	0	0	0	3	Chance	3	2	1	1	0	1
Jenkins	3	3	1	1	0	6	McGlothlin	2	1	0	0	0	2
Gibson	2	2	0	0	0	2	Peters	3	0	0	0	0	4
Short	2	0	0	0	1	1	Downing	2	2	0	0	0	2
Cuellar	2	1	0	0	0	2	Hunter (L)	5	4	1	1	0	4
Drysdale (W)	2	1	0	0	0	2							
Seaver	1	0	0	0	1	1							

(a) Singled for Chance in third. (b) Struck out for McGlothlin in fifth. (c) Struck out for Brock in sixth. (d) Singled for Peters in eighth. (e) Ran for Mincher in eighth. (f) Singled for Gibson in ninth. (g) Singled for Haller in tenth. (h) Hit into fielder's choice for Downing in tenth. (i) Singled for Short in eleventh. (j) Flied out for Cuellar in thirteenth. (k) Lined into double play for Drysdale in fifteenth. (l) Struck out for Hunter in fifteenth. Runs batted in—Allen, Perez, B. Robinson. Two-base hits—Yastrzemski, McCarver. Home runs—Allen, B. Robinson, Perez. Sacrifice hits—Fregosi, Freehan, Mazeroski. Double plays—B. Robinson, Carew, and Killebrew; McAuliffe and Killebrew. Stolen base—Aaron. Left on bases—Nationals 5, Americans 7.

Managers: Hank Bauer, Baltimore (A.L.); Walter Alston, Los Angeles (N.L.).

Umpires—Runge (A.L.), plate; Secory (N.L.), first base; DiMuro (A.L.), second base; Burkhart (N.L.), third base; Ashford (A.L.), left field line; Pelekoudas (N.L.), right field line. Time—3:41. Attendance—46,309.

July 9, 1968   At Astrodome, Houston (Night)

Americans	AB	R	H	PO	A	E	Nationals	AB	R	H	PO	A	E
Fregosi (Angels), ss ...	3	0	1	1	6	0	Mays (Giants), cf	4	1	1	0	0	0
Campaneris (Athletics),							Flood (Cardinals), lf	1	0	0	1	0	0
ss	1	0	0	1	0	0	M. Alou (Pirates), lf ...	1	0	1	1	0	0
Carew (Twins), 2b	3	0	0	2	2	0	Javier (Cardinals), 2b ..	0	0	0	0	0	0
Johnson (Orioles), 2b ..	1	0	0	1	1	0	McCovey (Giants), 1b ..	4	0	0	10	0	0
Yastrzemski (Red Sox),							Aaron (Braves), rf	3	0	1	1	0	0
cf-lf	4	0	0	0	0	0	Santo (Cubs), 3b	2	0	1	1	1	0
Howard (Senators), rf ..	2	0	0	0	0	0	Perez (Reds), 3b	0	0	0	0	1	0
Oliva (Twins), rf	1	0	1	2	0	0	Helms (Reds), 2b	3	0	1	1	2	0
Horton (Tigers), lf	2	0	0	1	0	0	Reed (Braves), p	0	0	0	0	0	0
Azcue (Indians), c	1	0	0	5	0	0	Koosman (Mets), p	0	0	0	0	0	0
Josephson (White Sox),							Grote (Mets), c	2	0	0	3	0	0
c	0	0	0	0	0	0	Carlton (Cardinals), p ..	0	0	0	0	1	0
Killebrew (Twins), 1b	1	0	0	4	0	1	(c)Staub (Astros)	1	0	0	0	0	0
Powell (Orioles), 1b	2	0	0	2	0	0	Seaver (Mets), p	0	0	0	0	0	0
Freehan (Tigers), c	2	0	0	4	0	0	F.Alou (Braves), lf	0	0	0	0	0	0
McClain (Tigers), p	0	0	0	0	0	0	Kessinger (Cubs), ss ...	2	0	0	0	1	0
McDowell (Indians), p ..	0	0	0	0	0	0	(d)Williams (Cubs), ss ..	1	0	0	0	0	0
(e)Mantle (Yankees) ...	1	0	0	0	0	0	Cardenas (Reds), ss ...	0	0	0	0	1	0
Stottlemyre (Yankees),							Drysdale (Dodgers), p ..	1	0	0	0	0	1
p	0	0	0	0	0	0	Marichal (Giants), p	0	0	0	0	0	0
John (White Sox), p ...	0	0	0	0	0	0	(b)Haller (Dodgers), c ..	2	0	0	6	0	0
Robinson (Orioles), 3b .	2	0	0	1	1	0	Bench (Reds), c	0	0	0	2	0	0
Wert (Tigers), 3b	1	0	1	1	0	0							
Tiant (Indians), p	0	0	0	0	0	0							
(a)Harrelson (Red Sox)	1	0	0	0	0	0							
Odom (Athletics), p	0	0	0	0	0	0							
Monday (Athletics), cf ..	2	0	0	0	0	0							
Totals	30	0	3	24	10	1	Totals	27	1	5	27	9	0

```
American League .................... 0  0  0    0  0  0    0  0  0—0
National League .................... 1  0  0    0  0  0    0  0  x—1
```

Pitching Summary

American League	IP	H	R	ER	BB	SO	National League	IP	H	R	ER	BB	SO
Tiant (L)	2	2	1	0	2	2	Drysdale (W)	3	1	0	0	0	0
Odom	2	0	0	0	2	2	Marichal	2	0	0	0	0	3
McClain	2	1	0	0	2	1	Carlton	1	0	0	0	0	1
McDowell	1	1	0	0	0	3	Seaver	2	2	0	0	0	5
Stottlemyre	⅓	0	0	0	0	1	Reed	⅔	0	0	0	0	1
John	⅔	1	0	0	0	1	Koosman	⅓	0	0	0	0	1

(a) Flied out for Tiant in third. (b) Flied out for Marichal in fifth. (c) Popped out for Carlton in sixth. (d) Flied out for Kessinger in sixth. (e) Struck out for McDowell in eighth. Two-base hits—Fregosi, Helms, Oliva, Wert. Stolen base—Aaron. Double plays—Carew, Fregosi, and Killebrew; Johnson and Powell. Wild pitch—Tiant. Left on bases—Americans 3, Nationals 8.

Managers: Dick Williams, Boston (A.L.); Al Schoendienst, St. Louis (N.L.).

Umpires—Crawford (N.L.), plate; Napp (A.L.), first base; Steiner (N.L.), second base; Kinnamon (A.L.), third base; Wendelstedt (N.L.), right field line; Odom (A.L.), left field line. Time—2:10. Attendance—48,321.

July 23, 1969   At Robert F. Kennedy Memorial Stadium, Washington

Nationals	AB	R	H	PO	A	E	Americans	AB	R	H	PO	A	E
Alou (Pirates), cf	4	1	2	5	0	0	Carew (Twins), 2b	3	0	0	0	2	0
Kessinger (Cubs), ss ...	3	0	0	0	0	0	Andrews (Red Sox), 2b	1	0	0	0	0	0
(e)Mays (Giants)	1	0	0	0	0	0	Jackson (Athletics),						
Menke (Astros), ss	1	0	0	1	0	0	cf-rf	2	0	0	2	0	0
Aaron (Braves), rf	4	1	1	0	0	0	Yastrzemski (Red Sox),						
Singer (Dodgers), p	0	0	0	0	0	0	lf	1	0	0	1	0	0
Beckert (Cubs), 2b	1	0	0	0	0	0	F.Robinson (Orioles), rf	2	0	0	0	0	0
McCovey (Giants), 1b ..	4	2	2	2	0	0	Blair (Orioles), cf	2	0	0	2	0	0
L.May (Reds), 1b	1	0	0	3	0	0	Powell (Orioles), 1b	4	0	1	9	1	0
Santo (Cubs), 3b	3	0	0	2	1	0	Howard (Senators), lf ..	1	1	1	0	0	1
Perez (Reds), 3b	1	0	0	1	1	0	(b)Smith (Red Sox), lf-rf	2	1	0	0	0	0
Jones (Mets), lf	4	2	2	3	0	0	Bando (Athletics), 3b ..	3	0	1	0	1	0
Rose (Reds), lf	1	0	0	2	0	0	Culp (Red Sox), p	0	0	0	0	0	0
Bench (Reds), c	3	2	2	4	0	0	(f)White (Yankees)	1	0	0	0	0	0
Hundley (Cubs), c	1	0	0	3	0	0	Petrocelli (Red Sox), ss	3	0	1	1	3	1
Millan (Braves), 2b	4	1	1	1	1	0	Fregosi (Angels), ss ...	1	0	0	0	0	0
Koosman (Mets), p	0	0	0	0	0	0	Freehan (Tigers), c ...	2	1	2	4	0	0
Dierker (Astros), p	0	0	0	0	0	0	Roseboro (Twins), c ...	1	0	0	6	0	0
Niekro (Braves), p	0	0	0	0	1	0	(g)C.May (White Sox) ..	1	0	0	0	0	0
Carlton (Cardinals), p ..	2	0	1	0	1	0	Stottlemyre (Yanks), p .	0	0	0	1	0	0
Gibson (Cardinals), p ..	0	0	0	0	0	0	Odom (Athletics), p	0	0	0	0	0	0
(d)Banks (Cubs)	1	0	0	0	0	0	Knowles (Senators), p .	0	0	0	0	0	0
Clemente (Pirates), rf ..	1	0	0	0	0	0	(a)Killebrew (Twins) ...	1	0	0	0	0	0
							McClain (Tigers), p	0	0	0	0	0	0
							(c)Mincher (Pilots)	1	0	0	0	0	0
							McNally (Orioles), p	0	0	0	0	0	0
							B.Robinson (Orioles),						
							3b	1	0	0	1	1	0
Totals	40	9	11	27	5	0	Totals	33	3	6	27	8	2

```
National League ...................... 1  2  5    1  0  0    0  0  0—9
American Legue ...................... 0  1  1    1  0  0    0  0  0—3
```

Pitching Summary

National League	IP	H	R	ER	BB	SO	American League	IP	H	R	ER	BB	SO
Carlton (W)	3	2	2	2	1	2	Stottlemyre (L)	2	4	3	2	0	1
Gibson	1	2	1	1	1	2	Odom	⅓	5	5	4	0	0
Singer	2	0	0	0	0	0	Knowles	⅔	0	0	0	0	0
Koosman	1⅔	1	0	0	0	1	McClain	1	1	1	1	2	2
Dierker	⅓	1	0	0	0	0	McNally	2	1	0	0	1	1
Niekro	1	0	0	0	0	2	McDowell	2	0	0	0	0	4
							Culp	1	0	0	0	0	2

(a) Flied out for Knowles in third. (b) Ran for Howard in fourth. (c) Struck out for McClain in fourth. (d) Lined out for Gibson in fifth. (e) Flied out for Kessinger in fifth. (f) Struck out for Culp in ninth. (g) Struck out for Roseboro in ninth. Runs batted in— Bench 2, Howard, McCovey 3, Millan 2, Carlton, Freehan 2. Two-base hits—Millan, Carlton, Petrocelli. Home runs—Bench, Howard, McCovey 2. Wild pitch—Stottlemyre. Left on bases—Nationals 7, Americans 5.

Managers: Mayo Smith, Detroit (A.L.); Al Schoendienst, St. Louis (N.L.).

Umpires—Flaherty (A.L.), plate; Donatelli (N.L.), first base; Stewart (A.L.), second base; Gorman (N.L.), third base; Springstead (A.L.), left field line; Venzon (N.L.), right field line. Time—2:38. Attendance—45,259.

July 14, 1970   At Riverfront Stadium, Cincinnati (Night)

Americans	AB	R	H	PO	A	E	Nationals	AB	R	H	PO	A	E
Aparicio (White Sox),							Mays (Giants), cf	3	0	0	3	0	0
ss	6	0	0	1	4	0	G. Perry (Giants), p	0	0	0	0	2	0
Yastrzemski (Red Sox),							(e)McCovey (Giants),						
cf-1b	6	1	4	8	0	0	1b	2	0	1	1	0	0
F.Robinson (Orioles), rf-							(g)Osteen (Dodgers), p	0	0	0	1	0	0
lf	3	0	0	1	0	0	(i)Torre (Cardinals)	1	0	0	0	0	0
Horton (Tigers), lf	2	1	2	1	0	0	Allen (Cardinals), 1b ...	3	0	0	4	0	0
Powell (Orioles), 1b	3	0	0	5	0	0	Gibson (Cardinals), p ..	0	0	0	0	0	0
Otis (Royals), cf	3	0	0	2	0	0	(h)Clemente (Pirates), rf	1	0	0	2	0	0
Killebrew (Twins), 3b ..	2	0	1	0	0	0	Aaron (Braves), rf	2	0	0	1	0	0
(b)Harper (Brewers), ..	0	0	0	0	0	0	Rose (Reds), rf-lf	3	1	1	3	0	0
B.Robinson (Orioles),							Perez (Reds), 3b	3	0	0	1	1	0
3b	3	1	2	1	1	0	Grabarkewitz (Dodgers),						
Howard (Senators), lf ..	2	0	0	0	0	0	3b	3	0	1	0	1	0
Oliva (Twins), rf	2	0	1	0	0	0	Carty (Braves), lf	1	0	0	0	0	0
D.Johnson (Orioles), 2b	5	0	1	5	1	0	Hickman (Cubs), lf-1b ..	4	0	1	6	1	0
Wright (Angels), p	0	0	0	0	0	0	Bench (Reds), c	3	0	0	5	1	0
Freehan (Tigers), c	1	0	0	4	0	0	Dietz (Giants), c	2	1	1	2	0	0
Fosse (Indians), c	2	1	1	7	0	0	Kessinger (Cubs), ss ...	2	0	2	0	0	0
Palmer (Orioles), p	1	0	0	0	0	0	Harrelson (Mets), ss ...	3	2	2	0	4	0
McDowell (Indians), p ..	1	0	0	0	3	0	Beckert (Cubs), 2b	2	0	0	2	1	0
(d)A.Johnson (Angels) .	1	0	0	0	0	0	Gaston (Padres), cf	2	0	0	2	0	0
J. Perry (Twins), p	0	0	0	0	0	0	Seaver (Mets), p	0	0	0	0	0	0
(f)Fregosi (Angels)	1	0	0	0	0	0	(a)Staub (Expos)	1	0	0	0	0	0
Hunter (Athletics), p ..	0	0	0	0	0	0	Merritt (Reds), p	0	0	0	0	0	0
Peterson (Yankees), p .	0	0	0	0	0	0	(c)Menke (Astros), 2b ..	0	0	0	2	1	0
Stottlemyre (Yankees),							Morgan (Astros), 2b ...	2	1	1	1	2	0
p	0	0	0	0	0	0							
Alomar (Angels), 2b ...	1	0	0	0	0	0							
Totals	44	4	12	35	11	0	Totals	43	5	10	36	14	0

```
American League  ..............  0 0 0   0 0 1   1 2 0   0 0 0—4
National League  ..............  0 0 0   0 0 0   1 0 3   0 0 1—5
```

Two out when winning run scored.

Pitching Summary

American League	IP	H	R	ER	BB	SO	National League	IP	H	R	ER	BB	SO
Palmer	3	1	0	0	1	3	Seaver	3	1	0	0	0	4
McDowell	3	1	0	3	3	3	Merritt	2	1	0	0	0	1
J. Perry	2	1	1	1	1	3	G. Perry	2	4	2	2	1	0
Hunter	⅓	3	3	3	0	0	Gibson	2	3	2	2	1	2
Peterson	0*	1	0	0	0	0	Osteen (W)	3	3	0	0	1	0
Stottlemyre	1⅔	0	0	0	0	2							
Wright (L)	1⅔	3	1	1	0	0							

* Pitched to one batter in ninth.

(a) Flied out for Seaver in third. (b) Ran for Killebrew in fifth. (c) Walked for Merritt in fifth. (d) Hit into force play for McDowell in seventh. (e) Grounded into double play for G. Perry in seventh. (f) Flied out for J. Perry in ninth. (g) Ran for McCovey in ninth. (h) Hit sacrifice fly for Gibson in ninth. (i) Grounded out for Osteen in twelfth. Runs batted in—Yastrzemski, Fosse, B. Robinson 2, Dietz, McCovey, Clemente, Hickman. Two-base hits—Oliva, Yastrzemski. Three-base hit—B. Robinson. Home run—Dietz. Sacrifice flies—Fosse, Clemente. Caught stealing—Harper. Hit by pitcher—By J. Perry (Menke). Left on bases—Americans 9, Nationals 10.

Managers: Earl Weaver, Baltimore (A.L.); Gil Hodges, New York (N.L.).

Umpires—Barlick (N.L.), plate; Rice (A.L.), first base; Secory (N.L.), second base; Haller (A.L.), third base; Dezelan (N.L.), left field; Goetz (A.L.), right field. Time—3:19. Attendance—51,838.

July 13, 1971   At Tiger Stadium, Detroit (Night)

Nationals	AB	R	H	PO	A	E	Americans	AB	R	H	PO	A	E
Mays (Giants), cf	2	0	0	0	0	0	Carew (Twins), 2b	1	1	0	1	2	0
Clemente (Pirates), rf ..	2	1	1	1	0	0	Rojas (Royals), 2b	1	0	0	1	1	0
Millan (Braves), 2b	0	0	0	1	1	0	Murcer (Yankees), cf ..	3	0	1	1	0	0
Aaron (Braves), rf	2	1	1	0	0	0	Cuellar (Orioles), p	0	0	0	0	0	0
May (Reds), 1b	1	0	0	6	0	0	(d)Buford (Orioles)	1	0	0	0	0	0
Torre (Cardinals), 3b ...	3	0	0	1	0	0	Lolich (Tigers), p	0	0	0	0	3	0
(f)Santo (Cubs), 3b	1	0	0	0	1	0	Yastrzemski (Red Sox),						
Stargell (Pirates), lf	2	1	0	2	0	0	lf	3	0	0	0	0	0
(g)Brock (Cardinals) ...	1	0	0	0	0	0	F.Robinson (Orioles), rf	2	1	1	2	0	0
McCovey (Giants), 1b ..	2	0	0	4	0	0	Kaline (Tigers), rf	2	1	1	2	0	0
Marichal (Giants), p	0	0	0	0	1	0	Cash (Tigers), 1b	2	0	0	7	0	0
Kessinger (Cubs), ss ..	2	0	0	1	1	0	Killebrew (Twins), 1b ..	2	1	1	4	0	0
Bench (Reds), c	4	1	2	5	0	0	B.Robinson (Orioles),						
Beckert (Cubs), 2b	3	0	0	0	5	0	3b	3	0	1	1	3	0
Rose (Reds), rf	0	0	0	0	0	0	Freehan (Tigers), c	3	0	0	6	1	0
Harrelson (Mets), ss ...	2	0	0	1	2	0	Munson (Yankees), cf ..	0	0	0	1	0	0
Jenkins (Cubs), p	0	0	0	0	0	0	Aparicio (Red Sox), ss .	3	1	1	1	2	0
(c)Colbert (Padres)	1	0	0	0	0	0	Blue (Athletics), p	0	0	0	0	0	0
Wilson (Astros), p	0	0	0	0	0	0	(a)Jackson (Athletics) ..	1	1	1	0	0	0
Ellis (Pirates), p	1	0	0	0	0	0	Palmer (Orioles), p	0	0	0	0	0	0
Davis (Dodgers), cf ...	1	0	1	2	0	0	(b)Howard (Senators) ..	1	0	0	0	0	0
(e)Bonds (Giants), cf ...	1	0	0	0	0	0	Otis (Royals), cf	1	0	0	0	0	0
Totals	31	4	5	24	11	0	Totals	29	6	7	27	12	0

```
National League .....................  0  2  1    0  0  0    0  1  0—4
American League ....................  0  0  4    0  0  2    0  0  x—6
```

Pitching Summary

National League	IP	H	R	ER	BB	SO	American League	IP	H	R	ER	BB	SO
Ellis (L)	3	4	4	4	1	2	Blue (W)	3	2	3	3	0	3
Marichal	2	0	0	0	1	1	Palmer	2	1	0	0	0	2
Jenkins	1	3	2	2	0	0	Cuellar	2	1	0	0	1	2
Wilson	2	0	0	0	1	2	Lolich	2	1	1	1	0	1

(a) Homered for Blue in third. (b) Grounded out for Palmer in fifth. (c) Struck out for Jenkins in seventh. (d) Struck out for Cuellar in seventh. (e) Struck out for Davis in eighth. (f) Grounded out for Torre in eighth. (g) Bunted for Stargell in ninth and was thrown out. Runs batted in—Bench 2, Jackson 2, F. Robinson 2, Aaron, Killebrew 2, Clemente. Home runs—Bench, Aaron, Jackson, F. Robinson, Killebrew, Clemente. Double plays—B. Robinson, Rojas, and Killebrew; Beckert, Kessinger, and May; Santo, Millan, and May. Hit by pitcher—By Blue (Stargell). Left on bases—Nationals 2, Americans 2.

Managers: Earl Weaver, Baltimore (A.L.); George "Sparky" Anderson, Cincinnati (N.L.).

Umpires—Umont (A.L.), plate; Pryor (N.L.), first base; O'Donnell (A.L.), second base; Harvey (N.L.), third base; Denkinger (A.L.), right field; Colosi (N.L.), left field. Time—2:05. Attendance—53,559.

July 23, 1972   At Atlanta Stadium, Atlanta (Night)

Americans	AB	R	H	PO	A	E	Nationals	AB	R	H	PO	A	E
Carew (Twins), 2b	2	0	1	2	3	0	Morgan (Reds), 2b	4	0	1	3	5	0
(c)Rojas (Royals), 2b ..	1	1	1	3	1	0	Mays (Mets), cf	2	0	0	2	0	0
Murcer (Yankees), cf ..	3	0	0	1	0	0	Cedeno (Astros), cf	2	1	1	0	0	0
Scheinblum (Royals), rf	1	0	0	1	0	0	Aaron (Braves), rf	3	1	1	0	0	0
Jackson (Athletics),							Oliver (Pirates), rf	1	0	0	0	0	0
rf-cf	4	0	2	5	0	0	Stargell (Pirates), lf	1	0	0	0	0	0
Allen (White Sox), 1b ..	3	0	0	4	0	0	Williams (Cubs), lf	2	1	1	0	0	0
Cash (Tigers), 1b	1	0	0	3	0	0	Bench (Reds), c	2	0	1	3	0	0
Yastrzemski (Red Sox),							Sanguillen (Pirates), c .	2	0	1	6	0	0
lf	3	0	0	3	0	0	May (Astros), 1b	4	0	1	13	2	0
Rudi (Athletics), lf	1	0	1	0	0	0	Torre (Cardinals), 3b ...	3	0	1	1	2	0
Grich (Orioles), ss	4	0	0	0	3	0	Santo (Cubs), 3b	1	0	0	0	0	0
Robinson (Orioles), 3b .	2	0	0	0	1	0	Kessinger (Cubs), ss ...	2	0	0	0	0	0
Bando (Athletics), 3b ..	2	0	0	1	1	0	Carlton (Phillies), p	0	0	0	0	0	0
Freehan (Tigers), c	1	1	0	3	0	0	Stoneman (Expos), p ..	1	0	0	0	0	0
Fisk (Red Sox), c	2	1	1	2	0	0	McGraw (Mets), p	0	0	0	0	0	0
Palmer (Orioles), p	0	0	0	0	0	0	(e)Colbert (Padres)	0	1	0	0	0	0
Lolich (Tigers), p	1	0	0	0	0	0	Gibson (Cardinals), p ..	0	0	0	1	0	0
Perry (Indians), p	0	0	0	0	0	0	Blass (Pirates), p	0	0	0	0	0	0
(b)Smith (Red Sox)	1	0	0	0	0	0	(a)Beckert (Cubs)	1	0	0	0	0	0
Wood (White Sox), p ...	0	0	0	0	0	0	Sutton (Dodgers), p	0	0	0	0	0	0
(d)Piniella (Royals)	1	0	0	0	0	0	Speier (Giants), ss	2	0	0	1	5	0
McNally (Royals), p	0	0	0	0	1	0							
Totals	33	3	6	28	10	0	Totals	33	4	8	30	14	0

```
American League ..................... 0 0 1   0 0 0   0 2 0   0—3
National League ...................... 0 0 0   0 0 2   0 0 1   1—4
```

One out when winning run scored.

Pitching Summary

American League	IP	H	R	ER	BB	SO	National League	IP	H	R	ER	BB	SO
Palmer	3	1	0	0	1	2	Gibson	2	1	0	0	0	0
Lolich	2	1	0	0	0	1	Blass	1	1	1	1	1	0
Perry	2	3	2	2	0	1	Sutton	2	1	0	0	0	2
Wood	2	2	1	1	1	1	Carlton	1	0	0	0	1	0
McNally (L)	⅓	1	1	1	1	0	Stoneman	2	2	2	2	0	2
							McGraw (W)	2	1	0	0	0	4

(a) Flied out for Blass in third. (b) Struck out for Perry in eighth. (c) Homered for Carew in eighth. (d) Grounded out for Wood in tenth. (e) Walked for McGraw in tenth. Runs batted in—Carew, Aaron 2, Rojas 2, May, Morgan. Two-base hits—Jackson, Rudi. Home runs—Aaron, Rojas. Sacrifice hits—Palmer, Speier. Stolen base—Morgan. Double plays—Carew and Allen; May unassisted; May, Speier, and May; Bando, Rojas, and Cash. Left on bases—Americans 3, Nationals 5.

Managers: Earl Weaver, Baltimore (A.L.); Danny Murtaugh, Pittsburgh (N.L.)

Umpires—Landes (N.L.), plate; DiMuro (A.L.), first base; Weyer (N.L.), second base; Neudecker (A.L.), third base; Dale (N.L.), left field; Kunkel (A.L.), right field. Time—2:26. Attendance—53,107.

July 24, 1973   At Royals Stadium, Kansas City (Night)

Nationals	AB	R	H	PO	A	E	Americans	AB	R	H	PO	A	E
Rose (Reds), lf	3	1	0	1	0	0	Campaneris (Athletics),						
Twitchell (Phillies), p ...	0	0	0	0	0	0	ss	3	0	0	1	2	0
Giusti (Pirates), p	0	0	0	0	0	0	Brinkman (Tigers), ss ..	1	0	0	1	1	0
(j)Mota (Dodgers), lf ...	1	0	0	0	0	0	Carew (Twins), 2b	3	0	0	5	1	0
Brewer (Dodgers), p ...	0	0	0	0	0	0	Rojas (Royals), 2b	0	0	0	1	1	0
Morgan (Reds), 2b	3	2	1	2	2	0	Mayberry (Royals), 1b ..	3	0	1	8	0	0
Johnson (Braves), 2b ..	1	0	0	1	1	0	Jackson (Athletics), rf ..	4	1	1	0	0	0
Cedeno (Astros), cf	3	0	1	3	0	0	Blair (Orioles), cf	0	0	0	1	0	0
Russell (Dodgers), ss ..	2	0	0	0	2	0	Otis (Royals), cf	2	0	2	0	0	0
Aaron (Braves), 1b	2	0	1	3	1	0	May (Brewers), cf-rf ...	2	0	0	0	0	0
Torre (Cards), 1b-3b ...	3	0	0	5	0	0	Murcer (Yankees), lf ...	3	0	0	0	1	0
Williams (Cubs), rf	2	0	1	0	0	0	Fisk (Red Sox), c	2	0	0	3	0	0
Bonds (Giants), rf	2	1	2	0	0	0	Munson (Yankees), c ..	2	0	0	5	1	0
Bench (Reds), c	3	1	1	3	0	0	Robinson (Orioles), 3b .	2	0	0	1	3	0
(f)Simmons (Cards), c ..	1	0	0	1	1	0	Bando (Athletics), 3b ..	1	0	0	0	1	0
Santo (Cubs), 3b	1	1	1	0	1	0	Nelson (Rangers), 3b ..	0	0	0	1	0	0
(h)Colbert (Padres)	1	0	0	0	0	0	(k)Horton (Tigers)	1	0	0	0	0	0
Fairly (Expos), 1b	0	0	0	4	0	0	Hunter (Athletics), p ...	0	0	0	0	0	0
Speier (Giants), ss	2	0	0	1	1	0	Holtzman (Athletics), p .	0	0	0	0	0	0
(d)Stargell (Pirates), lf ..	1	0	0	1	0	0	Blyleven (Twins), p	0	0	0	0	0	0
(i)Mays (Mets)	1	0	0	0	0	0	(b)Bell (Indians)	1	0	1	0	0	0
Seaver (Mets), p	0	0	0	0	1	0	Singer (Angels), p	0	0	0	0	1	0
Watson (Astros), lf	0	0	0	0	0	0	(c)Kelly (White Sox) ...	1	0	0	0	0	0
Wise (Cardinals), p	0	0	0	1	0	0	Ryan (Angels), p	0	0	0	0	0	0
(a)Evans (Braves)	0	0	0	0	0	0	(g)Spencer (Rangers) ..	1	0	0	0	0	0
Osteen (Dodgers), p ...	0	0	0	0	1	0	Lyle (Yankees), p	0	0	0	0	0	0
Sutton (Dodgers), p	0	0	0	0	1	0	Fingers (Athletics), p ...	0	0	0	0	0	0
(e)Davis (Dodgers), cf ..	2	1	2	2	1	0							
Totals	34	7	10	27	12	0	Totals	32	1	5	27	12	0

National League	0	0	2		1	2	2		0	0	0—7
American League	0	1	0		0	0	0		0	0	0—1

Pitching Summary

National League	IP	H	R	ER	BB	SO	American League	IP	H	R	ER	BB	SO
Wise (W)	2	2	1	0	1	1	Hunter	1⅓	1	0	0	0	1
Osteen	2	2	0	0	1	1	Holtzman	⅔	1	0	0	0	0
Sutton	1	0	0	0	0	0	Blyleven (L)	1	2	2	2	2	0
Twitchell	1	1	0	0	0	1	Singer	2	3	3	3	1	2
Giusti	1	0	0	0	0	0	Ryan	2	2	2	2	2	2
Seaver	1	0	0	0	1	0	Lyle	1	1	0	0	0	1
Brewer	1	0	0	0	1	2	Fingers	1	0	0	0	0	0

(a) Walked for Wise in third. (b) Tripled for Blyleven in third. (c) Popped out for Singer in fifth. (d) Struck out for Speier in sixth. (e) Homered for Sutton in sixth. (f) Called out on strikes for Bench in seventh. (g) Flied out for Ryan in seventh. (h) Fouled out for Santo in eighth. (i) Struck out for Stargell in eighth. (j) Grounded into force play for Giusti in eighth. (k) Struck out for Nelson in ninth. Runs batted in—Otis, Cedeno, Aaron, Bench, Bonds, Davis 2. Two-base hits—Jackson, Morgan, Mayberry. Three-base hit—Bell. Home runs—Bench, Bonds, Davis. Sacrifice hit—Osteen. Stolen base—Otis. Double play—Rojas, Brinkman, and Mayberry. Passed ball—Fisk. Left on bases—Nationals 6, Americans 7.

Managers: Dick Williams, Oakland (A.L.); George "Sparky" Anderson, Cincinnati (N.L.).

Umpires—Chylak (A.L.), plate; Burkhart (N.L.), first base; Barnett (A.L.), second base; W. Williams (N.L.), third base; Luciano (A.L.), left field line; Engel (N.L.), right field line. Time—2:45. Attendance—40,849.

July 23, 1974   At Three Rivers Stadium, Pittsburgh (Night)

Americans	AB	R	H	PO	A	E	Nationals	AB	R	H	PO	A	E
Carew (Twins), 2b	1	1	0	0	1	0	Rose (Reds), lf	2	0	0	1	0	0
Grich (Orioles), 2b	3	0	1	0	2	0	Brett (Pirates), p	0	0	0	0	0	0
Campaneris (Athletics),							(c)Brock (Cardinals) ...	1	1	1	0	0	0
ss	4	0	0	2	3	0	Smith (Cardinals), rf ...	2	1	1	2	0	0
Jackson (Athletics), rf ..	3	0	0	3	0	0	Morgan (Reds), 2b	2	0	1	3	4	0
Allen (White Sox), 1b ..	2	0	1	2	0	0	(g)Cash (Phillies), 2b ..	1	0	0	0	1	0
Yastrzemski (Red Sox),							Aaron (Braves), rf	2	0	0	0	0	0
1b	1	0	0	5	0	0	Cedeno (Astros), cf	2	0	0	2	0	0
Murcer (Yankees), cf ..	2	0	0	0	0	0	Bench (Reds), c	3	1	2	7	0	1
Hendrick (Indians), cf ..	2	0	1	3	0	0	Grote (Mets), c	0	0	0	1	0	0
Burroughs (Rangers), lf	0	0	0	1	0	0	Wynn (Dodgers), cf-rf ..	3	1	1	0	0	0
Rudi (Athletics), lf	2	0	0	1	0	0	Matlack (Mets), p	0	0	0	0	0	0
B.Robinson (Orioles), 3b							Grubb (Padres), lf	.1	0	0	0	0	0
....	3	0	0	0	0	0	Garvey (Dodgers), 1b ..	4	1	2	6	2	0
(h)Mayberry (Orioles) ..	1	0	0	0	0	0	Cey (Dodgers), 3b	2	0	1	0	0	0
Fingers (Athletics), p ...	0	0	0	0	0	0	(e)Schmidt (Phillies), 3b	0	1	0	0	1	0
Munson (Yankees), c ..	3	1	1	7	0	1	Bowa (Phillies), ss	2	0	0	2	0	0
Perry (Indians), p	0	0	0	0	0	0	(f)Perez (Reds)	1	0	0	0	0	0
(b)Kaline (Tigers)	1	0	0	0	0	0	Kessinger (Cubs), ss ...	1	1	1	1	0	0
Tiant (Red Sox), p	0	0	0	0	0	0	Messersmith (Dodgers),						
(d)F.Robinson (Angels)	1	0	0	0	0	0	p	0	0	0	2	1	0
Hunter (Athletics), p ...	0	0	0	0	0	0	(a)Garr (Braves), lf	3	0	0	0	0	0
Chalk (Angels), 3b	1	0	0	0	0	0	McGlothlen (Cardinals),						
							p	0	0	0	0	0	0
							Marshall (Dodgers), p ..	1	0	0	0	1	0
Totals	30	2	4	24	6	1	Totals	33	7	10	27	10	1

```
American League ..................... 0  0  2    0  0  0    0  0  0—2
National League  ..................... 0  1  0    2  1  0    1  2  x—7
```

Pitching Summary

American League	IP	H	R	ER	BB	SO	National League	IP	H	R	ER	BB	SO
Perry	3	3	1	1	0	4	Messersmith	3	2	2	2	3	4
Tiant (L)	2	4	3	2	1	0	Brett (W)..............	2	1	0	0	1	0
Hunter	2	2	1	1	1	3	Matlack	1	1	0	0	1	0
Fingers	1	1	2	2	1	0	McGlothlen	1	0	0	0	0	1
							Marshall	2	0	0	0	1	2

(a) Struck out for Messersmith in third. (b) Fouled out for Perry in fourth. (c) Singled for Brett in fifth. (d) Hit into force play for Tiant in sixth. (e) Walked for Cey in sixth. (f) Struck out for Bowa in sixth. (g) Flied out for Morgan in seventh. (h) Grounded out for B. Robinson in eighth. Runs batted in—Cey 2, Allen, Garvey, Morgan, Smith, Kessinger. Two-base hits—Cey, Munson, Morgan, Garvey. Three-base hit—Kessinger. Home run—Smith. Sacrifice fly—Morgan. Sacrifice hit—Perry. Stolen bases—Carew, Brock. Double plays—none. Wild pitch—Fingers. Left on bases— Americans 8, Nationals 6.

Managers: Dick Williams, California (A.L.); Lawrence "Yogi" Berra, New York (N.L.)

Umpires—Sudol (N.L.), plate; Frantz (A.L.), first base; Vargo (N.L.), second base; Anthony (A.L.), third base; Kibler (N.L.), left field; Maloney (A.L.), right field. Time— 2:37. Attendance—50,706.

July 15, 1975   At Milwaukee County Stadium, Milwaukee (Night)

Nationals	AB	R	H	PO	A	E	Americans	AB	R	H	PO	A	E
Rose (Reds), rf-lf	4	0	2	4	0	0	Bonds (Yankees), cf ...	3	0	0	0	1	0
Carter (Expos), lf	0	0	0	1	0	0	Scott (Brewers), 1b	2	0	0	5	0	0
Brock (Cardinals), lf ...	3	1	1	2	0	0	Carew (Twins), 2b	5	0	1	3	1	0
Murcer (Giants), rf	2	0	0	1	0	0	Munson (Yankees), c ..	2	0	1	1	1	0
Jones (Padres), p	0	0	0	0	1	0	(d)Washington						
Morgan (Reds), 2b	4	0	1	0	1	0	(Athletics), cf-lf	1	0	1	1	0	0
Cash (Phillies), 2b	1	0	0	0	0	0	Jackson (Athletics), rf ..	3	0	1	2	0	0
Bench (Reds), c	4	0	1	10	1	0	Dent (White Sox), ss ...	1	0	0	0	1	0
Garvey (Dodgers), 1b ..	3	1	2	4	1	0	Rudi (Athletics), lf	3	0	1	5	0	0
(i)Perez (Reds), 1b	1	0	0	1	1	0	(e)Hendrick (Indians), rf	1	1	1	0	0	0
Wynn (Dodgers), cf	2	1	1	1	0	0	Nettles (Yankees), 3b ..	4	0	1	2	2	0
Smith (Cardinals), cf-rf .	2	1	1	0	0	0	Tenace (Athletics), 1b-c	3	1	0	4	0	1
Cey (Dodgers), 3b	3	0	1	0	1	0	Campaneris (Athletics),						
Seaver (Mets), p	0	0	0	0	0	0	ss	2	0	2	3	2	0
Matlack (Mets), p	0	0	0	0	1	0	(f)Lynn (Red Sox), cf ..	2	0	0	1	0	0
(j)Oliver (Pirates), cf ...	1	1	1	0	0	0	Blue (Athletics), p	0	0	0	0	1	0
Concepcion (Reds), ss .	2	0	1	1	1	1	(a)Aaron (Brewers)	1	0	0	0	0	0
(h)Luzinski (Phillies) ...	1	0	0	0	0	0	Busby (Royals), p	0	0	0	0	0	0
Bowa (Phillies), ss	0	1	0	2	0	0	(c)Hargrove, (Rangers)	1	0	0	0	0	0
Reuss (Pirates), p	1	0	0	0	0	0	Kaat (White Sox), p	0	0	0	0	0	0
(b)Watson (Astros)	1	0	0	0	0	0	(g)Yastrzemski (Red						
Sutton (Dodgers), p	1	0	0	0	0	0	Sox)	1	1	1	0	0	0
Madlock (Cubs), 3b	2	0	1	0	0	0	Hunter (Yankees), p ...	0	0	0	0	0	0
							Gossage (White Sox), p	0	0	0	0	0	0
							(k)McRae (Royals)	1	0	0	0	0	0
Totals	37	6	13	27	6	1	Totals	36	3	10	27	9	1

National League	0	2	1	0	0	0	0	0	3—6
American League	0	0	0	0	0	3	0	0	0—3

Pitching Summary

National League	IP	H	R	ER	BB	SO	American League	IP	H	R	ER	BB	SO
Reuss	3	3	0	0	0	2	Blue	2	5	2	2	0	1
Sutton	2	3	0	0	0	1	Busby	2	4	1	1	0	0
Seaver	1	2	3	3	1	2	Kaat	2	0	0	0	0	0
Matlack (W)	2	2	0	0	0	4	Hunter (L)	2	3	2	2	0	2
Jones	1	0	0	0	0	1	Gossage	1	1	1	1	0	0

(a) Lined out for Blue in second. (b) Flied out for Reuss in fourth. (c) Flied out for Busby in fourth. (d) Ran for Munson in fifth. (e) Ran for Rudi in sixth. (f) Flied out for Campaneris in sixth. (g) Homered for Kaat in sixth. (h) Struck out for Concepcion in seventh. (i) Called out on strikes for Garvey in eighth. (j) Doubled for Matlack in ninth. (k) Grounded out for Gossage in ninth. Runs batted in—Garvey, Wynn, Bench, Yastrzemski 3, Madlock 2, Rose. Two-base hit—Oliver. Home runs—Garvey, Wynn, Yastrzemski. Sacrifice fly—Rose. Stolen bases—Brock, Washington, Hendrick, Nettles. Caught stealing—Concepcion, Washington. Hit by pitcher—By Reuss (Munson), by Gossage (Bowa). Balk—Busby. Passed ball—Bench. Double play—none. Left on bases—Nationals 6, Americans 8.

Managers: Alvin Dark, Oakland (A.L.); Walter Alston, Los Angeles (N.L.)

Umpires—Haller (A.L.), plate; Pelekoudas (N.L.), first base; Springstead (A.L.), second base; Froemming (N.L.), third base; Goetz (A.L.), left field; McSherry (N.L.), right field. Time—2:35. Attendance—51,480.

July 13, 1976   At Veterans Stadium, Philadelphia (Night)

Americans	AB	R	H	PO	A	E	Nationals	AB	R	H	PO	A	E
LeFlore (Tigers), lf	2	0	1	2	0	0	Rose (Reds), 3b	3	1	2	0	1	0
Yastrzemski (Red Sox),							Oliver (Pirates), rf-lf	1	0	0	1	0	0
lf	2	0	0	0	0	0	Garvey (Dodgers), 1b ..	3	1	1	6	0	0
Carew (Twins), 1b	3	0	0	9	2	0	Cash (Phillies), 2b	1	1	1	1	1	0
Brett (Royals), 3b	2	0	0	0	1	0	Morgan (Reds), 2b	3	1	1	2	3	0
Money (Brewers), 3b ...	1	0	0	0	1	0	Perez (Reds), 1b	0	0	0	2	0	0
Munson (Yankees), c ..	2	0	0	4	0	0	Foster (Reds), cf-rf	3	1	1	3	0	0
Fisk (Red Sox), c	1	0	0	1	0	0	Montefusco (Giants), p .	0	0	0	0	0	0
(d)Chambliss (Yankees)	1	0	0	0	0	0	Russell (Dodgers), ss ..	1	0	0	1	2	0
Lynn (Red Sox), cf	3	1	1	0	0	0	Luzinski (Phillies), lf ...	3	0	0	0	0	0
(e)Otis (Royals)	1	0	0	0	0	0	Griffey (Reds), rf	1	1	1	1	0	0
Harrah (Rangers), ss ...	2	0	0	0	0	0	Bench (Reds), c	2	0	1	1	0	0
Belanger (Orioles), ss ..	1	0	0	1	1	0	Cedeno (Astros), cf	2	1	1	1	0	0
Patek (Royals), ss	0	0	0	0	1	0	Kingman (Mets), rf	2	0	0	1	0	0
Staub (Tigers), rf	2	0	2	1	0	0	Boone (Phillies), c	2	0	0	5	0	0
Tiant (Red Sox), p	0	0	0	0	0	0	Concepcion (Reds), ss .	2	0	1	2	3	0
(c)Wynegar (Twins)	0	0	0	0	0	0	Bowa (Phillies), ss	1	0	0	2	1	0
Tanana (Angels), p	0	0	0	1	0	0	Rhoden (Dodgers), p ..	0	0	0	0	0	0
Grich (Orioles), 2b	2	0	0	1	1	0	Cey (Dodgers), 3b	0	0	0	0	0	0
Garner (Athletics), 2b ..	1	0	0	1	1	0	Jones (Padres), p	1	0	0	1	1	0
Fidrych (Tigers), p	0	0	0	1	0	0	Seaver (Mets), p	1	0	0	0	0	0
(a)McRae (Royals)	1	0	0	0	0	0	Schmidt (Phillies), 3b ..	1	0	0	0	0	0
Hunter (Yankees), p ...	0	0	0	0	0	0	Forsch (Astros), p	0	0	0	0	0	0
(b)Rivers (Yankees), rf .	2	0	1	2	0	0							
Totals	29	1	5	24	8	0	Totals	33	7	10	27	12	0

American League	0 0 0	1 0 0	0 0 0—1
National League	2 0 2	0 0 0	0 3 x—7

Pitching Summary

American League	IP	H	R	ER	BB	SO	National League	IP	H	R	ER	BB	SO
Fidrych (L)	2	4	2	2	0	1	Jones (W)	3	2	0	0	1	1
Hunter	2	2	2	2	0	3	Seaver	2	2	1	1	0	1
Tiant	2	1	0	0	0	1	Montefusco	2	0	0	0	2	2
Tanana	2	3	3	3	1	0	Rhoden	1	1	0	0	0	0
							Forsch	1	0	0	0	0	1

(a) Grounded out for Fidrych in third. (b) Struck out for Hunter in fifth. (c) Walked for Tiant in seventh. (d) Grounded out for Fisk in ninth. (e) Struck out for Lynn in ninth. Runs batted in—Garvey, Foster 3, Lynn, Griffey, Cedeno 2. Three-base hits—Garvey, Rose. Home runs—Foster, Lynn, Cedeno. Stolen base—Carew. Double plays—Morgan, Concepcion, and Garvey; Morgan, Bowa, and Garvey; Cash, Russell, and Perez; Money, Garner, and Carew. Passed ball—Munson. Left on bases—Americans 4, Nationals 3.

Managers: Darrell Johnson, Boston (A.L.); George "Sparky" Anderson, Cincinnati (N.L.)

Umpires—Wendelstedt (N.L.), plate; Neudecker (A.L.), first base; Olsen (N.L.), second base; Denkinger (A.L.), third base; Davidson (N.L.), left field; Evans (A.L.), right field. Time—2:12. Attendance—63,974.

July 19, 1977   At Yankee Stadium, New York (Night)

Nationals	AB	R	H	PO	A	E
Morgan (Reds), 2b	4	1	1	1	0	0
Trillo (Cubs), 2b	1	0	0	0	1	0
Garvey (Dodgers), 1b ..	3	1	1	1	0	0
Montanez (Braves), 1b .	2	0	0	6	1	0
Parker (Pirates), rf	3	1	1	2	0	0
Templeton (Cardinals),						
ss	1	1	1	1	2	1
Foster (Reds), cf	3	1	1	2	0	1
Morales (Cubs), cf	0	1	0	1	0	0
Luzinski (Phillies), lf ...	2	1	1	2	0	0
Winfield (Padres), lf ...	2	0	2	1	0	0
Cey (Dodgers), 3b	2	0	0	0	0	0
Seaver (Reds), p	0	0	0	0	1	0
(e)Smith (Dodgers)	1	0	1	0	0	0
(f)Schmidt (Phillies)	0	0	0	0	0	0
R.Reuschel (Cubs), p ..	0	0	0	0	0	0
Stearns (Mets), c	0	0	0	2	0	0
Bench (Reds), c	2	0	0	4	0	0
Lavelle (Giants), p	0	0	0	0	0	0
(c)Rose (Reds), 3b	2	0	0	0	1	0
Concepcion (Reds), ss .	1	0	0	1	1	0
Valentine (Expos), rf ...	1	0	0	0	0	0
Sutton (Dodgers), p	0	0	0	0	1	0
Simmons (Cardinals), c	3	0	0	5	0	0
Gossage (Pirates), p ...	0	0	0	0	0	0
Totals	33	7	9	27	8	1

Americans	AB	R	H	PO	A	E
Carew (Twins), 1b	3	1	1	7	0	0
Scott (Red Sox), 1b	2	1	1	4	0	0
Randolph (Yankees),						
2b	5	0	1	2	6	0
Brett (Royals), 3b	2	0	0	2	1	0
Campbell (Red Sox), p ..	0	0	0	0	0	0
(d)Fairly (Blue Jays) ...	1	0	0	0	0	0
Lyle (Yankees), p	0	0	0	0	0	0
(g)Munson (Yankees) ..	1	0	0	0	0	0
Yastrzemski (Red Sox),						
cf	2	0	0	0	0	0
Lynn (Red Sox), cf	1	1	0	2	0	0
Zisk (White Sox), lf	3	0	2	0	0	0
Singleton (Orioles), rf ..	0	0	0	0	0	0
Jackson (Yankees), rf ..	2	0	1	0	0	0
Rice (Red Sox), rf-lf ..	2	0	1	1	0	0
Fisk (Red Sox), c	2	0	0	6	1	0
Wynegar (Twins), c	2	1	1	3	0	0
Burleson (Red Sox), ss	2	0	0	0	0	0
Campaneris (Rangers),						
ss	1	1	0	0	1	0
Palmer (Orioles), p	0	0	0	0	0	0
Kern (Indians), p	0	0	0	0	0	0
(a)Jones (Mariners)	1	0	0	0	0	0
Eckersley (Indians), p ..	0	0	0	0	1	0
(b)Hisle (Twins)	1	0	0	0	0	0
LaRoche (Angels), p ...	0	0	0	0	0	0
Nettles (Yankees), 3b ..	2	0	0	0	1	0
Totals	35	5	8	27	11	0

```
National League ....................  4 0 1   0 0 0   0 2 0—7
American League ....................  0 0 0   0 0 2   1 0 2—5
```

Pitching Summary

National League	IP	H	R	ER	BB	SO
Sutton (W)	3	1	0	0	1	4
Lavelle	2	1	0	0	0	2
Seaver	2	4	3	2	1	2
R. Reuschel	1	1	0	0	0	0
Gossage	1	1	2	2	1	2

American League	IP	H	R	ER	BB	SO
Palmer (L)	2*	5	5	5	1	3
Kern	1	0	0	0	0	2
Eckersley	2	0	0	0	0	1
LaRoche	1	1	0	0	1	0
Campbell	1	0	0	0	1	2
Lyle	2	3	2	2	0	1

* Pitched to one batter in third.

(a) Flied out for Kern in third. (b) Flied out for Eckersley in fifth. (c) Flied out for Lavelle in sixth. (d) Struck out for Campbell in seventh. (e) Singled for Seaver in eighth. (f) Ran for Smith in eighth. (g) Struck out for Lyle in ninth. Runs batted in—Morgan, Foster, Luzinski, 2, Garvey, Zisk 2, Randolph, Winfield 2, Scott 2. Two-base hits—Foster, Winfield, Zisk, Templeton. Home runs—Morgan, Luzinski, Garvey, Scott. Sacrifice hit—Sutton. Caught stealing—Concepcion. Double plays—Randolph and Scott; Montanez, Templeton, and Montanez. Wild pitches—Palmer, Lyle. Hit by pitch—By Lyle (Morales), by R. Reuschel (Singleton). Left on bases—Nationals 4, Americans 7.

Managers: Billy Martin, New York (A.L.); George "Sparky" Anderson, Cincinnati (N.L.)

Umpires—Kunkel (A.L.), plate; Harvey (N.L.), first base; Phillips (A.L.), second base; Stello (N.L.), third base; Pulli (N.L.), left field; Brinkman (A.L.), right field. Time—2:34. Attendance—56,683.

July 11, 1978   At San Diego Stadium, San Diego (Night)

Americans	AB	R	H	PO	A	E	Nationals	AB	R	H	PO	A	E
Carew (Twins), 1b	4	2	2	6	1	0	Rose (Reds), 3b	4	0	1	1	0	0
Brett (Royals), 3b	3	1	2	0	2	0	(d)Lopes (Dodgers), 2b	1	0	1	0	1	0
Gossage (Yankees), p .	0	0	0	0	0	0	Morgan (Reds), 2b	3	1	0	2	1	0
Rice (Red Sox), lf	4	0	0	2	0	0	Clark (Giants), rf	1	0	0	0	0	0
Lemon (White Sox), lf ..	0	0	0	0	0	1	Foster (Reds), cf	2	1	0	2	0	0
Zisk (Rangers), rf	2	0	1	0	0	0	Luzinski (Phillies), lf ...	2	0	1	0	0	0
Evans (Red Sox), rf	1	0	0	3	0	0	Fingers (Padres), p	1	0	0	0	1	0
Sundberg (Rangers), c .	0	0	0	2	1	0	(e)Stargell (Pirates)	1	0	0	0	0	0
(f)Thompson (Tigers) ..	1	0	0	0	0	0	Sutter (Cubs), p	0	0	0	0	0	0
Lynn (Red Sox), cf	4	0	1	3	0	0	Niekro (Braves), p	0	0	0	0	0	0
Money (Brewers), 2b ...	2	0	0	1	1	0	Garvey (Dodgers), 1b ..	3	1	2	7	1	0
White (Royals), 2b	1	0	0	1	2	0	Simmons (Cardinals), c	3	0	1	4	1	0
(g)Porter (Royals)	1	0	0	0	0	0	Concepcion (Reds), ss .	0	1	0	2	0	0
Patek (Royals), ss	3	0	1	1	1	0	Monday (Dodgers), rf ..	2	0	0	1	0	0
Palmer (Orioles), p	1	0	0	1	0	0	Rogers (Expos), p	0	0	0	0	0	0
Keough (Athletics), p ..	0	0	0	0	0	0	Winfield (Padres), lf	2	1	1	1	0	0
(b)Howell (Blue Jays) ..	1	0	0	0	0	0	Bowa (Phillies), ss	3	1	2	2	4	0
Sorenson (Brewers), p .	0	0	0	0	1	0	Boone (Phillies), c	1	1	1	3	1	0
(c)Hisle (Brewers)	1	0	1	0	0	0	Pocoroba (Braves), c ..	0	0	0	0	0	0
Kern (Indians),p	0	0	0	0	0	0	Blue (Giants), p	0	0	0	0	1	0
Guidry (Yankees), p ...	0	0	0	0	0	0	(a)Smith (Dodgers), rf ..	3	0	0	1	0	0
Nettles (Yankees), 3b ..	0	0	0	0	1	0	Cey (Dodgers), 3b	1	0	0	1	0	0
Totals	31	3	8	24	10	1	Totals	32	7	10	27	11	0

American League .... 2 0 1   0 0 0   0 0 0—3
National League .... 0 0 3   0 0 0   0 4 x—7

Pitching Summary

American League	IP	H	R	ER	BB	SO	National League	IP	H	R	ER	BB	SO
Palmer	2⅔	3	3	3	4	4	Blue	3	5	3	3	1	2
Keough	⅓	1	0	0	0	0	Rogers	2	2	0	0	0	2
Sorenson	3	1	0	0	0	0	Fingers	2	1	0	0	0	1
Kern	⅔	1	0	0	0	0	Sutter (W)	1⅔	0	0	0	0	2
Guidry	⅓	0	0	0	0	0	Niekro	⅓	0	0	0	0	0
Gossage (L)	1	4	4	4	1	1							

(a) Struck out for Blue in third. (b) Grounded out for Keough in fourth. (c) Singled for Sorenson in seventh. (d) Ran for Rose in seventh. (e) Flied out for Fingers in seventh. (f) Flied out for Sundberg in ninth. (g) Fouled out for White in ninth. Runs batted in—Brett 2, Luzinski, Garvey 2, Fisk, Boone 2, Lopes 1. Two-base hits—Brett, Rose. Three-base hits—Carew 2, Garvey. Sacrifice flies—Fisk, Brett. Stolen bases—Bowa, Brett. Caught stealing—Zisk, Carew, Lopes. Double play—Brett, Money, and Carew. Wild pitches—Rogers, Gossage. Passed ball—Sundberg. Left on bases—Americans 4, Nationals 7.

Managers: Billy Martin, New York (A.L.); Tom Lasorda, Los Angeles (N.L.).

Umpires—Pryor (N.L.), plate; Chylak (A.L.), first base; Tata (N.L.), second base; Deegan (A.L.), third base; Runge (N.L.), left field, McCoy (A.L.), right field. Time—2:37. Attendance—51,549.

July 17, 1979   At Kingdome, Seattle (Night)

Nationals	AB	R	H	PO	A	E
Lopes (Dodgers), 2b ...	3	0	1	4	1	0
(i)Morgan (Reds), 2b ...	1	1	0	1	1	0
Parker (Pirates), rf	3	0	1	0	2	0
Garvey (Dodgers), 1b ..	2	1	0	5	0	0
Perry (Padres), p	0	0	0	0	0	0
Sambito (Astros), p ...	0	0	0	0	0	0
Reynolds (Astros), ss ..	2	0	0	0	1	0
Schmidt (Phillies), 3b ..	3	2	2	1	1	1
Cey (Dodgers), 3b	1	0	0	2	1	0
Parrish (Expos), 3b	0	0	0	0	0	0
Foster (Reds), lf	1	0	1	0	0	0
Matthews (Braves), lf ..	2	0	0	2	0	0
(j)Mazzilli (Mets), cf	1	1	1	0	0	0
Winfield (Padres), cf-lf .	5	1	1	3	0	0
Boone (Phillies), c	2	1	1	0	0	0
Carter (Expos), c	2	0	1	6	1	0
Bowa (Phillies), ss	2	0	0	1	3	0
LaCoss (Reds), p	0	0	0	0	0	0
(k)Hernandez						
(Cardinals)	1	0	0	0	0	0
Sutter (Cubs), p	0	0	0	0	1	0
Carlton (Phillies), p	0	0	0	0	0	0
(a)Brock (Cardinals) ...	1	0	1	0	0	0
Andujar (Astros), p	0	0	0	0	0	0
(c)Clark (Giants)	1	0	0	0	0	0
Rogers (Expos), p	0	0	0	0	0	0
(e)Rose (Phillies), 1b ...	2	0	0	2	0	0
Totals	35	7	10	27	12	1

Americans	AB	R	H	PO	A	E
Smalley (Twins), ss	3	0	0	2	2	0
Grich (Angels), 2b	1	0	0	2	0	0
Brett (Royals), 3b	3	1	0	1	2	0
Nettles (Yanks), 3b	1	0	1	1	2	0
Baylor (Angels), lf	4	2	2	1	0	0
Kern (Rangers), p	0	0	0	0	0	0
Guidry (Yanks), p	0	0	0	0	0	0
(l)Singleton (Orioles) ...	1	0	0	0	0	0
Rice (Red Sox), rf-lf ...	5	0	1	3	0	0
Lynn (Red Sox), cf	1	1	1	0	0	0
Lemon (White Sox), cf .	2	1	0	2	0	0
Yastrzemski (Red Sox),						
1b	3	0	2	5	1	0
(f)Burleson (Red Sox),						
ss	2	1	0	0	1	0
Porter (Royals), c	3	0	1	2	0	0
Downing (Angels), c ...	1	0	1	3	0	0
White (Royals), 2b	2	0	0	2	2	0
(g)Bochte (Mariners),						
1b	1	0	1	2	0	0
Ryan (Angels), p	0	0	0	0	0	0
(b)Cooper (Brewers) ...	0	0	0	0	0	0
Stanley (Red Sox), p ...	0	0	0	1	0	0
(d)Kemp (Tigers)	1	0	0	0	0	0
Clear (Angels), p	0	0	0	0	0	0
(h)Jackson (Yanks), rf .	1	0	0	0	0	0
Totals	35	6	10	27	10	0

```
National League .....................  2  1  1   0  0  1   0  1  1—7
American League .....................  3  0  2   0  0  1   0  0  0—6
```

Pitching Summary

National League	IP	H	R	ER	BB	SO
Carlton	1	2	3	3	1	0
Andujar	2	2	2	1	1	0
Rogers	2	0	0	0	0	2
Perry	0*	3	1	1	0	0
Sambito	⅔	0	0	0	1	0
LaCoss	1⅓	1	0	0	0	0
Sutter (W)	2	2	0	0	2	3

American League	IP	H	R	ER	BB	SO
Ryan	2	5	3	3	1	2
Stanley	2	1	1	1	0	0
Clear	2	2	1	1	1	0
Kern (L)	2⅔	2	2	2	3	3
Guidry	⅓	0	0	1	1	0

* Pitched to three batters in sixth.

(a) Singled for Carlton in second. (b) Walked for Ryan in second. (c) Grounded out for Andujar in fourth. (d) Lined out for Stanley in fourth. (e) Grounded into double play for Rogers in sixth. (f) Ran for Yastrzemski in sixth. (g) Singled for White in sixth. (h) Grounded into force play for Clear in sixth. (i) Struck out for Lopes in seventh. (j) Homered for Matthews in eighth. (k) Struck out for LaCoss in eighth. (l) Grounded out for Guidry in ninth. Runs batted in—Schmidt, Foster, Baylor, Lynn 2, Parker, Winfield, Yastrzemski, Carter, Bochte, Mazzilli 2. Two-base hits—Foster, Baylor, Schmidt, Winfield, Porter, Rice. Three-base hit—Schmidt. Home runs—Lynn, Mazzilli. Sacrifice hit—Bochte. Sacrifice fly—Parker. Double plays—Brett, White, and Yastrzemski; White, Smalley, and Yastrzemski. Wild pitch—Andujar. Hit by pitcher— By Andujar (Lemon). Balk—Kern. Left on bases—Nationals 8, Americans 9.

Managers: Bob Lemon, New York (A.L.); Tom Lasorda, Los Angeles (N.L.)

Umpires—Maloney (A.L.), plate; Weyer (N.L.), first base; Bremigan (A.L.), second base; W. Williams (N.L.), third base; Cooney (A.L.), left field; Rennert (N.L.), right field. Time—3:11. Attendance—58,905.

Bibliography

Butler, Hal. *Baseball All-Star Game Thrills.* New York: Julian Messner, 1968.

Danzig, Allison, and Reichler, Joe. *The History of Baseball: Its Great Players, Teams and Managers.* Englewood Cliffs, New Jersey: Prentice-Hall, Inc., 1959.

Durant, John. *The Story of Baseball in Words and Pictures.* New York: Hastings House, 1947.

Graham, Frank. *The New York Yankees, An Informal History.* New York: G.P. Putnam's Sons, 1948.

Musial, Stan, and Broeg, Bob. *Stan Musial: "The Man's" Own Story.* New York: Doubleday & Co., Inc., 1964.

Smith, Robert. *Baseball's Hall of Fame.* New York: Grosset & Dunlap, Inc., 1965.

Walsh, Christy, ed. *Baseball's Greatest Lineup.* New York: A. S. Barnes & Co., 1952.

Whiting, Robert. *The Chrysanthemum and the Bat: Baseball Samurai Style.* New York: Dodd, Mead & Co., 1977.

Williams, Ted, and Underwood, John. *My Turn at Bat: The Story of My Life.* New York: Simon & Schuster, 1969.

I've also used various books, guides, and other material issued by The Sporting News Publishing Co. of St. Louis, including the annual *Sporting News Official Baseball Guide, Official Baseball Register,* and *Baseball Dope Book,* as well as many editions of *The Sporting News,* which for several generations now has been called "The Bible of Baseball."

I must also give a general citation to all those players, managers, and coaches who took time out from their batting practice, infield drills, wind sprints, and fungo hitting in order to answer questions about the All-Star Game.

Index

Aaron, Hank, 67, 71, 74, 75, 76, 79, 84, 85, 86, 87, 88, 91, 94, 96, 97, 115, 116, 120
Adcock, Joe, 76
Aguirre, Hank, 82
Allen, Johnny, 30
Allen, Richie, 89
Almon, Bill, 108
Alou, Felipe, 81
Alou, Matty, 91
Alston, Walter, 62–63, 69, 70, 77, 86, 123
Altman, George, 78
Alvis, Max, 87
Anderson, George (Sparky), 97–98, 100, 101, 116, 125
Andujar, Joaquin, 112
Antonelli, Johnny, 63–64, 69, 74
Aparicio, Luis, 79, 80, 81
Appling, Luke, 22, 23, 25, 35, 50
Ashburn, Richie, 52, 58, 59, 61
Autry, Gene, 124
Averill, Earl, 8, 10, 15, 22, 25, 27–28, 98
Avila, Bobby, 60, 63, 64

Bagby, Jim, Jr., 43
Bailey, Ed, 70, 84
Baker, Del, 37, 40
Bando, Sal, 91
Banks, Ernie, 71–72, 74, 76, 86
Bartell, Dick, 8
Battey, Earl, 80, 81, 84, 87
Bavasi, E. J. (Buzzy), 110

Baylor, Don, 112
Bell, Gary, 77
Bell, Gus, 61, 64, 70, 71
Bench, Johnny, 91, 94, 97, 98, 99, 100, 101, 116, 117, 118, 120, 122
Benton, Al, 43
Berger, Wally, 8, 19
Bergman, Ron, 114
Berra, Lawrence (Yogi), 54, 58, 62, 65, 66, 67, 70, 72, 75, 82, 120–21
Bickford, Vern, 54
Blackwell, Ewell, 48, 50, 58
Blanton, Cy, 28
Blue, Vida, 94, 99, 103, 106
Bochte, Bruce, 113
Bolling, Frank, 80
Bonds, Bobby, 97–98, 116, 118
Bonham, Ernie, 44
Boone, Bob, 104, 112
Boone, Ray, 69
Borowy, Hank, 45
Boudreau, Lou, 36, 38, 42, 50, 51, 52, 53, 55
Bowa, Larry, 100, 104
Boyer, Ken, 68, 69, 74, 77, 79, 85, 86
Branca, Ralph, 52, 55
Brecheen, Harry, 50
Brett, George, 103, 106–07, 112, 120, 121
Brewer, Tom, 69
Bridges, Tommy, 28, 33
Brissie, Lou, 54
Brock, Lou, 99, 112, 120, 122

Brown, Mace, 31
Buck, Jack, 124
Buhl, Bob, 76
Bunning, Jim, 74, 79, 80, 84
Burdette, Lou, 70, 74
Burgess, Forrest (Smoky), 78, 79
Burleson, Rick, 113, 114
Busby, Steve, 99

Callison, Johnny, xi, 85–86
Campanella, Roy, 52, 57, 61
Campaneris, Bert, 102
Carew, Rod, 6, 90, 94, 96, 102, 103, 115, 126–27
Carlton, Steve, 91, 112, 122
Carresquel, Chico, 58, 61, 67
Carter, Gary, 113–14
Carty, Rico, 6
Case, George, 44
Cash, Norman, 78
- Cavarretta, Phil, 45–46, 48, 49, 51
Cedeno, Cesar, 29, 96, 101, 116
Cepeda, Orlando, 79–80, 85
Cey, Ron, 98, 99, 104, 114, 118
Chance, Dean, 89
Chandler, A. B. (Happy), 56
Chandler, Spurgeon (Spud), 43, 44
Chapman, Ben, 8, 11, 22
Chapman, Sam, 48
Clark, Jack, 104, 108
Clemente, Roberto, 78, 79, 80, 87, 88, 89, 93, 95, 120
Cochrane, Mickey, 19, 20, 22, 42, 43
Colavito, Rocky, 75, 78, 79, 81, 82, 86
Colbert, Nate, 97
Coleman, Jerry, 57
Coleman, Joe, 52
Collins, James (Rip), 22, 23
Concepcion, Dave, 100, 104
Conley, Gene, 67–68
Cooper, Mort, 42, 44
Cooper, Walker, 46, 48, 52
Coscarart, Pete, 34
Crandall, Del, 74, 76
Cronin, Joe, 8, 9, 10, 12–13, 14, 15, 19, 28, 30, 31, 33, 36, 51, 98
Crosetti, Frankie, 26, 32
Crowder, Alvin (General), 8, 10
Cuccinello, Tony, 8

Daley, Arthur, 16
Danning, Harry, 35
Danzansky, Joseph, 110

Dark, Alvin, 58, 59, 62, 64, 100
Davenport, Jim, 81
Davalillo, Vic, 87
Davis, Curt, 25
Davis, Tommy, 84
Davis, Willie, 116
Dean, Dizzy, 22, 23, 27–29
Demaree, Frank, 23, 24
Derringer, Paul, 35
Dickey, Bill, 8, 15, 22, 25, 27, 28, 31, 32, 33, 44, 49, 98
Dickson, Murry, 61
Dietz, Dick, 92–93
Dillinger, Bob, 54
DiMaggio, Dom, 39, 45, 47, 48, 53, 54, 57, 59
DiMaggio, Joe, 22–26, 27, 31, 32, 33, 36, 38, 39, 40, 42, 45, 50, 51, 52, 53, 54, 55, 58, 59, 109–10
DiMaggio, Vince, 44–45
Doby, Larry, 52, 54, 57, 61, 63, 64
Doerr, Bobby, 44, 45, 46, 47, 50, 51
Donovan, Dick, 78
Downing, Brian, 113, 114
Dressen, Chuck, 62
Drysdale, Don, 74–75, 80, 89, 90, 114, 120
Duren, Ryne, 74
Durocher, Leo, 22, 24, 25, 30–31, 43, 52, 65, 67
Dyer, Eddie, 50, 51
Dykes, Jimmy, 8, 9, 10

Early, Jake, 44
Edwards, Johnny, 85
Elliot, Bob, 37–38
Ellis, Dock, 94
English, Woody, 8
Ennis, Del, 68
Erskine, Carl, 64
Estrada, Chuck, 76
Everett, Marj, 110
Evers, Walter (Hoot), 52
Ewell, Jim (Doc), 29, 76, 88

Face, Roy, 74, 76, 78
Fain, Ferris, 58, 61
Farrell, Dick, 81
Feeney, Charles S. (Chub), 119, 124
Feller, Bob, 33, 34, 35, 37, 43, 48, 49
Ferrell, Rick, 8, 9, 10, 22, 25
Ferrell, Wes, 8
Fidrych, Mark, 29, 101, 102
Fingers, Rollie, 104, 108

Mathews, Eddie, 61, 67, 71, 74, 76, 77, 79, 80, 82
Mathewson, Christy, 17
Matthews, Gary, 113
May, Lee, 96, 97
Mays, Willie, xi, 67, 68, 70, 71, 74, 76, 77, 78, 79, 80–81, 83–84, 85, 86–87, 88, 89, 90, 91, 120, 127
Mazeroski, Bill, 72, 74, 76
Mazzilli, Lee, 113
Medwick, Joe (Ducky), 15, 22, 24, 28, 35, 46
Messersmith, Andy, 99
Meyer, Buddy, 20
Michaels, Cass, 53, 57
Millan, Felix, 91
Miller, Eddie, 39
Miller, Stuart (Stu), 78, 79
Minoso, Orestes (Minnie), 60, 61, 64, 70, 71
Mize, Johnny, 28, 35, 38, 50, 51, 52, 53, 61
Monbouquette, Bill, 76
Moore, Terry, 38
Morales, Jerry, 102
Moran, Billy, 80, 81
Morgan, Joe, 93, 97, 98, 99, 100, 101, 103, 104, 114, 116, 119, 120, 122
Moriarty, George, 18
Mossi, Don, 71
Mullin, Pat, 52
Muncrief, Bob, 46
Mungo, Van Lingle, 15, 28
Murcer, Bobby, 94, 98, 99
Murphy, Johnny, 32
Murtaugh, Danny, 78
Musial, Stan, 44, 46, 51, 53, 57, 58–59, 60, 68, 69, 70, 71, 72, 77, 80, 84, 115, 119

Narleski, Ray, 72
Neal, Charlie, 76
Nettles, Graig, 113–14, 115
Newcombe, Don, 52, 53–54, 57, 59
Newhouser, Hal, 45, 46, 48, 49, 50, 51
Newsom, Buck, 35
Nicholson, Bill, 45
Niekro, Phil, 104–05
Nixon, President Richard M., 72, 75
Nuxhall, Joe, 67

O'Dell, Billy, 72, 75
Odom, John (Blue Moon), 91
O'Doul, Frank (Lefty), 8, 10
Oliva, Tony, 87
Oliver, Al, 100
O'Neill, Steve, 49–50

Osteen, Claude, 93
Otis, Amos, 93, 97
Ott, Mel, 22, 30, 33, 35
Owen, Mickey, 42

Pafko, Andy, 51, 52, 54, 57
Page, Joe, 51
Paige, Leroy (Satchel), 61
Palmer, Jim, 101, 102, 103–04
Pappas, Milt, 82, 86
Parker, Dave, 101, 113–14
Parnell, Mel, 53
Pascual, Camilo, 79, 80
Passeau, Claude, 38, 39, 40, 42, 48
Patek, Fred, 104, 118–19
Pearson, Albie, 84
Pepitone, Joe, 84, 85, 87
Perez, Tony, 89, 100
Perry, Gaylord, 88, 92, 96, 98, 113
Perry, Jim, 92
Pesky, Johnny, 47, 121–22
Peters, Hank, 124–25
Peterson, Fritz, 93
Petrocelli, Rico, 91
Pierce, Billy, 61, 66, 67, 69, 70, 71
Podres, Johnny, 77, 81
Pollet, Howie, 54
Porter, Darrell, 112
Post, Wally, 70
Prell, Ed, 3
Purkey, Bob, 79

Radatz, Dick, 84, 85, 86
Raffensberger, Ken, 46
Randolph, Willie, 102
Raschi, Vic, 52, 53, 56, 57, 60
Reese, Harold (Pee Wee), 50, 52, 53, 54, 61
Reidenbaugh, Lowell, 106
Reiser, Harold (Pete), 37, 38
Reynolds, Allie, 57, 61
Reynolds, Craig, 114
Rice, Jim, 103, 109, 112, 113, 114, 115, 121
Richards, Paul, 78
Richardson, Bobby, 82, 84, 85
Richert, Pete, 88
Rickey, Branch, 125
Rizzuto, Phil, 57
Roberts, Robin, 56, 58, 61, 63, 66
Robinson, Brooks, 76, 81, 85, 87, 88, 89, 90, 92, 118, 120, 126
Robinson, Eddie, 53, 54, 60
Robinson, Frank, 75, 94–95, 117
Robinson, Jackie, 52–53, 57, 59, 60, 125

Rogers, Steve, 104
Rojas, Octavio (Cookie), 96
Rolfe, Robert (Red), 27, 28, 33
Rollins, Rich, 80
Romano, John, 81
Roosevelt, President Franklin D., 27, 41
Rosar, Buddy, 48, 50
Rose, Pete, 86, 90, 92–93, 99, 100, 101, 105, 115, 116, 118, 119, 120, 122
Roseboro, John, 82
Rosen, Al, xi, 49, 60, 62–64, 67, 68
Rowe, Lynwood (Schoolboy), 24
Rudi, Joe, 99
Ruffing, Charles (Red), 32, 35
Runnels, Pete, 81, 122
Rush, Bob, 60
Ruth, George Herman (Babe), 5, 7–12, 15, 16, 40, 68
Ryan, Connie, 45, 46, 120
Ryan, Nolan, 98, 102, 112, 123

Sain, Johnny, 50, 51
Sambito, Joe, 113
Sanford, Jack, 70
Sanguillen, Manny, 96
Santo, Ron, 84, 87, 88, 92, 97, 98, 116
Sauer, Hank, 56, 57, 60
Sawyer, Eddie, 58
Schmidt, Mike, 112, 118
Schmitz, Johnny, 52
Schoendienst, Albert (Red), 48, 58, 64–65, 67, 70
Schumacher, Hal, 8, 19–20
Schwall, Don, 80
Scott, George, 88, 102, 123
Seaver, Tom, 89, 99–100, 120, 121
Selkirk, George, 25, 32, 33
Seminick, Andy, 53
Sewell, Truett (Rip), 45, 46, 48–49
Shantz, Bobby, 60
Shaw, Bob, 81
Shea, Frank (Spec), 50
Shotton, Burt, 56, 57, 58
Simmons, Al, 8, 10, 11, 15
Simmons, Curt, 60, 70
Simmons, Ted, 116
Singer, Bill, 98
Singleton, Ken, 114
Skinner, Bob, 72, 76
Skowron, Bill, 70
Slaughter, Enos, 38, 51, 52, 56, 57, 60–61
Smalley, Roy, Jr., 112
Smith, C. Arnholt, 110, 111

Smith, Edgar, 38, 39
Smith, Mayo, 90, 91
Smith, Ozzie, 108
Smith, Reggie, 92, 99, 100
Snider, Duke, 57, 61, 64
Sorenson, Lary, 109
Southworth, Billy, 44, 53, 55
Spahn, Warren, 53, 55, 61, 64, 69, 72
Spence, Stan, 48, 50, 51
Splittorf, Paul, 118
Stargell, Willie, 86, 94, 105, 109, 116
Staub, Daniel (Rusty), 101
Steinbrenner, George, 124
Stengel, Casey, 31, 57, 62, 63, 70, 71, 75, 78, 88
Stephens, Vern, 44, 45, 46, 48, 49
Stewart, Bill, 65
Stirnweiss, George (Snuffy), 48–49
Stone, Dean, 64–65
Stoneman, Bill, 96
Stottlemyre, Mel, 91, 93
Sullivan, Frank, 67
Summers, Bill, 39
Sutter, Bruce, 104, 113, 115
Sutton, Don, 102, 116

Tanana, Frank, 101, 102, 123
Tebbetts, George (Birdie), 52, 53
Temple, Johnny, 68, 75
Templeton, Garry, 102
Tenace, Gene, 99
Terry, Bill, 8, 14, 20, 27, 28, 30, 31
Thomas, Frank, 72
Thompson, Jason, 121
Tiant, Luis, 90, 99
Tobin, Jim, 46
Torre, Joe, 86, 87, 93, 120
Travis, Cecil, 37, 38, 39
Traynor, Harold (Pie), 8
Tresh, Tommy, 81
Triandos, Gus, 72, 74
Trucks, Virgil (Fire), 53
Turley, Bob, 71, 72

Vander Meer, John, 30, 31, 42, 44, 58
Vaughan, Floyd (Arky), 20, 33, 35, 38–39
Veeck, Bill, 123–24
Vernon, Mickey, 52, 63, 66, 67, 68, 123
Versalles, Zoilo, 87
Virdon, Bill, 117
Vosmik, Joe, 19–20

Wagner, Hal, 47
Wagner, Leon 81
Wakefield, Dick, 44
Walker, Bill, 19
Walker, Fred (Dixie), 45
Walker, Jerry, 75
Walters, William (Bucky), 35, 38, 42, 45
Waner, Paul, 8
Ward, Arch, 1–5, 13
Warneke, Lon, 8, 9, 10, 11, 15, 22, 25, 26
Washington, Claudell, 100
Watson, Bob, 116
Weaver, Earl, 83, 93, 94, 116–17
Welch, Bob, 106
Wertz, Vic, 53, 59, 70
West, Max, 35
West, Sammy, 8, 28
White, Bill, 78, 79, 80, 84
White, Frank, 113
Whitney, Arthur (Pinky), 23, 24
Wilhelm, Hoyt, 79
Williams, Billy, 86, 96–97, 116
Williams, Dick, 99
Williams, Stan, 77

Williams, Ted, xi, 28, 35, 37–40, 42, 47–50,
   51, 53, 56, 57, 62, 66, 69, 70, 71, 72, 77, 85,
   88
Wills, Maury, 78, 80–81, 86, 88
Wilson, Jimmy, 8
Winfield, Dave, 102, 104, 107–08, 112, 114
Wood, Wilbur, 96, 97
Wright, Clyde, 93
Wyatt, Whitlow, 35, 37
Wynn, Early, 67, 70, 72, 74, 75
Wynn, Jim, 99
Wynegar, Harold (Butch), 102
Wyrostek, Johnny, 57

Yastrzemski, Carl, 90, 92, 93, 94, 99–100,
   103, 112, 113, 115
York, Rudy, 42, 44, 47, 48
Yost, Eddie, 122
Young, Dick, 103
Yount, Robin, 118

Zachry, Pat, 108
Zimmer, Don, 79, 103, 120
Zisk, Richie, 102, 104, 109, 117